4/09

The Man Who Emptied Death Row

The Elmer H. Johnson and Carol Holmes Johnson Series in Criminology

The Man Who Emptied Death Row

Governor George Ryan and the Politics of Crime

James L. Merriner

Southern Illinois University Press / *Carbondale*

Copyright © 2008 by the Board of Trustees,
Southern Illinois University
All rights reserved
Printed in the United States of America

11 10 09 08   4 3 2 1

Publication of this book has been underwritten by The
Elmer H. Johnson and Carol Holmes Johnson Series
in Criminology fund.

Library of Congress Cataloging-in-Publication Data
Merriner, James L., 1947–
   The man who emptied death row : Governor George
Ryan and the politics of crime / James L. Merriner.
      p. cm.—(The Elmer H. Johnson and Carol
Holmes Johnson series in criminology)
   Includes bibliographical references and index.
   ISBN-13: 978-0-8093-2865-9 (cloth : alk. paper)
   ISBN-10: 0-8093-2865-8 (cloth : alk. paper)
   1. Political corruption—Illinois. 2. Capital
punishment—Political aspects—Illinois. 3. Ryan,
George H. 4. Governors—Illinois—Biography.
I. Title.
JK5745.M47 2008
977.3′044092—dc22
[B]   2008000566

Printed on recycled paper. ♻
The paper used in this publication meets the minimum
requirements of American National Standard for Information Sciences—Permanence of Paper for Printed
Library Materials, ANSI Z39.48-1992. ∞

For Charles Marvin Merriner and Sharon Ann Merriner Davis

Contents

Illustrations

Preface

I never made a conscious decision to stake my career on writing about political corruption. Now I find myself writing my fifth book about politics and history, all focused largely on corruption and its countervailing reforms. Perhaps some background will help explain why I believe a biography of George H. Ryan is a much bigger story than just an account of another crooked politician who got caught.

President Jimmy Carter's budget director, Bert Lance, was forced to resign under fire for some unethical banking deals. At the time, I was political editor of the *Atlanta Constitution* and had known Lance since he had run for governor of Georgia in 1974. Lance told me privately after resigning in disgrace, "Look, if they come after you, if they really want to get you, they can always find something." I did not really agree, figuring, "Well, Bert, that's just your self-vindication."

In 1980, I was hired by the *Chicago Sun-Times*. Shortly before I left Atlanta, an Atlanta alderman was indicted for some infraction of the election laws. It was front-page news, of course. Then, soon after I arrived in Chicago, a Chicago alderman was indicted for something or other—and it did not even make the front page! Amazed, I asked my editor, "Is it routine news around here for aldermen to get indicted?" He said, "Well, um, yeah."

So as a political writer and editor, I covered the investigations, indictments, convictions, and appeals of many aldermen, city officials, state legislators, state officials, judges, congressmen, and two former governors. In 1995, I left the *Sun-Times* to write a biography of Dan Rostenkowski, the Chicago congressman who chaired the House Ways and Means Committee for many years. "Rosty" was indicted for misusing public and campaign monies, was defeated for reelection in 1994, eventually pleaded guilty to two counts of mail fraud, and went to prison. Before his plea and sentence, he told me privately, in so many words, just what Lance had said—if those in the U.S. Justice Department, with all its power and resources, come after you, if they want to get you, they can always find something to hang you on; all of us have violated some regulation or statute or other. Again, I thought Rosty had committed serious crimes against the public trust and did not really believe him.

Still, I wondered why public corruption seemed more pervasive in Chicago and Illinois than elsewhere. I explored that question in *Grafters and Goo Goos: Corruption and Reform in Chicago, 1833–2003,* published in 2004. At that time, former Illinois governor Ryan was under indictment on corruption charges. My publisher suggested that I write a political history of Chicago public schools. Without thinking, I said, "No, that's not the story. George Ryan is the story." Actually, I had not written about Ryan's case and had scarcely even thought about it.

This book ensued. Ryan never explicitly raised the Lance/Rostenkowski defense, at least not in public or to me, but his supporters have said as much: If they come after you, they can always find something to get you on. The feds have ruined Ryan, he will lose his pension, lose his house, they have bankrupted his kids, he is an old man who will rot in jail, his wife is in despair; that's too much, even if he is guilty of some political practices that used to be legal, or at least winked at, when George was coming up.

Ryan is nearly a generation older than I, but I thought I understood him. That is, I grew up in small towns in the Midwest. I knew people like Ryan—small-town businessmen who think that they run everything, that they have every right to run everything, and that they have every right to profit from running things. Sometimes the profiteering crosses the line into illegality, sometimes egregiously so. I believed that some of Ryan's transgressions were egregious.

But I was not naive about the political ambitions of some prosecutors. During the 1980s, I covered Governor Jim Thompson, who had made his name by putting a former governor, Otto Kerner, in jail. Governor Thompson arranged to name his colleague Dan K. Webb as U.S. attorney in Chicago. Webb eagerly prosecuted Cook County judges in the Operation Greylord investigation, the largest judicial scandal in U.S. history. Eventually, Thompson and Webb left public office and joined a Chicago law firm, Winston and Strawn. When Ryan was indicted, that firm defended him free of charge.

If the incumbent U.S. attorney thinks Ryan is so wicked, I wondered, why are two predecessor U.S. attorneys, Thompson and Webb, defending him? And all these people—the incumbent U.S. attorney, the two former ones, and the former governor—were Republicans, or at least placed in office by Republicans. Defense attorneys could hardly argue that Ryan was the victim of a spiteful partisan prosecution. The case was complex, based on circumstantial evidence. How could ordinary citizens, let alone Ryan's jurors, possibly determine what constitutes public corruption these days?

Defenders of Ryan and many other indicted officials complain that we have criminalized politics, passing so many reformist laws and regulations that nothing substantive can get done because our politicians constantly fear that a U.S. attorney is looking over their shoulders. I agree that since the Bert Lance era, many laws and regulations have been written, some of them wrongheaded, but then, is it a bad thing that politicians are worried about prosecutorial oversight? We need somebody to try to keep them honest—voters apparently do not.

Shortly before he left office as governor, months before he was indicted, Ryan pardoned or commuted the sentences of every convict on death row in Illinois. This was a stunning and unprecedented act. Some liberal reformers who normally would hunger for the prosecution of a crooked Republican hailed Ryan as a moral hero. They said his courage in this matter eclipsed whatever petty legalities he might have violated.

Really? I wondered. Does moral courage in one area trump offenses in another? And is Ryan really a crook, or just a small-town political hack? Have we criminalized politics? Harry Truman was, after all, a Kansas City courthouse machine hack, despised by the clerisy, but his presidency is now a happy national memory.

This book is an effort to address these questions.

"I should like to thank . . ." At this point, one normally stops reading, but I want to declare that, having written five books, I still am amazed at how willing most people are to help an author do his research.

A word about technique. All interviews for this book were conducted on the record with a couple of exceptions. The exceptions provided no uncorroborated account of anyone's thoughts, statements, or actions. Also, I relied on primary sources—interviews, memoirs, and court documents—over secondary sources to the extent possible.

In the summer of 1998, I worked briefly for Glenn Poshard's campaign against Ryan for governor. No inside information from that stint was used in this book.

Some people offered information and insights about Ryan's career not found on the public record, as voluminous as that record is. At the risk of omitting someone, I extend many thanks to Phil Angelo, David Axelrod, James Burns, Patrick Collins, Terry Cosgrove, William Dart, Tyrone Fahner, Peter Fitzgerald, Paul Green, Larry Horist, Jerome Joyce, Richard Juliano, Mike Lawrence, Paul Lis, Marcena Love, Sheila Murphy, Mike Robinson, Tom Roeser, Larry Sabato, Cal Skinner, James Thompson, Anthony Valukas, Dan Walker, Charles Wheeler, and Rich Williams. Some were Ryan's friends, some his enemies, and some indifferent, but all were candid. Any errors of fact or interpretation are mine alone.

Thanks also to George Ryan. During his prosecution, conviction, and appeal, he was legally constrained from talking with me. So I suggested taking the legal case off the table but interviewing him about the rest of his life story. He agreed and answered every question I put to him, not always to my satisfaction, but with his customary bluntness.

Introduction

> Politics is a hard thing, said the Romans (*politica est res dura*), and they meant that it is a dangerous enterprise not suited for the sentimentalist and romantic.
>
> —Carl J. Friedrich, *The Pathology of Politics*

George Homer Ryan Sr. was a small-town druggist who became one of the most important state governors in U.S. history. Shortly before leaving office in January 2003, he pardoned four Illinois death row prisoners and commuted the sentences of all 167 others—171 convicted killers in all. This action was widely hailed as a moral sunburst. It won him worldwide acclaim and nominations for the Nobel Peace Prize.

At the same time, Ryan was a crook. In 2006, he was convicted of eighteen counts of official wrongdoing. Under Ryan, the state of Illinois itself was, the federal government alleged, a racketeering enterprise.

The paradox of a petty and ruthless grafter who was also a moral entrepreneur against capital punishment makes a story that might challenge a Dostoyevsky. Ryan's motives and character in both areas, the moralist and the thief, are hidden in the corkscrew of the human heart. Maybe he emptied out death row from honest revulsion regarding the failures of a criminal justice system that had sentenced some innocent people to die. Or maybe he devised a spectacular public relations ploy, the ultimate grand gesture, to divert attention from the sheriff's posse riding after him. Maybe, too, he wanted to build a case in his defense that prosecutors simply cannot be trusted. If they would hound innocent people to the gallows, surely they would persecute a governor for mere political reasons.

Ryan's motives might be puzzling, but they are not opaque. The key to understanding George Ryan is that he is the son of a political machine. A machine runs on an intricate system of rewards and coercions, based on the values of loyalty and tribalism. To outsiders, a machine can appear to be insulated from reality. Ryan's machine was located in Kankakee, Illinois, where he grew up.

Many political scientists hold that such machines are dead. They were nationalized, eclipsed, made irrelevant by the New Deal and the subsequent expansion of the welfare state. And by television, of course. Television is the new precinct captain and all that.

1

Perhaps these political scientists should visit Chicago. Somebody should buy them tickets to O'Hare International Airport. There they might notice boutiques in the terminals and bulldozers plowing runways out on the field. These businesses won city contracts under a Democratic machine run by a mayor named Daley. Then put the professors in a rental car and have them drive an hour south on Interstate 57 to Kankakee. There they might observe a parallel, though smaller in scale, Republican machine.

"Will it play in Peoria?" was an old vaudeville saying and a slogan of the Nixon White House. It might just as well have been "Will it carry in Kankakee?" Both are small cities downstate from Chicago, farming and decaying industrial communities holding all the fabled virtues and vices of the heartland.

In Kankakee, industrial rust so encrusted the city that in 1999, the acme of the national dot-com economic boom, the *Places Rated Almanac* judged it to be the worst place to live among 354 metropolitan areas in the United States and Canada.[1] Naturally, the city fathers denounced this ranking as execrably erroneous. Still, it seems clear that the baggage of old political machines is unhelpful to cities seeking to modernize.

The old machine had kept Kankakee corrupt for generations. A former member of the Kankakee County board of supervisors, Len Small, became governor of Illinois during the era of Prohibition gangsterism in the 1920s. Small was indicted for embezzling a million dollars of state interest money. After he was acquitted, jury-tampering was alleged. Two of his associates were subpoenaed but fled the state to evade indictment for tampering with the jury. Then Governor Small pardoned them. (George Ryan was the fifth incumbent or former Illinois governor to be indicted on corruption charges in eighty-one years.)

In the early 1960s, the Kankakee County sheriff was indicted for allowing prisoners to escape, making false claims for expenses, and conspiring to operate whorehouses. The sheriff pleaded guilty but soon won a do-nothing state patronage job as a meat and poultry inspector. Such was the culture in which George Ryan entered public life as a member of the Kankakee County board of supervisors in 1966.

Ryan's political sponsor Edward M. McBroom showed him how patronage jobs were awarded at the Manteno Mental Health Center. Through unwritten agreements under the informal welfare system of political machines, people who wanted Manteno jobs first had to buy a car from McBroom's Cadillac lot. Sometimes McBroom would have a new car driven to the mental hospital to persuade the favored payroller that it was time to trade up. If the payroller had a blue-collar job and could not afford a Cadillac, he still was expected to buy his toasters and other household items at McBroom's hardware store. In like manner, Kankakee city employees were expected to get their prescriptions filled at Ryan's pharmacy. The matrix of coercions and favors, the handshake deals behind closed doors—that is how things often get done in our democracy. Ryan always kept a sharp eye out for making a deal, achieving a compromise, assuring that every friend got rewarded and every enemy was punished.

Throughout its seven-year investigation of Ryan's actions in office, the U.S. Justice Department never directly accused him of extorting cash for specific favors. Rather, he and his friends took care of one another in an exchange of loyalties and gains.

Exactly what constitutes public corruption remains an unsettled question. Ryan and many other indicted public officials have offered the defense that ordinary political transactions have been unjustly criminalized under an excess of reformist zeal. This defense, however self-serving, has some merit, which this book will try to assess. Anticorruption endeavors feature their own excesses and abuses.

Whatever the issues of public policy and criminal justice at stake, George Ryan's improbable path from Kankakee to the governor's mansion directly helped or harmed the lives of many people along the way. The stories of three truck drivers and three accused murderers might help to explain much about his career.

The first truck driver, whose name is not recorded, was a Kankakee city employee. He merrily drove a city truck along the streets, carrying nothing but an old chair in the back, in a do-nothing patronage job. A resident, Russell Johnson, noticed and grew angry enough at such "ghost payrolling" to run for mayor. In 1985, he upset Republican mayor Thomas Ryan, George's older brother, who had served in that office for twenty years. After two terms, Democratic mayor Johnson himself was ousted as the local Republican machine regained control. (Upon George Ryan's conviction in 2006, Johnson remarked, "The things they accused him of happen every day in Kankakee."[2])

The second truck driver, unlike the anonymous Kankakee payroller who so incensed Russell Johnson, has a known name: Ricardo Guzman. A Mexican native, he obtained a truck driver's license through a bribe paid to an examiner for the Illinois secretary of state's office. Such bribes were funneled into Secretary of State George Ryan's campaign fund. After all, that was how things always seemed to be done in Kankakee—and Chicago and all over Illinois.

On November 8, 1994, Ryan was reelected secretary of state. That same day, Guzman was driving a truck on I-94 near Milwaukee. A bracket over a mud flap/taillight assembly dangled dangerously from the rear of the vehicle. Other truckers tried to warn Guzman over CB radio, but he did not understand English. The metal assembly fell off the truck onto the pavement.

Following in a Plymouth Grand Voyager were the Reverend Duane "Scott" Willis, his wife, Janet, and six of their nine children. The debris from Guzman's truck punctured the van's gas tank. A spark caused an explosion that killed the children, five of them in an instant. The eldest, twelve-year-old Benjamin, managed to extricate himself from the van along with his seriously burned parents, but he died the next day.

That horror provoked the Better Government Association of Chicago to investigate the secretary of state's office. An attorney for the Willises and the U.S. Justice Department likewise investigated. By 2005, as Ryan's racketeering trial loomed, the government's "Operation Safe Road" probe had netted seventy-two convictions or guilty pleas with no acquittals. Ryan continued to maintain his innocence.

The news media naturally focused on the political implications of the Operation Safe Road scandal, but as the name of the investigation suggests, unqualified truck drivers who obtained licenses by bribery threatened public safety. Just in the first year of Operation Safe Road and just at one licensing facility in Melrose Park, a Chicago suburb, supervisors admitted taking bribes from more than two hundred truckers. Only nine months after the scandal broke, the *Chicago Sun-Times* reported that, apart from the Willis family tragedy (not then directly linked to the scandal), falsely licensed Illinois truckers had caused fifty-nine accidents that injured at least twenty people. Two truckers died in their own fatal accidents. Eventually, federal investigators estimated "very conservatively" that nine people were killed in accidents involving falsely licensed truckers (my count is eleven). No truck drivers were indicted, because federal extortion laws treat them as victims of a bribery scheme, not its perpetrators.

The third trucker, Miodrag Dobrosavljevich, was not exactly a driver but the owner of a truck repair business. He is named here because he was the first trucking industry figure to be indicted in Operation Safe Road.

Safe Road became public knowledge soon after state and federal officers raided the Melrose Park office in September 1998. Such publicized raids against centers of vice and crime are a staple of Chicago-area history, dating at least to 1857. The Melrose Park raid prompted some of Secretary of State Ryan's associates to shred documents frantically and try to burn others over a barbecue grill.

Dobrosavljevich was indicted in October 1998 for racketeering conspiracy, extortion conspiracy, and mail fraud. He pleaded guilty to racketeering and was sentenced to fourteen months in prison and a fine of $4,000. For the next seven years, grand juries were impaneled, U.S. attorneys called news conferences, indictments were issued, the scandal steadily expanded, more people were indicted, more headlines blared.

Ryan's successor as secretary of state ordered the retesting of 550 holders of dubiously obtained Commercial Driver's Licenses. One driver stopped at green lights instead of red. Another did not know how to start his car. Of the 550, only 171 passed the test. Many others, including Guzman, simply did not show up for the examination, and their licenses were voided. Eventually, the state demanded retesting of more than 1,200 truckers.

Dobrosavljevich, Guzman, and the anonymous Kankakee trucker all had their connections to George Ryan, though he might never have met any of them. Toward the end of his four-year term as governor, the Illinois political community was convinced that Ryan would be indicted before he left office in January 2003 because an incumbent governor presents a bigger scalp to prosecutors than a mere retired hack. In the way that investigations of public corruption now seem to take forever, this belief was premature. Ryan was not indicted until December of that year. By that time, even many of his enemies recognized how tough he was, how he stood up under the punishment, took the blows.

The first murderer for our consideration is J. B. Hairston Sr. of Kankakee. He was convicted in 1974 of killing his girlfriend. She cowered in a public restroom while he fired a fatal shot through the door. Hairston then cradled her in his arms and, when police arrived, admitted his guilt.

At the time, Ryan was a state representative. The imprisoned Hairston appealed to him for clemency. Ryan wrote letters to state officials supporting the appeal. After all, Ryan explained, Hairston had been a customer of his pharmacy. Further, he knew him to be "hard-working and conscientious."[3] Later, while running for governor, Ryan proposed legislation mandating an automatic life sentence for anyone who shoots somebody during the commission of a crime. Challenged about Hairston while pushing that bill, Ryan said he did not remember the case. As for Hairston, clemency was denied, but he was released from prison in 1982.

The second alleged murderer—he was falsely accused—is Anthony Porter. During his 1983 trial for a double murder in Chicago, Porter's defense attorney fell asleep. The trial judge woke him up. (That judge, upholding a tradition of the Cook County judiciary, later was caught in an unrelated financial scandal and resigned.)

Porter came within fifty hours of execution. His family made funeral arrangements. But the Illinois Supreme Court granted a reprieve in late 1998 because Porter scored so low on an IQ test (51) that he probably did not understand what would soon happen to him or why. The delay gave the Center on Wrongful Convictions at Northwestern University Law School and Northwestern journalism students time to investigate Porter's case. Incredibly, the real killer soon confessed to the Northwestern team. Porter was released from prison on February 5, 1999. George Ryan had just become governor.

The first capital case to cross Ryan's desk was that of Andrew Kokoraleis. His crimes were so ghastly that they scarcely bear thought. He confessed to killing as many as eighteen women as part of a four-member satanic cult that kidnapped them, stabbed them with knives or ice picks, mutilated the corpses, and hid the remains. Sometimes they amputated a victim's breast with piano wire, masturbated on it, then ate the breast. Arrested in 1982, Kokoraleis was sentenced to life in prison for one murder and sentenced to death for another.

The most feverish advocate of the death penalty could hardly invent a seemingly more worthy candidate for the ultimate punishment than Kokoraleis. His appeals were exhausted in 1999. However, early that year, the *Chicago Tribune* published a five-part series documenting 381 cases in the United States, dating to 1963, in which courts had reversed murder convictions because of prosecutorial misconduct or errors. Of those cases, forty-six were in Illinois.

By March 1999, eleven men sentenced to death in Illinois had been cleared since the state had reinstated capital punishment in 1977. The new capital punishment law had been supported by then-representative George Ryan.

Governor Ryan agonized over whether the state should kill Kokoraleis. Ryan had never been much concerned with the issue of capital punishment—he was "for" it in the sense that it was a solid plank in the Republican law-and-order platform. After Anthony Porter and the *Tribune* revelations, though, capital punishment suddenly had a face. It was that of Kokoraleis, a shaved-headed, mustachioed, olive-skinned fiend whose life or death was in Ryan's hands. Ryan directed an aide to write the papers for a ninety-day stay of execution. At length, he decided that the law had been duly followed and the murderer was undoubtedly guilty. Kokoraleis was taken to a new super-maximum-security prison in Tamms in deep southern Illinois. To the last minute, he apparently believed that Ryan would grant a reprieve. He spent his final day praying with his brother. When the lethal shot was injected, he sighed three times and muttered softly to himself before he died on March 17, 1999, at the age of thirty-five. He was the last person to be executed in Illinois. Even after Ryan was sentenced to seventy-eight months in prison, he said, "I guess if I have any regrets as my time as Governor, it's that I executed a guy."[4]

Hairston, Porter, Kokoraleis—again with their connections to George Ryan. What do Ryan, the truckers, and the accused killers have in common? The politics of crime—or in a larger sense, the operations of the criminal justice system and of American democracy. The rise and fall of George Ryan might tell us much about how our democracy works and how it stumbles.

On the last working day of his administration, Friday, January 10, 2003, Ryan went to DePaul University Law School in Chicago to announce the pardons of four death row inmates. Their murder confessions allegedly had been tortured out of them by Chicago police. One of the favored torture techniques was called "bagging," covering the victim's head with a plastic typewriter cover until he struggled for breath and then lost consciousness. In this manner there were no visible marks of abuse on the body. Other methods included electric shocks to the genitals and plain, old-fashioned beatings.

Bill Kurtis, a noted television journalist and producer of documentaries, described the scene at DePaul in a book published in 2004, *The Death Penalty on Trial*. "Ryan looked up at their eager faces," Kurtis wrote. "He was an approachable, jolly sort of man. His short-cropped gray-white hair topped a round face giving him the warm look of a beloved grandfather. But today his face was rigid and serious. He frowned down at his notes. Then George Ryan took a deep breath and made history."[5]

A reader might wonder whether Kurtis ever met Ryan. "Beloved grandfather" indeed. Ryan's public persona was not that of a kindly grandfather. Instead, he seemed to be always grumpy and sour, appearing to frown even when smiling. He looked like the old man on your block who, when you were a kid, always yelled at you to keep off his lawn and don't touch his rose bushes. Ryan grew progressively crabbier as Operation Safe Road inflated.

Political consultants normally resent it whenever the opposing candidate gets "free media," his face and statements on television news. Advisers to Ryan's Democratic opponent in the gubernatorial election of 1998 actually were gleeful whenever Ryan got free media. They figured that his public image as a mean old man could only put voters off.

Even so, Ryan's persona was also that of a regular guy, an ordinary businessman-politician, a Kankakee everyman who talked straight—not one of what former U.S. representative Dan Rostenkowski of Chicago called "the blow-dried guys," those modern media politicians afraid to say anything unless it is first tested by polls and focus groups conducted by expensive consultants. Ryan's unpolished persona as a regular guy, just like you and me, might well have contributed to his popularity with voters during his thirty-six years in public office. He was, after all, the longest-serving public officer in Illinois. He never lost an election, at least not until a jury voted him down.

Ryan's defenders describe him, for all his gruffness, as a sentimental fellow at heart, a teddy bear underneath the belligerence, a softie who made late-night visits to his pharmacy customers to make sure they were all right. Two men who were no friends of Ryan's—one a journalist, the other a powerful Democrat—told me that Ryan had intervened to rescue their seriously ill family members from the health care bureaucracy and never asked for a payback. That is what Ryan loved: being a big shot, getting things done, building allegiances.

Ryan apparently was part of what sociologist David Riesman famously called "the lonely crowd." As a politician, Ryan was lonely because he had few true friends, only fellow politicians obsessed with their calculations of self-advancement. Apparently, there was no friend to tell him that what he was doing, scamming all this money, was wrong—or, if there was, Ryan could not hear him.

In any case, Ryan said at DePaul:

Three years ago, I was faced with startling information. We had exonerated not one, not two, but thirteen men [by that date] from Death Row.
They were found innocent. Innocent of charges for which they were sentenced to die. Can you imagine? We nearly killed innocent people. We
nearly injected them with a cocktail of deadly poisons so that they could
die in front of witnesses on a gurney. . . .

Half of the nearly 300 capital cases in Illinois had been reversed for
a new trial or re-sentencing. Nearly half! Thirty-three of the Death Row
inmates were represented at trial by an attorney who had been disbarred
or at some point suspended from practicing law.

I'm not a lawyer, but I don't think you need to be one to be appalled by
those statistics. I have one question: How does that happen?[6]

Notice how he presented his dilemma not as a governor, a high public official,
but as just an ordinary man from the heartland confronted by a broken system
that seemingly could not be fixed. One can imagine Ryan thinking, They want
me to put people to death? When the number of exonerated inmates on Illinois death row (thirteen) now exceeds the number of people we have executed
(twelve) since 1977? No way. I am going to pardon or commute the sentences
of each and every one. Okay, the families of the murder victims are going to go
ballistic. So be it. Let them revile me. And meanwhile, let the federal government
come after me for Operation Safe Road. They can't prove that I ever pocketed a
dishonest dollar. My conscience is clear. I sleep well at night.

1 See Kankakee for a Dime

Tom Ryan Sr. was an Irish Catholic, born in Maquoketa, Iowa, in 1900. The town lies on the Mississippi River at the center of the snout of eastern Iowa that presses against Illinois. To marry a local girl, Jeanette Bowman, Tom converted to Protestantism. Tom's father was a railroad worker; Jeanette's family was in the cattle business.

The couple's second son, George Homer Ryan, was born in Maquoketa on February 24, 1934. Eventually George would be kidded by the Illinois General Assembly, which passed a resolution in his "honor" stating that his family abandoned the town because he could never figure out how to pronounce it (it's Muh-COKE-eh-tuh).[1]

Tom Ryan earned a pharmacy degree. When George was one year old, Walgreens transferred his father from Maquoketa to Chicago. The family moved to Seventy-ninth Street and Cottage Grove Avenue, but Tom never actually lived there because the children contracted scarlet fever and the home was quarantined. After less than a year, Walgreens moved the Ryans to Kankakee, population then about 55,000. This was in the depths of the Great Depression, when bread was eight cents a loaf and the yearly average household income was $1,672.

Young George visited the Bowmans' farm in Maquoketa during the summers. "I'd stay with my grandfather and my uncles," he remembered. "They had a big cattle sale barn, and I'd go around with my uncle; he'd talk to all the farmers around the area and buy their cattle and get them to bring them into his sale barn on Saturday morning. I was maybe eight, nine years old. That's where I learned to drive. He let me drive the Chevy truck; I could hardly reach the pedals. I could drive it through the fields. They had me cut thistles. For a kid, it was a great job. [I'd] sort of help to sort cattle—they'd give me a whip, I'd run the gate."[2]

During the winters, George's chore at home was to wait for the coal truck to unload into the bin in the basement, then shovel coal into the stoker and take out the clinkers. Meanwhile, his father was hired away from Walgreens by an independent druggist and prospered. In 1948, Tom Ryan opened his first drugstore, at Dearborn and Court streets downtown. George, fourteen years old, started working there after school, sweeping up and jerking sodas. The experience of the Depression seared George, as it did nearly every member of his generation, yet his family was, for the time and place, upper-middle class. They had a maid, an almost unheard-of luxury, at their home at 904 Cobb Boulevard.

"Whatever [George] thought, he said," recalled the maid, Mary Frances Crossley, who lived to age 102. "He was just like his mother. She didn't keep nothing in. But they all treated me like I was one of the family."[3] Crossley helped to care for George, his older brother, Tom Jr., a sister, Kathleen, and an adopted sister, Elizabeth, called "Nancy." Harry Schrey, a friend of Tom and Jeanette's, had died in 1947, a year after his wife died, leaving their daughter an orphan. The Ryans took fifteen-year-old Nancy into their household, although she was not legally adopted.

That George caught Lura Lynn Lowe's eye—or vice versa, it was never clear which—in freshman English class at Kankakee High School became a staple of newspaper personality profiles of the Ryans. Lura Lynn was born in a rural community called Aroma Park on the southeast border of Kankakee on July 5, 1934, the daughter of a hybrid seed merchant. Her father and grandfather had developed a variety of hybrid corn sold across the country, but then the business was lost in a fire. In high school, Lura Lynn and George, a letterman in football and basketball, dated steadily. They were graduated in 1952.

Kankakee seemed to exemplify the national prosperity of the 1950s, just as later it hunkered on the leading edge of the Rust Belt economic plunge of the 1980s. Local firms manufactured furniture, stoves, hot water heaters, and ladders (all those plants are gone now). The population jumped from 73,524 in 1950 to 92,063 in 1960. The 1950s also birthed two major features of modern American life—the shopping mall and the interstate highway system. Kankakee opened its first mall, called Meadowview, in 1955. Tom Ryan's drugstore was one of the original tenants. Sons Tom and George helped stock the shelves.

Business was so good that downtown traffic congestion was a problem. Especially irritating were the clogged streets on football weekends when Northwestern University in Evanston, north of Chicago, played the University of Illinois at Urbana, south of Kankakee. Partly to get all that once-a-year football traffic out of town, city fathers routed the new Interstate 57 more than a mile east of Kankakee in 1959. The harm thereby visited on the downtown business district might seem obvious now, but it was not in 1959.

The 1950s also was the decade of the so-called Silent Generation, complacent conformists unlike the hell-raising rebels who followed in the 1960s. It was the era of *The Organization Man,* a 1956 book based on a sociological study of the postwar Chicago suburb of Park Forest. The silent organization man meekly followed the beaten paths of the businesses and professions. Both of these myths, the Silent Generation and the Organization Man, are doubtless exaggerated. In the case of young George Ryan, he certainly was no rebel, but like many young men of all times, he seems to have fumbled a bit for a career. After high school, he spent a restless year taking pharmacy classes at Butler University in Indianapolis while waiting to get drafted.

The U.S. Army came calling in 1954 and sent twenty-year-old draftee Ryan to Korea a year after the war there had ended. "When he was in Korea," his criminal defense attorney said many years later, "in his free time he devoted himself to feeding starving Korean kids who he discovered were going to a garbage dump looking for food."[4] Ryan himself remembered this episode a bit more modestly. "When the army found out that I had some background in pharmacy, they assigned me to the air force in Korea, to run the pharmacy at the air force base hospital," he said. "For thirteen months that's what I did. So during the course of my service, I got involved with the local people that came in the hospital. . . . I got to know kids that worked there, civilian kids that worked on the base, in the kitchens. We took care of them, gave them shots, gave them medicines when they needed it. They would come in and say, 'Oh, my son is very sick,' and medical care wasn't the best outside of the base. We'd help them when we could."[5]

When Ryan got home, he married Lura Lynn Lowe in the First Methodist Church of Kankakee on June 10, 1956. Ryan said he had dated a couple of girls when he was at Butler University, but Lura Lynn was his only real girlfriend. She had been working in the MacCarthy Tractor Sales office. Her sister was her matron of honor, and Tom Ryan Jr. was George's best man. The couple honeymooned in Wisconsin. Their first child, Nancy, was born a year later. By then, George was attending Ferris State College in Big Rapids, Michigan.

George, Lura Lynn, George's sister Kathleen, and her husband, Duane Dean, lived together in Big Rapids while both men studied pharmacy. George's older brother, Tom, already had a pharmacy degree; George earned his in 1961, shortly after his daughter Lynda was born. The Ryans moved to Aroma Park to live with Lura Lynn's grandparents. The next year, the Ryans had triplet girls—Julie, Joanne, and Jeanette. That was the year young pharmacist George served as campaign manager for state senator Edward McBroom. In 1964, the Ryans had their last child, a son, George Homer Jr.

"A drugstore is a good training place" for a politician, Ryan said. "Even when I was in the Illinois House, I used to come home and work the pharmacy on weekends. You deal with a lot of people. They come in, young mothers, elderly people, they want to get straightened out with their medicines. You get a chance to talk to them about their kids and themselves."[6]

In 1965, the Ryans bought a house at 912 South Greenwood Avenue. It was called the Mann House after a former mayor, Fred Mann, who had built the house in 1911. The Ryans paid $34,000 for it, and it is still their residence. At the time, the median house price in the United States was $21,500. Like many American politicians, Ryan likes to speak of his humble origins, but they were not so humble. Their large, red-brick house was in a designated historical district a block away from Polk Park, which sits on the bank of the Kankakee River.

The town name retains a minor but real place in American popular culture. Steve Goodman noted in his 1971 song about a train called "City of New Orleans" that it headed south from Kankakee. That happened to be the same year the Illinois Central Railroad stopped running passengers on that train, giving way to Amtrak and the ongoing decline of passenger service.

Illinois Central workers, with the help of vote fraud, had pretty much created the city and county of Kankakee back in the 1850s. An effort to carve Kankakee County out of Will and Iroquois counties failed in an 1851 referendum. Two years later, residents tried again, and Kankakee County was christened with the help of 360 votes from a settlement named Limestone. Oddly, Limestone had cast only 92 votes for the measure in 1851. Anticipating a long history of alleged vote fraud in Illinois, an outcry was raised, an appeal was filed, and nothing came of it. Then the issue was which town, Momence or Kankakee, should be the county seat. Kankakee at the time comprised a railroad right-of-way, a store, and one abandoned log cabin. Illinois Central work gangs cast multiple votes, Limestone's returns were reliably 250 to 0 in favor of Kankakee, and thus the city and county seat were born. Coveted railroad rights-of-way brought prosperity to many localities in that era.

In the twentieth century, the McBrooms helped build the town. In 1908, brothers Victor, Stanley, and Vernon McBroom bought a bankrupt restaurant on Schuyler Avenue. In 1915, Victor was elected assistant supervisor of Kankakee Township. In 1920, he joined the firm of his father-in-law, E. A. Jeffers. That business became the Cadillac dealership on Washington Avenue just south of the Kankakee River. It was the epicenter of local Republican politics for six decades. The family supported a local politician, Lennington Small.

The career of Len Small (1862–1936) was almost banal both in its steady ascent of Illinois politics and in its corruption. Born a farm boy on the edge of Kankakee, Small became clerk of the circuit court, a Republican state committeeman, and a trustee of the original Kankakee State Hospital. His name was first smudged with scandal in 1902 with revelations that his hospital patronage workers were forced to give money to Republican candidates.

Small served two terms as state treasurer. He apparently was so corrupt that after each term, laws were passed to tighten the regulation of public funds, extraordinary acts for the Illinois General Assembly, normally indifferent to such matters. By the time he was elected governor in 1920, Small was a farmer, banker, and publisher of the *Kankakee Daily Journal*.

Effective control of the local press meant that machine politicians received favorable coverage no matter what they did. When Ryan was governor, he seemed largely unconcerned with what newspapers said about him except for the *Daily Journal*. That is how parochial he was, even though as governor he made unprecedented trips to Cuba and South Africa.

Governor Small placed his two sons and a son-in-law in high-level jobs in his administration. In 1921, the state's attorney general indicted Small on charges of laundering money during his time as treasurer. Small allegedly had deposited state funds in a Kankakee bank, lent the money to Chicago meatpackers, and collected interest at 6 percent. He reimbursed the state at 2 or 3 percent. Almost certainly, the jury that acquitted Small was bribed. He and his wife, Ida Moore Small, were celebrating his acquittal that evening when Ida suffered a stroke. She died the next day.

The attorney general next charged Small in a civil suit. In the 1924 election, Small ousted that attorney general with a candidate of his own. In 1927, the state supreme court upheld a judgment of $1,025,424 against Small. The governor's new attorney general reduced that sum to $650,000 and declared that Small had not taken money illegally. Small continued in cahoots with Chicago mayor "Big Bill" Thompson and Al Capone, but apparently he had angered even Illinois voters, who are hard to displease when it comes to corruption. Small lost the 1928 Republican gubernatorial primary.

Kankakee was not thereby cleaned up, though. A locally famed madam named Nell Clark was first arrested in 1913. She spent so much time being pampered in the city jail that her corner cell was called the "bridal suite." Clark was still operating her brothel at 367 West Avenue when she died in 1942.

The government of Kankakee was for sale, a fact metaphorically expressed by Groucho Marx in the song "Lydia the Tattooed Lady" in the 1939 Marx Brothers movie *At the Circus*. Lydia, the song said, would expose her epidermis, displaying Kankakee and other worldly sights, for a dime. Maybe Groucho intended no comment at all on the culture of Kankakee and merely found an obscure and faintly comical, Indian-derived, three-syllable place name to fill the meter of the lyric. Even if unwittingly, though, the line suggests that Kankakee was for sale and a bit salacious. According to local lore, Kankakee was given a choice of hosting a state hospital for the insane or the University of Illinois. The town chose the hospital because it offered more opportunities for patronage jobs. The legend is apocryphal—the university was placed in Urbana ten years before the hospital came to Kankakee—but like many legends it expresses an underlying truth.

In any case, the McBrooms more or less ran Kankakee until Victor's grandson Edward died in 1990. There was even a movie star McBroom—Marden "Andy" McBroom, Victor's nephew. Using the stage name David Bruce and wearing a pencil-thin mustache in vogue at the time, Marden acted in seventy-two Hollywood movies and in television during the 1940s and 1950s. He had minor roles in war movies such as *Sergeant York* and *Sands of Iwo Jima* and larger roles in horror films such as *The Mad Ghoul*. (The actor Fred MacMurray, a leading man during the same era, also was born in Kankakee.) Marden McBroom's sister, Amanda, was a singer and songwriter in Los Angeles. She composed "The Rose," a 1979 hit for Bette Midler. (Another civic claim to fame: singer Barry Manilow got his first solo job as a cocktail pianist at The Little Corporal in Kankakee.)

As all dynasties must, the McBrooms' withered away. The Manteno Mental Health Center, where the McBrooms famously controlled patronage, closed in 1985—very hard times in general for Kankakee—and lost its last 876 jobs. Edward McBroom, born in 1925, had joined his father's Jeffers and McBroom Company at age twenty-one. At his funeral in 1990, the eulogy was given by Lieutenant Governor George Ryan, whom Edward had recruited into politics. An honorary pallbearer was Tom Ryan Jr., whom Edward had made mayor of Kankakee. The *Daily Journal* noted that McBroom's mother was a Republican precinct committeewoman and that his maternal grandfather, Jeffers, had served on the GOP committee under Governor Small. Small's great-grandson still controlled the *Daily Journal*. Again like many dynasties, the McBrooms had their family dysfunctions. Edward was so estranged from a son that the son was not even listed as a survivor in the *Daily Journal*'s obituary. Edward believed that this son's wife was, literally, a witch. Edward's death terminated the dynasty, which yielded to the Ryans.

According to George, the Ryans had a terrible time trying to decide whether to get involved in politics. In 1961, Kankakee committed heresy—it elected a Democratic mayor, Ray Nourie. The McBrooms were not about to see him reelected and slated George's brother, Tom Jr., for mayor in 1965. George Ryan said, "My father had retired and gone to Phoenix. We never had been involved in politics, and the second thing was, our business was growing. Some people said, 'Aw, you get involved in politics and your business will go to hell.' Another guy says, 'Aw, come on, you have a civic obligation to do it.'" The brothers worked for the family business, Ryan Pharmacies, Incorporated. Although they were doing well, they could not afford to hire another pharmacist to allow time off for campaigning. "In the end," Ryan said, "we decided that it was an obligation that we had to do."[7] George was Tom's campaign manager.

Tom was a navy veteran and past president of the Kankakee Shrine Club, while his wife, Stella, belonged to the Eastern Star. Such lodge connections are highly important in small-town politics. Also, Tom was a good baseball player for an American Legion team—in those days, small towns fielded amateur teams against neighboring towns; today, ubiquitous media distractions have killed off such recreations. The *Daily Journal* called Tom's 55 percent share of the mayoral vote "overwhelming." Twenty years later, he was defeated by a Democrat, Russell Johnson. Honoring tradition, Tom then took a do-nothing "ghost payroller" job with the state Department of Transportation.

In 1966, the county supervisor from George's district became a judge, opening a vacancy on the county board. Ed McBroom had George Ryan appointed to the post. "It was an easy job to take," Ryan said, "because once a week you went down to the courthouse and had a few meetings. Spend a few hours and that was it, didn't take a lot of time." He was elected in his own right in 1968 and in 1970 was selected as board president. "It was another good training ground," Ryan said, "especially to learn about—hell, I didn't know anything about what the General Assembly was about. I was working, had a bunch of kids."[8]

Indeed, the Ryans made their contribution to the postwar baby boom. They had six children under the age of eight—actually, five were still in diapers—when they moved into the place on South Greenwood Avenue. Lura Lynn ran two washers and two dryers in the basement almost around the clock. She was a housewife while George was the breadwinner in the style of the prerevolution. A man of his times, George was not exceptionally helpful with household chores. Instead, he developed his business and political careers.

When Lura Lynn could not take it anymore, she would ask George to book a weekend at the old Water Tower or Sherman hotel in downtown Chicago, then leave the kids with a family friend. "We'd check into the hotel," Lura Lynn remembered. "I'd go to bed and sleep. He'd bring all the reading material and things he wanted to catch up on and do that while I was sleeping. George would order food to the room, wake me up. I'd eat it, then go back to sleep."[9]

One time when Lura Lynn had had enough was a Christmas Eve. An elderly woman called George to say she suddenly had a bright idea to give her cat catnip as a Christmas present and wanted him to bring some to her. George dutifully put on his coat to go to the pharmacy over Lura Lynn's objections to leaving his family on Christmas Eve. "Honey, I have to," George said. "You see, her cat is all she has."[10] Even many of Ryan's enemies conceded that, whatever his flaws, he sincerely wanted to help people. How a man so tender-hearted also could be so venal remains a puzzle.

In 1972, Ryan was slated for the state House of Representatives. The *Chicago Tribune,* then and now a Republican-leaning publication, endorsed Ryan for Kankakee voters. By his third term, Ryan was the House Republican leader. He rose to become Speaker of the House, lieutenant governor, secretary of state, and governor. He never perceived that the Kankakee way of politics was outdated, let alone unethical. Throughout his career, political scientists and journalists were writing obituaries of urban political machines. If Ryan ever noticed these writings, he would have scorned them. When Ryan was sentenced to prison in 2006, his friends said he still did not think he had done anything wrong. He had told the *Kankakee Daily Journal* as much earlier that summer. The jury just made a mistake, he said, and we'll get it fixed on appeal. Sentencing judges normally want to hear some expression of contrition from the convict, but Ryan apparently was oblivious of that.

2 Smell the Meat a-Cookin'

Nearly four decades after the event, the word "shoebox" remains a metonym for political corruption in Illinois. Democratic secretary of state Paul Powell died in October 1970. Two days later, the executor of his estate found $800,419 in cash in a shoebox, briefcases, and strongboxes in his residence in a Springfield hotel. Also stored were forty-nine cases of whiskey, fourteen transistor radios, and, inexplicably, two cases of creamed corn. One shoebox could hardly hold $800,000 in cash, but the mythical "$800,000 shoebox" captured the public imagination and, indeed, enchanted the news media across the nation. The actual shoebox was displayed each May at Powell Day in his hometown for many years until the widow of the executor of Powell's estate decided that it was falling apart.

The parallels between the careers of Paul Powell and George Ryan seemingly were invented by a novelist seeking implausible coincidences. Powell became his party's leader in the House, then Speaker, then a two-term secretary of state.

In the interest of geographical ticket-balancing, Chicago Democrats backed Powell, from Vienna in the hills of deep southern Illinois, for secretary of state in 1964. They promised to give $300,000 to his campaign, big money at the time. Powell insisted he wanted no checks or pledges, just cash. He told a friend, "Old Paul is going to have some of this money left over when this race is done, 'cause I'm not going to spend it all."[1] Throughout his tenure, citizens paying their driver's license fees wrote the checks, not to a state agency, but to Paul Powell personally. This practice was eliminated after Powell's term, just as reforms followed Len Small's time as state treasurer and Ryan's as secretary of state.

"I can smell the meat a-cookin'," Powell said after Democrats took over the state House in 1948, the year Harry Truman was elected president and Adlai Stevenson governor. Like Powell's shoebox, that olfactory observation of his became part of Illinois lore. Powell was elected Speaker even without Stevenson's support. Like Ryan, he favored carrying large amounts of cash yet was a notorious moocher. Even so, again like Ryan, he tipped big. He was wont to hand over $100 bills to visitors in his office, urge them to buy a $100 U.S. savings bond for $87.50, and spend the rest on a good steak dinner (this was before the double-digit inflation of the 1970s). His state salary never exceeded $30,000, but Powell's estate was settled at $4.6 million. A young lawyer named Jayne Carr worked on a case against Powell's estate; she later became Governor James R. Thompson's wife.

Powell's was far from the first example of spectacular political thievery in the state. In 1956, the press revealed that Republican state auditor Orville E. Hodge had stolen $2,500,008. Like Powell and Ryan, Hodge was a high-living man about town, the sort who was everybody's pal. He was especially friendly with members of the so-called West Side Bloc, Republicans from Chicago's West Side who protected the interests of organized crime. (By the 1980s, this breed was nearly extinct yet still potent enough to help pass some of Governor Thompson's bills unrelated to crime.) In 1955, the House, with only two nays, voted Hodge's office an emergency appropriation of $525,000. He stole every nickel of it.

Governor during this time was William G. Stratton, elected in 1952 at age thirty-eight as a "boy wonder" Republican. The Hodge scandal threatened to sink the Republican ticket in 1956, so Chicago mayor Richard J. Daley obligingly fielded a patsy as Stratton's Democratic opponent. Still another fixture of Illinois political lore is that Democratic mayors of Chicago actually prefer Republican governors to Democratic ones. This arrangement secures the mayor's status as the state's most powerful Democrat while inviting deal-making with Spring-field. Democratic mayors and Republican governors tend to strike deals, adding weight to the cynical thought that politicians always sell out, so you should vote for your opponent because he will sell out to you. Stratton and Daley cut a deal to raise state and city sales taxes. Later, Daley and Governor Richard Ogilvie struck a deal to impose a state income tax. Still later, James Thompson made deals with Mayor Harold Washington in the 1980s, as did George Ryan with Daley's son, Mayor Richard M. Daley, in 1998 and after. In many ways, Ryan's career was commonplace in Illinois.

Governor Stratton, like his predecessor Small and successors Ogilvie, Thompson, Ryan, and others, was preoccupied with patronage. Awarding sinecures and jobs to the politically worthy while denying them to the unworthy was an accepted practice. When the governor's office changed parties, many state workers of the other party routinely were fired. Shortly after Stratton took office, a bureaucrat in the state agriculture department wanted to fire an employee who had been a Democratic candidate for office. He worried, though, that civil service regulations might protect the worker. "What do you have to do to justify a discharge under Civil Service? Is a conviction and sentence for murder necessary?" the bureaucrat asked a Stratton aide.[2] The bureaucrat's memo did not specify whether he thought that, on the scale of felonies, running as a Democrat was a greater or lesser crime than homicide. Later, Thompson avidly promoted patronage to the extent that the U.S. Supreme Court slapped him down with an antipatronage ruling in 1990.

Two other things that Governors Small, Stratton, Kerner, Ogilvie, Thompson, Ryan, and others had in common were (1) the lavish provision of road-building and other pork-barrel projects and (2) the enthusiastic collection of campaign contributions from interest groups. After leaving office, Stratton was indicted for tax evasion for not reporting the personal use of campaign funds, but he was acquitted in 1965. This case established that Illinois politicians may spend campaign funds for personal matters, a practice now outlawed.

As for the General Assembly, it was notoriously bought off by lobbies, in particular the racing and trucking industries. State senator Paul Simon, later a U.S. senator and presidential hopeful, wrote in *Harper's* that in Springfield, "cold cash passes directly from one hand to another."[3] For his trouble, his colleagues voted him a "Benedict Arnold Award." Such was the legislature that Ryan joined in 1973.

Patronage; collection of funds from interest groups and the concealment thereof; a reputation for chronic corruption and pork barrel; a Chicago-downstate, urban-rural political axis—the pattern of Ryan's governorship was ingrained long before he took that office. As Ryan was growing up in politics in Kankakee, he knew about the Len Small scandal, the Orville Hodge scandal, the William Stratton scandal, and the Paul Powell shoebox, not to mention perennial prosecutions of sundry aldermen, circuit judges, and state legislators. In Kankakee itself, Sheriff Carl McNutt allowed prisoners to escape and used another as a chauffeur. A jury at first cleared McNutt, but he pleaded guilty to two other charges in 1962, briefly took a state ghost payroller job, and died. Then, as Ryan was preparing to run for the state House in 1972, U.S. attorney James R. Thompson was battering former governor Otto Kerner and Mayor Daley's machine with indictments.

Thompson was perhaps the most important political figure in Ryan's career, though it would be an error to see theirs as a mentor-protégé relationship. Their relationship was much more complicated. As governor, Thompson never particularly hungered for Ryan to be his Speaker of the House, lieutenant governor, or secretary of state. When Ryan was a freshman legislator, "Big Jim" Thompson (somehow Illinois politicians are never nicknamed "Little") was a young U.S. attorney who had the Chicago Democratic machine on the run.

Even earlier, the Republican sheriff of Cook County, Richard Ogilvie, had been giving local Democrats fits. Ogilvie was elected governor in 1968, and both Thompson and Ryan launched their careers during his administration. A nearly overlooked irony is that Ryan arose under Republican governors—Ogilvie and Thompson—who both had reputations for putting crooked politicians in jail.

For that matter, the Democratic governor from 1961 to 1967, Otto Kerner, was himself a former U.S. attorney in Chicago. His record in battling corruption was not stellar, though. During one of Chicago's periodic spasms of reform, he insisted, "There is no such thing as organized crime or syndicated crime or gambling. It is only newspaper talk."[4]

President Lyndon B. Johnson named Governor Kerner to head a national commission to study the urban riots of the 1960s. Partly as a reward for that service, Johnson appointed Kerner to the federal appeals court in 1967. (The lieutenant governor who served the rest of Kerner's term, Samuel H. Shapiro, was from Kankakee; young George had served Shapiro milkshakes at his dad's drugstore.) Kerner's elevation to the bench would profoundly change the lives of Thompson and Ryan in ways they could not have foreseen. Indeed, the fallout from that seemingly routine presidential appointment to the judiciary would alter the national polity in a manner still not completely understood.

Ogilvie served one term as governor, 1969–73. He openly strove to build a state Republican patronage machine to rival Daley's Chicago and Cook County Democratic machine. The battle between Ogilvie's Republican pragmatists and Republican conservative ideologues still is being fought. Pragmatic, moderate governors such as Dick Ogilvie, Jim Thompson, Jim Edgar, and George Ryan made conservatives gnash their teeth. Why the religious right wing never captured the state GOP in Illinois as it did in many other states is a question that might profitably be explored. One theory is that the wealthy businessmen who financed right-wing campaigns in Illinois were inept political amateurs.[5] Ryan honed his pragmatism in the 1968 Ogilvie campaign and never was a member of the religious right, though he sometimes pretended to be.

Midpoint in Ogilvie's term, voters approved a new Illinois state constitution. One provision of it gave governors an "amendatory veto" to rewrite statutes, subject to legislative approval. Intended merely to streamline governmental processes, this seemingly technical clause much enhanced the power of Ogilvie's Democratic successor, Dan Walker, followed by Republicans Thompson, Edgar, and Ryan.

There are two major legends about Ogilvie. The first is that he was incorruptible. Ogilvie had been a rackets-busting Cook County sheriff. In fact, there is some evidence that Ogilvie had made accommodations with organized crime to get elected sheriff.[6] The second legend is that he was defeated for reelection as governor in 1972 because he had the guts to pass an Illinois income tax to rescue state finances. He sacrificed his political career for the public good. Maybe so, but Ogilvie also had signed a law banning household leaf-burning, an unpopular antipollution measure at the time. Worse, he sent state police on raids against American Legion halls in southern Illinois that housed illegal slot machines in the back rooms. (In the early 1950s, Democratic governor Adlai Stevenson likewise had dispatched raids against gambling dens downstate, but not those in Cook County.) There is a saying in Illinois politics that downstate cannot elect you, but it can beat you. Whatever the electoral consequences of the income tax, Democratic mayor Daley in Chicago and American Legionnaires downstate helped to defeat Ogilvie.

20

Meanwhile, Jim Thompson was the U.S. attorney in Chicago under President Nixon's administration. Thompson maintains that he never really wanted that job. The previous U.S. attorney, William Bauer, happened to watch Thompson argue a case before the state supreme court. He tendered Thompson a job offer: first assistant U.S. attorney.

But Thompson had the notion that he would follow in Ogilvie's footsteps by being elected Cook County sheriff and then governor. Dismayed by Bauer's offer, Thompson called Governor Ogilvie in Springfield, drove there in a rainstorm, and begged to be slated for Cook County sheriff.

"Why on earth would you want to be sheriff of Cook County?"

"Because I want to be governor."

"That's the craziest idea I ever heard."[7]

Yet that was the very path Ogilvie had tramped to the governor's mansion. Big Jim returned to Chicago and asked the county Republican central committee to slate him for sheriff. They listened politely, then slated Thompson's alderman instead (he lost).

U.S. attorney Bauer persisted, inviting Ogilvie and Thompson to lunch at the Union League Club in Chicago, a storied venue of political deal-making since shortly after the Civil War. Still no sale, Thompson said. So then Bauer hauled him to a nearby restaurant. "He kept ordering double martinis for me. And at four o'clock in the afternoon I agreed to be the first assistant U.S. attorney. About a year later [in 1971] I became U.S. attorney."[8]

This is a story that Thompson likes to tell. Surely, though, he was not unaware of the political benefits of the publicity surrounding his prosecutions of Daley machine members. Another story Thompson likes to tell is that he indicted two-thirds of the Republican members of the Chicago city council—there were three of them then (out of fifty), and he indicted two.

A shambling, imposing six-foot-six, Thompson became a natural Republican candidate for governor in 1976. Daley feared, though, that he really wanted to run for the larger, in Daley's eyes, office of mayor. Thompson had announced in 1943 at age seven that when he grew up he wanted to be president of the United States. Even so, he started out as a shy, awkward campaigner. His 1976 campaign consultants told him he should lose weight, get married, and get a dog. Thompson complied with all three directives and became a brilliant, cornpone campaigner.

He was the longest-serving governor of Illinois, fourteen years. In 1990, he stepped down to become a rainmaker partner in a Chicago law firm. Thompson, the former fighting prosecutor, provided the defense counsel for George Ryan. Thompson's law firm, Winston and Strawn, gave Ryan an estimated $20 million worth of legal defense for free. People thought, wow, those guys, Thompson and Ryan, must be the best friends in the world. The larger irony was mostly unnoticed. Thompson had pioneered the very legal theory under which Ryan later was prosecuted.

A racing impresario, Marjorie Lindheimer Everett, gave sweetheart stock deals to Governor Kerner and his top aide during the 1960s. Everett then deducted the value of those stocks from her income tax returns, reasoning that bribery was an ordinary and necessary business expense in Illinois. The Internal Revenue Service frowned on this interpretation of the tax laws. In due course, the IRS referred the matter to the Nixon Justice Department.

"Marje" Everett had, if not a legal, at least a commonsense argument. In Illinois, the sport of kings was the sport of crooks. When payoffs were offered, politicians came spinning out of the turn as eagerly as the racehorses themselves. Paul Powell's estate had included nearly $1 million in racing stocks—racing payoffs helped to stuff, metaphorically, his shoebox.

In Kerner's case, though, U.S. attorney William Bauer had trouble finding a law that the former governor might have broken. Kerner had not directly stolen any money from private persons or taxpayers. He merely had accepted a sweetheart stock deal from Everett, then rewarded her with favorable racing dates and other boons from state government.

An assistant U.S. attorney dusted off an 1872 mail fraud statute and said Kerner might be indicted for depriving the citizens of Illinois of his "loyal and honest service" in office. The young lawyer's boss, Bauer, scoffed. "Do you mean to tell me if some guy sends a love letter to his mistress he's defrauded his wife of his loyal service?"[9]

Don't laugh—the "honest service" provision of mail fraud has been applied so broadly since then, that might happen. The definition of "honest service" has tied U.S. courts in knots for decades. Bauer's successor, Jim Thompson, aggressively pressed honest-service cases against Kerner and many others. Shortly before Christmas in 1972, U.S. attorney Thompson and his first assistant, Samuel K. Skinner (later White House chief of staff for President George H. W. Bush), visited Kerner in his judge's chambers to inform him that a grand jury would return an indictment against him the next day. "A fine Christmas present that is," Kerner said bitterly.

At trial, Kerner's stiff-necked, how-dare-you-impugn-my-integrity demeanor did not aid his defense. He was convicted of mail fraud, conspiracy, tax evasion, and perjury and sentenced to three years in prison. Kerner was the first U.S. appellate judge ever convicted of felonies. When doctors discovered he had lung cancer, Thompson joined in signing a legal petition that won Kerner's release for ill health. He died in 1975.

Although Thompson later was elected governor four times, his national influence in championing honest-service cases to stamp out both public and private corruption still is not properly appreciated. He fathered an epidemic of indictments of public officials in the Watergate era of the 1970s and after. Thirty years later, Thompson defended Ryan against those very same honest-service charges. In an interview with me, Thompson expressed no regrets about his pioneering the honest-service, mail-fraud attack that the criminal defense bar, civil libertarians, and some judges have said has produced overzealous prosecution in an age of overexcited reform. Whatever one thinks of politicians, there really is such a thing as overzealous prosecution.

George Ryan, for one, felt the prosecution of him was overzealous. Like Kerner, he had not directly embezzled money or taken bribes. Ryan surely thought, They are outlawing ordinary political transactions now? Is this what we have come to? How can anything get done? Ed McBroom took care of me and my brother Tom, and then I took care of Tom with a state job, and all the time—this is the point—we served our constituents well. Don't they understand?

The paradox that Ryan was a sentimental, sweethearted guy at the same time that he was depressingly petty in his venality already has been posed. Another mystery is why Illinois politicians keep taking dirty money, no matter how many ethics laws get passed and how many officeholders hear jailhouse doors clanging behind them. Will they never learn? It cannot be something in the water because, as a wit has noted, Wisconsin also borders Lake Michigan, but that state has a longstanding reputation for clean government. One point that seems clear is that Ryan did not properly heed Section 1346 of the U.S. mail fraud statute: "honest service" is required of public officials.

The feds went on to investigate Ryan's Democratic successor as governor, Rod Blagojevich, elected on an anticorruption platform in 2002, for allegedly corrupt acts. In one indictment of an influence peddler, Blagojevich was thinly veiled as "Public Official A," just as Ryan had been early in Operation Safe Road. Nevertheless, Illinois voters reelected Blagojevich in 2006.

3 What Can I Do for You?

The election of legislative leaders normally is a sedate formality, the leaders already having been chosen in the proverbial smoke-filled rooms of party caucuses. It happened that George Ryan in his early legislative years witnessed three explosively prolonged elections of leaders. The first was an eight-ballot contest for Speaker in 1973, the second a ninety-three-ballot fight for Speaker in 1975, and the third a 186-ballot war for president of the Illinois Senate in 1977. These struggles schooled him in how tough intraparty politics can get, if he needed any such instruction.

A Democrat, Daniel Walker, had upset Ogilvie for governor in 1972. Still, Republicans held on to the General Assembly by one vote in the House, 89–88, and one in the Senate, 30–29. This was the drill for Ryan's first day as a state representative, January 10, 1973:

Secretary of State Michael J. Howlett called the House to order at noon. The House adopted Resolution 1, ordaining that the secretary of state call upon the Illinois Supreme Court to request that one of the justices administer the oath of office to the members-elect, whereupon Justice Howard Ryan came and duly swore them in. The House then adopted Resolution 2, requiring the election of a Speaker. After this ceremonial rigmarole, the House fell into an uproar for the next nine hours.

The Republican contenders were Henry Hyde, then of Park Ridge, a suburb on the Northwest Side of Chicago, and W. Robert Blair, of Park Forest, a new postwar-planned town south of Chicago. (Park Ridge is the hometown of Hillary Rodham Clinton, Park Forest the locale of William H. Whyte's classic sociological study of 1956, *The Organization Man*.) Hyde was a conservative true believer, Blair a pragmatic practitioner of patronage. Whom did George Ryan support? The practical pol.

Senator Ed McBroom called Ryan and asked, "Who you gonna be for Speaker?"

"I don't know, I kinda like Hyde."

"Well, lemme tell you, Hyde comes from up north. Bob Blair is in our neighboring county [his district included part of Will County], and we do things together. . . . Blair is in our best interests to be Speaker, governmentally, politically."[1] Ryan thereupon voted for Blair.

Observers often see such leadership elections as personality contests or ideological clashes. In fact, this one was geographical as much as anything. It reflected the eternal regional split between Cook County and downstate.

Also, Blair was then a better politician than Hyde, although Hyde went on to become a powerful U.S. congressman, indeed the leader of the House prosecution of President Clinton in the Senate impeachment trial of 1999. In 1973, Blair outfoxed Hyde by cutting deals with Republicans and Democrats alike. Since Republicans had just a one-vote majority, Democrats were ripe for striking deals to help elect a Republican Speaker.

The Speaker would appoint legislative committee chairs, control the flow of legislation, and hand out patronage. Understanding that power, not ideology, was at stake, Blair agreed to allow Hyde's supporters to name four-tenths of the committee chairs. Moreover, Blair signed a pact agreeing not to retaliate against Republicans who had fought against him—and a politician putting such agreements in writing is a rarity. Blair expressed indignation at having to sign the deal, objecting that doing so impugned his integrity. He quickly double-crossed on the deal anyway. Blair also did not scruple to cut deals with the aforementioned West Side Bloc of Chicago Republicans beholden to organized crime.

On the other side of the aisle, Blair consorted with a powerful Democrat such that certain representatives stayed off the floor, at least in the early ballots. Democrats had their own liberal-conservative split, and some of their conservatives wanted Hyde. At 10:05 P.M., Blair was elected on the eighth ballot with all eighty-nine Republican votes for him, none for Hyde. Blair promised Hyde he could continue to serve as majority leader, then reneged. The new majority leader was William Walsh, who would loom large in Ryan's later career. Some of Hyde's backers were so enraged that they threatened to caucus separately and hire their own staff. In the way that pragmatism trumps ideology in Illinois, their apostasy soon came to nothing. Blair proceeded to spend $838,000 to renovate the House, expanded the floor by carving out space under the rear gallery, and exiled Representative Hyde's seat to that cavern.

For all that, Ryan, the master politician, made no enemy of Hyde. "He was a very nice man, cordial, friendly. He always closed a phone conversation with, 'What can I do for you?'" Hyde remembered.[2]

These intricate maneuvers of many years ago have been reviewed in some detail because they formed the midlevel course work in Ryan's political academy. Blair was, so to speak, Whyte's organization man, not an idealist, not a rebel or reformer. Nor was his supporter Ryan. Blair and Ryan might have personified another sociological type as members of "the lonely crowd." Calculations of career advancement drove Blair's and Ryan's actions at the expense of other values.

In a bow to protocol, Speaker Blair invited his major Democratic opponent to join him at the rostrum, saying, "This is not the old Blair speaking, it is the new Blair."[3] Despite such amity, the new Blair drove Governor Walker nuts. Probably not so much, though, as Walker's own Democrats did.

The American political landscape is littered with such as Daniel Walker, gifted politicians who wanted to be president but somehow fell short of their potential. An ambitious young Chicago lawyer, Walker had sought Mayor Daley's blessing to be slated as the Democratic candidate for state attorney general in 1960. Daley ardently sought the election that year of his fellow Irish Catholic, John F. Kennedy, as president. Lest the Illinois ticket be too top-heavy with Catholics, Daley made sure a Protestant, Otto Kerner, was slated for governor.

The Cook County Democratic Central Committee asked three questions of candidates seeking its backing: (1) How much money can you raise? (2) Will you pledge to support the entire Democratic ticket? (3) Would you consent to run for some other office if the committee sees fit to slate you for it? After these interviews, Daley would repair to Delphi, where he inscrutably would construct an ethnically jumbled statewide slate.

When Walker made his pitch for attorney general, he failed one of the three tests by saying he was not interested in running for any other office. Daley merely nodded to a lieutenant, who escorted Walker out of the room.

Soon a Daley pal, the state Democratic chairman, emerged and threw his arm over Walker's shoulders. "Good presentation," he said. Then he lowered his voice. "Dan, you gotta be realistic. There's a bunch of Catholics on the ticket this year from Kennedy on down, and one more will be hard for Daley to swing."

Walker protested that he was not a Catholic.

"Doesn't matter, Dan. With all those [seven] children, everyone'll think you are."[4]

Much later, Walker authored the investigative report that labeled the disorder at the 1968 Democratic National Convention in Chicago a "police riot." That was more than enough to earn Daley's permanent enmity, but then Walker ran against Daley's chosen candidate for governor in 1972. Walker hiked twelve hundred miles across the entire state—at the time, a novel political stunt—and defeated Daley's man, Paul Simon.

Walker, a confrontational sort who tended to view himself as the only honest man in town, found his legislative programs blocked by an alliance of Daley's Democrats with Republicans. The divide was not just political but personal, even ethnocultural. Walker's top aide observed, "I knew from the beginning that every time Daley looked at Walker, he saw the Church of England and the British suppression of the Irish, and when Dan would look at Daley, he would see the quintessential politician who was only interested in political gain."[5]

In sum, the state government that freshman representative George Ryan encountered in 1973 was personal, ethnic, regional, rancorous, ruthless. He entered politics in troubled times, locally and nationally. Ryan first put his name on a piece of legislation known as House Joint Resolution 4. It opposed amnesty for Vietnam War draft evaders and deserters. Along with that standard Republican tough-on-national-security measure, he joined Senator McBroom in sponsoring a Republican tough-on-crime bill. The two from Kankakee proposed that Illinois judges run for reelection in partisan contests. That would replace the system, still in place, of having judges run unopposed for retention in office. McBroom said the pressure of facing outright elections would force lenient judges to stop coddling criminals. In part, this proposal was yet another Republican effort to upset the Democratic machine's control of the Cook County judiciary. Neither Republican nor Democratic leaders supported the bill, though. Republicans did not want to cede control of the judiciary in their own counties. McBroom and Ryan withdrew the bill. Perhaps Ryan drew a lesson about what happens when you try to "reform" Illinois government. On balance, it was not an auspicious first year in office for him.

Within two years, thirteen incumbent or former members of the Illinois General Assembly had been indicted on criminal charges.

Speaker W. Robert Blair was not a well-liked man, even among his own party. The most popular Republican in the state was William J. Scott, the attorney general (Scott would be convicted in 1980 of income tax fraud). Scott proposed a statewide grand jury, a tough-on-crime bill perennially smothered by the West Side Bloc. Blair took a walk when Scott's bill came to a vote in the House, thereby ensuring its defeat. Scott promised to destroy Blair's career.

Actually, he might not have needed to make an effort. In the post-Watergate Republican rout of 1974, Blair failed even to win reelection to his House seat. Republicans, who had prevailed in the House by one vote, now found themselves in a 101–76 minority. The election of a Democratic Speaker seemingly would be automatic.

Not, though, while Daley and Walker despised each other. Daley's candidate for Speaker was Clyde Choate, from far downstate Anna, a recipient of the Medal of Honor in World War II and a protégé of Paul Powell. Walker's forces opposed Choate. The Daley and Walker camps tried to outwit each other through ninety-two ballots. "Legislators took frequent breaks, often going out drinking," Walker recalled. Whenever one side saw they might have enough votes on the floor to win, the other side frantically used stalling tactics while rounding up their stray members from the bars. Once, a member was carried unconscious onto the House floor. At length, Daley had had enough. He called Walker and said, "You said Choate could not be trusted and you're right. He promised repeatedly he could deliver some Republican votes and he lied. So I cannot support him."[6] Walker suggested William Redmond, from the Chicago suburb of Bensenville, as a compromise. Redmond duly was elected on the ninety-third ballot with some Republican help. Then he effectively turned over his power to Daley's man, Gerald Shea, the House majority leader from the Chicago suburb of Riverside.

Another man Daley sent to Springfield was his son, Richard M. Daley. As chairman of the Senate Judiciary Committee in 1975, young Daley supported his father against the governor so avidly that Senator Dawn Clark Netsch, a liberal Chicago Democrat, called him "dirty little Richie"; the *Chicago Tribune* noted "charges that he is arrogant, ruthless, vindictive, and downright mean."[7] A quarter-century later, the junior Daley was mayor himself and worked closely with Republican governor Ryan.

For all the opposition of the Daleys, Walker had some notable achievements as governor. During a national recession in 1975, he broadly expanded the state's unemployment and workers' compensation benefits. This issue, an unsexy one, drew little media attention then or later, but corporate interests considered the costs so onerous that they spent years trying to undo the legislation. In fact, that lingering issue played a hidden role in George Ryan's eventual election as Speaker.

Walker also passed the state's first campaign financial disclosure law, signed into law a state lottery, and helped to create the Regional Transportation Administration with taxation powers for public transit in the Chicago area. Still, Mayor Daley wanted him out. Daley assigned the popular secretary of state Michael J. Howlett to oppose Walker in the 1976 Democratic primary. The trouble was, Howlett was a good friend of the Republican candidate, James Thompson, and did not want to run. Indeed, when Thompson first opened his campaign office, Howlett had contributed the office furnishings. Daley assigned deputies to tell Howlett that he owed it to his party to run. So Howlett ran, defeated Walker for the gubernatorial nomination in March, and then lost to Thompson in the November election.

The first official action of a new Illinois governor after taking the oath of office is to preside over the election of the president of the Illinois Senate. Normally this is a brief ceremonial duty, but the election early in 1977 took 186 ballots and five weeks. Thompson presided the whole time, never even occupying the governor's office but working out of a small Senate office just steps behind the rostrum. The former prosecutor remembered the event as an invaluable education in politics: "It was maybe the best thing that ever happened to me because I had no government experience, I certainly had no legislative experience."[8] Thompson quickly learned both the formal procedures and the informal folkways of a legislative body. Thereafter he won passage of nearly all his major programs, even in Democratic legislatures. He probably knew as much about legislating as George Ryan did.

But then, Ryan helped to teach him. Early in Thompson's term, "several of my members picked up the paper in the morning and saw the governor playing racquetball or jogging or someplace with his dogs," Ryan said. "They'd come to me and say, 'Geez, what's with this guy? We can't get in to see him.' So I went to the governor and sat down with him and said, 'Governor, what I think you've got to do, especially when the [legislative] session's in, is to be at your desk in your office and be ready to receive some of these folks.'"[9]

In the Senate, Democrats held thirty-four of fifty-nine seats, but they were split into three factions—"regular Democrats," machine members mostly controlled by Daley; independent Democrats; and a four-member black caucus. At 5:40 A.M. on February 16, 1977, after a sixteen-hour session, regular Democrats finally elected Daley's candidate, Thomas C. Hynes.

Over in the House, the Republican minority leader was Ryan, also chosen amid rancor. Representative William Walsh of La Grange Park, a suburb west of Chicago, had twelve years of House seniority on Ryan. Late in 1976, he won pledges from thirteen members who had been uncommitted, giving him a near-lock of thirty-eight out of the forty-two votes needed to lead the Republican minority. However, the McBrooms were pushing Ryan for the post.

On December 6, 1976, Walsh accused Ryan supporters of trying to buy the election with campaign contributions and consulting contracts channeled through Representative James "Bud" Washburn, the incumbent minority leader. Washburn was retiring from his district in Morris, near Kankakee, and backing Ryan. The next day, House Republicans caucused at a Holiday Inn. Ryan was elected over Walsh on a 46–37 vote by secret ballot. The political ritual is for the winner and the loser to appear arm-in-arm, say nice things about each other, and pledge party unity. Walsh refused Ryan's request to do this dance. When the traditional motion was offered to make the vote unanimous, six supporters of Walsh stormed out of the room. Ryan named a leadership team that included two liberal Chicago Republicans but no members from the Cook County suburbs. Such a maneuver was heretical in the Illinois GOP, but Ryan did not act merely from spite. The suburbs supported Walsh, and by the time Ryan had gathered enough votes by cutting deals with downstate members, he had nothing left to give the suburbs. Governor Thompson kept his hands off the Ryan-Walsh feud but worried that the GOP split would cause trouble for his administration. Meanwhile, Walsh's accusation that Ryan effectively had bought the election made a one-day story in the press and then disappeared. Before long, though, charges that Ryan misused campaign contributions and consulting contracts became thematic in his career.

Ryan went to bed the night of the November 1978 elections believing Republicans had won a one-seat majority of the Illinois House, only to awaken the next morning to learn that a computer glitch had caused a miscount in a downstate county. Ryan had hoped to be elevated to majority leader, but at least he had the consolation of winning reelection as minority leader.

Legislators waited until the election was safely past—twenty-two days past—then, on November 29, 1978, voted to give themselves a 40 percent pay raise. The resulting public uproar caused a profound structural change in the General Assembly. Voters were so angry that in 1980 they passed an amendment to the state constitution cutting the size of the House from 177 to 118 members. Like the "amendatory veto," this might seem to be a change in the mere mechanics of government, of interest mostly to political scientists. In fact, the so-called Cutback Amendment was another reform that backfired. It was supposed to reduce the influence of machine politics but enhanced it instead.

Governor Thompson promptly vetoed the legislative pay raise, but that was just part of the scam. He dictated a veto message while on vacation at Kiawah Island, South Carolina, and ordered it signed by autopen back in Springfield. By acting at once, Thompson enabled the General Assembly to vote that same day to override his veto. The vote to override was 110–56 in the House (Ryan voted with the majority) and 37–21 in the Senate. Had the governor sat on the bill, it would have died when the legislative session expired on January 10, 1979. The package included pay raises for Thompson himself, the five other statewide elected officials, and judges. Legislative leaders said Thompson was in on the deal from the start, although for the record he denied it.

President Jimmy Carter denounced the pay raises for Illinois legislators, and also for Cook County commissioners and Chicago aldermen, because they busted his 7 percent wage inflation guidelines. Carter was angry that elected officials had not set the right example. "This is a standard for everyone to follow—everyone. As far as I am concerned, every business, every union, every professional group—every individual in this country—has no excuse not to adhere to these standards," Carter complained.[10]

It was an era of high inflation and of a so-called taxpayers' revolt sparked by the Proposition 13 initiative against property tax increases in California. Illinois lawmakers insisted they deserved their 40 percent boost to $28,000 because their last raise, three years before, had been for just 14 percent. Still, the public outcry was such that the legislature met again in special session in January to phase in the raise over two years.

That action hardly quelled the protests. A Chicago reformer named Patrick Quinn, later the state treasurer and lieutenant governor, launched a petition drive to cut the size of the House by one-third. Moreover, each member would be elected from a single-member district.

Uniquely in the nation, each Illinois House district elected three members—by longstanding practice, two from one party and the third from another. Thereby, Democratic districts in Chicago sent liberal Republicans to Springfield; downstate Republican districts sent independent Democrats. Even DuPage County, the Republican stronghold west of Cook County, elected some Democrats under the system known as "cumulative voting" or "bullet voting." Each voter cast three votes to split as he or she wished—one vote for each of three candidates, one and a half for each of two, or three for one.

Patrick Quinn urged voters to send tea bags to the governor, reminiscent of the Boston Tea Party, to protest the raise. Forty thousand people sent them to Thompson and legislators alike. The Cutback Amendment won 64 percent of the vote, thus killing off the liberal Republicans and ornery independents. The amendment embittered a generation of Illinois politicians who detest Quinn to this day. Ryan's chief of staff told him in 1979, "The session began with your unanimous re-election as Minority Leader—and ended with a great deal of bitterness and rancor. . . . Suburban disaffection appears to remain."[11] After the amendment passed in 1980, the chief of staff asked about a parallel issue to limit the number of terms a lawmaker could serve. The snarl is almost audible in Ryan's reply: "Since the public expressed its desire to reduce the size of the House, the limitations on the number of terms is something they don't deserve. They gave no thought to the quality of those that might be left to serve them."[12]

The smaller the legislative body, the easier it is for the leadership to control. This adage is not just a political theory but empirically demonstrated. For example, Massachusetts had reduced the size of its state House from 240 to 160 members in 1979. The change curtailed the independence of representatives and actually cost taxpayers money because fewer legislators demanded more staff to handle the load.

In Illinois, the Democratic and Republican leaders of the House and Senate are called the Four Tops, after the Motown singing group of the 1960s. Two pillars of the establishment—Jim Edgar, a Republican former governor, and Abner Mikva, a Democratic former federal appeals judge and White House counsel—headed a seventy-member study group in 2001. It had a ponderous title, the University of Illinois Task Force on Political Representation and Alternative Electoral Systems. Its job was to study the effect of the Cutback Amendment. It concluded that the amendment had enhanced the power of the Four Tops, and of the special interests that finance them, at the expense of voters. The study did not exactly say so, but legislators now seem mostly just to sit around waiting for the Four Tops and the governor to cut their deals. Then they vote as told. If not, they do not get the crucial endorsements and campaign cash for the next election. No longer is there much of the old coalition-building of liberals, conservatives, and independents to pass a bill. To this day, Ryan and many others regard the amendment as an antidemocratic blunder. The Edgar-Mikva task force recommended going back to the old system. Voter groups occasionally circulate petitions for a constitutional amendment to do so, but to no avail. The power of the Four Tops much vexed Governors Thompson, Edgar, and Ryan. As with his bill to change judicial elections, perhaps Ryan drew a lesson about what happens when reformers get excited and try to clean up Illinois politics. Ryan was Speaker of the last 177-member "Big House" from 1981 to 1983.[13]

When Ryan went to bed on election night of 1980, Republicans actually had won a House majority by six seats. It happened amid the landslide election of President Reagan. Indeed, that was the only time that Thompson's party enjoyed a majority of either chamber during his fourteen-year governorship. At the same time, Democratic secretary of state Alan J. Dixon was elected to the U.S. Senate. Thompson would appoint Dixon's successor as secretary of state. Ryan wanted to be named secretary of state because it offered a straight shot to the governor's mansion, but he became Speaker instead.

Illinois business interests favored Ryan for Speaker. His record was that of a solidly pro-business Republican. In particular, he kept fighting the 1975 expansion under Governor Walker of unemployment benefits and workers' compensation. The pro-business *Chicago Tribune* reported in 1977 that the system was the nation's costliest and beset with fraud. Ryan, noting that Illinois had lost 200,000 manufacturing jobs in ten years, in 1978 proposed a seven-point plan to improve the climate for industry in the state. "Businesses are being taxed so heavily that operating in Illinois is, in many cases, becoming unprofitable. As businesses leave, unemployment increases. That strains the budget of the unemployment compensation program while the number of businesses paying for the program is shrinking," Ryan said.[14] The *Tribune* published a letter from Ryan on February 26, 1980, suggesting that the governor, Democratic lawmakers, and the media all at last had seen the light on the need to reform workers' compensation. By July, all House Republicans were unified on the issue—the first such GOP unanimity since Blair was Speaker in the early 1970s. But then, Democrats killed Ryan's bill in committee.

Ryan was not an ideal legislator. His chief of staff scolded, "You have never really utilized staff effectively. You must take more time to study a problem and increase your understanding of issues. You rely too much on quick cram sessions without developing a general overall understanding of a problem. This wastes the staff's expertise and leaves you with only a shallow knowledge of the issue at hand. You are great on legislative and political maneuvering, but we need to complement that ability with more issue understanding."[15]

You are great on legislative and political maneuvering.

Then Alan Dixon went to the U.S. Senate and Thompson said, "It has long been George's dream to be speaker and it has long been an ambition of mine to see him in that spot, but it's up to George to decide."[16] That statement was disingenuous, meant to save face for Ryan. In fact, Thompson wanted a young aide named Jim Edgar in Dixon's old job as secretary of state. Thompson later explained, "I thought that Jim would be most electable, and I thought that one day Jim would succeed me as governor. The secretary of state's office would be a stepping-stone for that. In fact, on the day I hired him to be a member of my staff [as legislative lobbyist, after Edgar was elected to a second term in the House in 1978], I brought him into my office, sat him down on the couch and offered him the job. I said, 'While you're thinking about this you might want to talk to [your wife] Brenda, and you might also mention to her that someday you'll be the governor of the state of Illinois after I've served long enough.' And he was just flabbergasted by that."[17]

So on November 23, 1980, Ryan "withdrew" as a candidate for secretary of state. At the time, William Dart was the lobbyist for the Illinois Manufacturers Association, a powerful interest group. Dart had dinner one evening with Senator John Friedland of Elgin. Friedland mentioned that former representative R. Bruce Waddell of Dundee was so popular in the House that whoever would promise to bring Waddell back into a spot in the leadership would be elected Speaker. Normally, Dart observed, lobbyists "never get involved" in leadership fights "because it was dangerous if the wrong guy got in"—the guy you had not supported. "I decided to tread there. . . . We really needed some legislation to move, unemployment comp and workmen's comp. They were still taxing [sales of] manufacturing equipment; we were still trying to get rid of that tax."

Late that evening, Dart called William Walsh, Ryan's foe in the 1976 fight for minority leader, "who would have been my choice [for Speaker], a very principled guy." For some reason, Walsh "was very offended by the idea" of giving Waddell a leadership post as part of a deal to become Speaker, Dart said.

"The next call we made was to Ryan. Ryan didn't hesitate." Throughout his term, "he returned in every way our [the Illinois Manufacturers Association's] fidelity because he knew we got him in. That started a good relationship that lasted a long time." Later, though, Ryan and Dart had a bitter falling out.[18]

4 I Push This Button Right Here

On December 3, 1980, House Republicans reelected George Ryan as their leader by acclamation, thus assuring his formal election as Speaker in January. Ryan still maintains that the Speaker and the president of the Senate actually are more powerful than the governor. Ryan candidly sought, exercised, and enjoyed power—he never pretended, in the way of some politicians, to be diffident about it. "I used to say to people, you know, I even control the drapes in the House chamber," Ryan said.

> I want them open, I push this button right here and they open. I want them closed, I close 'em. If that guy out there is speaking and I don't like what he's saying, I tell the guy down there to shut off his mic.
>
> But that wasn't where the power was. The power was the flow of legislation, the makeup of committees. . . . You want a bill to come out of committee, you send it to a committee you're pretty sure you can get it out of.[1]

Still, Speaker Ryan was duly loyal to Governor Thompson. One time the governor backed a bill affecting pharmacies, but Ryan, a pharmacist, was against it. Thompson recalled:

> It was one of those things where your staff is saying, "We gotta have this bill, we gotta have this bill."
>
> "Well, go out on the floor and pass it."
>
> "No, goddamn it, George is against it, grrrrr."
>
> I was leaving my office to go somewhere, driving out to the Springfield airport, [and I] picked up the phone and called George on the Speaker's rostrum. I said, "George, I have to have this bill. It's personal. And you need to pass it for me."
>
> He said, 'Well, I'm against this bill."
>
> I said, "I don't care, I'm asking you to pass the bill, I'm the governor, you're my Speaker, pass the bill!"
>
> And he said [giving a creditable imitation of Ryan's growl], "Oh, all right!," and he passed the bill.[2]

But on one major issue, the proposed Equal Rights Amendment, Ryan defied Thompson. The passage of decades has dulled the memory of how emotional the struggle over the ERA really was. Supporters of the proposed amendment to the U.S. Constitution, guaranteeing equality of rights between the sexes, faced a ratification deadline of June 30, 1982. Approval of three more states was needed, and Illinois was a particular target of pro-ERA forces. Unfortunately for them, in Illinois a three-fifths legislative vote was needed to ratify a constitutional amendment. Supporters sought a change in the rules to allow approval by a simple majority. Ryan, as Speaker, refused.

Thompson supported the ERA but said the three-fifths rule was legislative business, and he would not try to overturn it. Actually, Thompson and Ryan probably have received more blame for the failure of the ERA than they deserve. The truth is that the Democratic-controlled Illinois Senate would not pass it either, but the activists' fire was turned on the two Republican officials. Ryan at least agreed to put the matter to a vote by the full body, which the Senate was loath to do. Ryan sent out a form letter: "I have consistently voted against this issue and I do not intend to reconsider my position on same. We have found that the root cause of prejudice and discrimination can only be combated by changing the attitudes of people and additional laws are really not the answer."[3]

For weeks in the spring of 1982, seven women conducted a hunger strike in the Capitol rotunda in support of the ERA. Opponents merrily stood before them and chomped on cheeseburgers and candy bars. Another group of ERA backers chained themselves for four days to the brass circular railing on the second floor under the rotunda. When that did not avail, they entered the House chamber and sat on the floor, instantly halting proceedings. As legislators stepped over the protesters to exit, Representative James Kelley of Rockford allegedly kicked one or two of them. "I'm not a gazelle," explained Kelley, who weighed 293 pounds, "and I stepped on one of them."[4] Meanwhile, Ryan pointedly refused to ask police to remove the protesters or arrest them. "That's what they wanted," he said.[5]

Tactics grew fiercer. Thirteen ERA militants blocked the entrance to Thompson's office and were removed by police. In late June, nine women were arrested after they splattered animal blood outside the governor's office and the legislative chambers. They scrawled the names of Thompson and Ryan in blood. According to Thompson, public disgust with that action killed the ERA.

In an interview in 2006, Thompson called the ERA "the most hypocritical, bullshit issue of my time." He noted that a governor has no power to sign or veto a constitutional amendment. "All I could do was, quote, support it and fight for it in the legislature, which I did, exceedingly, time after time. And of course all the pro-ERA forces figured I could get it passed. . . . The Democrats, especially the downstate Democrats and the West Side of Chicago [African American] Democrats, were just as much against ERA as conservative Republicans." Thompson added, "That was just such a goofy issue, you know. I'd have the opponents come in and they'd say, 'Unisex bathrooms!' I said, 'Did you every fly on an airplane?' 'Yeah.' 'Are there men and women's bathrooms on airplanes?' 'Well, uh, no, but, uh . . .'"[6] The Equal Rights Amendment was never ratified.

The first major George Ryan scandal erupted in 1982 when he was running for lieutenant governor. As with later scandals, Ryan and his political patrons and clients seemed not to grasp what the fuss was all about. Ryan set a pattern: he did not deny the essential facts, only an invidious interpretation of them. Had he not merely done a service for a constituent, an ordinary political transaction? So the reformers are saying that even that is illegal now? As usual for the times, charges were hurled and denied, a federal grand jury was impaneled, an official investigation took many months—and in the end it all came to nothing.

Revelations of frightful conditions in nursing homes and mental hospitals are something of a staple of investigative journalism. In the early 1970s, charges of nursing home fraud and abuse were investigated by the Better Government Association of Chicago (BGA) and then U.S. attorney Jim Thompson. By 1982, Thompson was seeking reelection as governor with Ryan as his running mate. The press then was exposing mistreatment of patients at Illinois nursing homes directed and partly owned by Morris I. Esformes.

On June 11, 1981, state health officials received complaints that an eighty-year-old woman in Elmhurst Terrace Convalescent Center suffered a "severely infected" bedsore "large enough to accommodate two clenched fists."[7] Esformes was the convalescent center's managing partner. Illinois Public Health director William L. Kempiners fined the facility, which had a history of violations, $8,525.

At the same time, Esformes bought control of another nursing home, Westview Terrace in Kankakee. That nursing home had been one of the best customers of Ryan's family business, Meadowview Pharmacy. Suddenly, Westview Terrace stopped filling its Medicaid prescriptions at Meadowview.

Soon, on July 16, Ryan set up a meeting among Esformes, public health director Kempiners, and himself. Ryan then regained Westview's Medicaid business, worth about $60,000 a year. Following a second meeting between Esformes and state health officials, charges against the Elmhurst Terrace nursing home were reduced and then dropped. Violations cited at a third Esformes nursing home were never pursued.

Journalists and prosecutors often hear and know more than they can report or prove. Apart from the Esformes matter, sources alleged that some nursing homes overcharged the federal government for Medicaid prescriptions, then kicked back part of the extra payments to Ryan's pharmacies. If the nursing homes refused, they might find themselves harassed by state and local inspectors. This particular allegation was not made public except by a newspaper columnist after Ryan was convicted of unrelated charges in 2006: "The investigation quietly disappeared after Ryan was elected Jim Thompson's lieutenant governor in 1982, and many of us hoped that Ryan would be scared straight by the experience."[8] The point is not that Ryan was guilty of such Medicaid offenses but that by that time so much sleaze had covered his boots that his opponents were willing to believe almost anything against him.

On November 9, 1981, Speaker Ryan hosted a campaign fund-raiser at the Illinois Athletic Club attended by nursing home operators. On that day, though, Ryan received only $750. There was $3,050 more, but it was held back until Ryan set up a meeting in his Springfield office of state officials and several nursing home operators. Soon, the state dropped a proposed regulation that would financially penalize nursing homes for understaffing. The remainder of the contributions then flowed to Ryan.

The BGA and the *Chicago Sun-Times* collaborated in investigating these incidents and broke the story on July 11, 1982. Ryan explained that Esformes "didn't feel he had a fair shake" on the bedsore charges. "The guy said he couldn't get anybody to listen to his complaints and wanted to know if I'd set him up with the [public health] director, and I said, 'Absolutely.' That's just the way I am. You want a meeting with somebody—I'll set you up. I get paid $38,000 a year [as Speaker] to look after the people's business."

Ryan said he did not know details of the case against Esformes, other than that it might "cost him a license or they were going to shut down his home." Ryan allowed that he probably mentioned his pharmacy business to Kempiners because "Bill's an old friend." However, "I put no pressure on anybody to do anything for Esformes, and I defy you to find the guy that says I did. I never asked for any more than a meeting with Esformes and Billy Kempiners."

As for Kempiners, he recalled that at the first meeting in question, Esformes "was going wild—yelling and screaming about my department and the people in it." Kempiners said, though, that he saw some merit in Esformes's defense against the state charges. In addition, Kempiners confirmed that Ryan had told him he was trying to keep Esformes's Medicaid business at his own pharmacy.[9]

Governor Thompson seemed unconcerned about his running mate's apparent conflict of interest. He said Ryan "simply put a constituent together with a department head so that the constituent could present his case. . . . I've done it. Republicans do it. Democrats do it. Unless they bring improper influence to bear, there's nothing wrong."[10] Perhaps Thompson missed the larger ethical point. At the time, Thompson was being criticized for accepting South African gold coins, artwork, cash, and other valuable gifts from people with state government interests. People knew about such gifts only because Thompson openly reported them. Early in his term, he was criticized for taking a free trip to the Kentucky

Derby. Thompson, alert to prevent a U.S. attorney from potentially doing to him what he had done to Otto Kerner, then created a "gift book" listing everything from T-shirts and cowboy hats to gold coins and priceless antiques.

Anyway, Ryan issued a defiant statement: "Each and every accusation is an outright, damnable lie. I welcome any investigation by a proper authority."[11] Consider whether authorities were eager to launch such an investigation. The state's attorneys in DuPage and Kankakee counties, where the nursing homes were located, and in Sangamon County, where the Springfield meetings occurred, were loyal Republicans. The Illinois attorney general, Ty Fahner, was a Thompson protégé. The U.S. attorney in Chicago, Dan K. Webb, was a Thompson protégé.

Three days after the allegations against Ryan surfaced, Thompson called him to center stage at a fund-raiser at Navy Pier in Chicago. He said they had "worked hand in hand, side by side, for the last six years to help the people of the state. We're going to continue to do that for the next four years." Ryan did not speak to the crowd, but he muttered to a reporter, "Are you still screwing all your friends lately, if you have any left?"[12]

Within a month, a federal grand jury subpoenaed state records relating to the nursing home allegations. U.S. attorney Webb removed himself from the case because of his closeness to Thompson, so it fell to his assistant, Gregory C. Jones. In October 1984, Jones announced that there was insufficient evidence to file criminal charges against Ryan. Years later, Governor Ryan named Jones to the state gaming board. Webb by then was Ryan's defense attorney in the Operation Safe Road investigation.

A jury eventually convicted Ryan in Safe Road, perhaps reflecting a major shift in what the public regards as corruption. The political machine's matrix of favors and coercions and the self-enriching manipulations of governmental processes were no longer just ordinary transactions but illegal and punishable. It is tempting to speculate that if Ryan actually had been indicted for his nursing home interventions a quarter-century ago, he would have been acquitted. Black-letter statutes and regulations against corruption, along with prosecutors' and jurors' attitudes, have evolved since then.

By July 2005, there was a Democratic attorney general in Illinois, Lisa Madigan. She forced the owners of a nursing home in the Chicago suburb of Evergreen Park to surrender their license because, among other misdeeds, a patient had traded sex for cigarettes and ended up pregnant. The majority owner of that nursing home was Morris Esformes.

In August 1981, Thompson's lieutenant governor, Dave O'Neal, resigned on the ground that the job gave him nothing to do. In Illinois parlance, the office is called "lite gov." It remained vacant for seventeen months.

Democrats controlled the legislative redistricting that followed the 1980 census, and President Reagan was in a midterm slump in 1982. Therefore, Republicans knew their chances to keep control of the new "Little House" mandated by the Cutback Amendment were slim. So Speaker Ryan sought to succeed O'Neal as lite gov. He had to fight and win a tough Republican primary to get the job.

Ty Fahner, the attorney general, also was running on the Republican ticket in 1982. Fahner and Ryan thought they might help each other by passing a bill to set up statewide grand juries, a perennial anticrime measure. It always met the same fate as the repeated efforts to change the way judges are chosen—recall what happened when Ryan and McBroom tried to legislate that reform in 1973. The grand jury bill failed in a nearly farcical illustration of how Illinois politics is, first, personal; second, regional; and third, partisan. The actual merits of the issue come in fourth.

Narcotics rings and gambling operations often overlapped county lines, so some Republicans and liberal Democrats kept saying that statewide grand juries were needed. Attorney general Fahner thought he could make this issue part of the Republican law-and-order platform. However, state's attorneys in 102 Illinois counties did not want outside prosecutors looking over their shoulders. Many machine politicians all over Illinois also had reasons of their own to resist enhancing the state's investigative powers. To combat this embedded parochialism, Fahner proposed authorizing statewide grand juries only for drug trafficking, hazardous waste dumping, and various consumer frauds. Moreover, the Illinois Supreme Court would have to green-light any such grand jury. Ryan's pal, House Majority leader Arthur Telcser, sponsored Fahner's bill.

"George couldn't have worked any harder," Fahner recalled. "He would bring people into his office. They would say they would not vote for it, and George being George would say, 'Well, you son of a bitch, I'm going to remember that.'"[13]

Then the parochialism really hit the fan. Chicago mayor Jane M. Byrne, a Democrat, opposed the bill. She was Governor Thompson's enemy. Democratic state's attorney Richard M. Daley of Cook County supported the bill. He was Byrne's enemy. Thompson and Ryan went to work corralling Republican votes. Democratic leaders, sensing the election-year publicity bonanza the bill might give Thompson, Ryan, and Fahner, rounded up Democratic votes in opposition. The *Chicago Tribune*, which supported Fahner, editorialized, "Wavering lawmakers were pressured, threatened, and wooed; jobs for friends and relatives were practically auctioned off for votes."[14]

The bill failed in part because of, of all irrelevant issues, the Equal Rights Amendment. Two Republican representatives refused to support Fahner's legislation unless Ryan dumped the three-fifths rule for passing the ERA, which of course he would not do.

Yet a critical reason that the Fahner bill died was never reported. Opposition came from, of all Republican-leaning organizations, the Illinois Manufacturers Association. Normally the group supported Thompson, but to conservatives the governor was a "tax and spend Republican." During fourteen years in office, he tripled the state budget. In 1983, Thompson proposed and the legislature passed an increase in the state sales tax. Ryan wrote Thompson a "private" letter opposing the tax and leaked it to the media. Another time, Ryan was conspicuously "neutral" on a gasoline tax hike urged by Thompson. So Ryan and the state's antitax industrialists got along well.

Still, the IMA had no particular reason to want statewide grand juries. "We just figured it as a nuisance, so we opposed it," said the IMA's lobbyist, William Dart. A legislator's husband had lunch with a prominent judge; that judge expounded on the wondrous things a statewide grand jury would enable. Those remarks found their way into a *Chicago Sun-Times* article. Dart took the newspaper clipping to the House Democratic leader, Michael J. Madigan of Chicago. Madigan, a shrewd infighter, saw right away that the prospect of overzealous prosecutors and judges would drive more legislators away from the bill.

"It blew up," Dart said. "It was George's plan. George asked [Dart's wife, also a lobbyist], 'Where's your husband? Tell him I want to talk with him!' George was screaming and yelling. . . . He really got tough, but my reputation was similar. I spent four years in the Marine Corps."

At bottom, as usual in politics, the conflict was irreducibly personal. Fahner had hired one of Dart's former interns to work for statewide grand juries and Fahner's campaign. "I can't let an intern beat me; that would look bad," Dart figured.[15]

The statewide grand jury contretemps was no scandal, but neither did it help Ryan's campaign for lieutenant governor. His Republican opponents were Don Totten, a hard-line suburban conservative, and Susan Catania, a Chicago liberal. Thompson backed Ryan, not that the governor especially wanted Ryan on the ticket. He definitely did not want Totten or Catania. Totten was close to the Reagan White House, which Thompson was not, and a rival for influence in the Illinois GOP. Catania was, in the eyes of mainstream Illinois Republicans, as radical as Leon Trotsky. The party redistricted her out of her House seat under the Cutback Amendment, and Ryan even tried to dump her from the state Commission on the Status of Women.

Ryan won the March 17, 1982, primary with a plurality of 43 percent of the vote against 33 percent for Catania and 24 percent for Totten. Although Thompson later denied it, there followed an effort to dump Ryan from the ticket in favor of a candidate for lite gov who favored the ERA and was not smudged by charges of nursing home scams. Some of Thompson's associates at least dangled carrots and brandished sticks in trying to persuade Ryan to quit. "I have no intention of dropping out of the race unless I die or something," he grumped.[16] Ryan remained a tempting target for Democrats. Grace Mary Stern, the Democratic nominee for lieutenant governor, called him "an abrasive, sexist state legislator who has risen to the top like scum on cocoa."[17]

The Democratic candidate for governor was Adlai Stevenson, a former U.S. senator and the son of his party's nominee for president against Dwight D. Eisenhower in 1952 and 1956. The Thompson-Ryan ticket was expected to beat Stevenson and Stern handily. But Thompson won by only 5,074 votes, or one-tenth of a percentage point. Charges that vote fraud had turned the election were made as expected. In reality, Stevenson owed his heavy Democratic vote to the fact that African American leaders had registered hundreds of thousands of new black voters in anticipation of nominating a black mayor of Chicago in February 1983. In any event, although Thompson denied that Ryan had been a drag on the Republican ticket, some of his associates believed he was. Ryan bristled that he actually had helped the ticket by attracting conservative voters disenchanted with Thompson. Thereby was planted another wobbly plank in the strained platform of the Thompson-Ryan relationship. At the time, neither dreamed that Thompson and his protégé Webb eventually would defend Ryan against criminal charges.

5 Cut Ribbons and Hand Out Money

Governor Thompson put George Ryan in charge of economic development in downstate Illinois, a traditional lite-gov task. Ryan summed up his job: "Cut ribbons and hand out money."[1] These duties acquired extra urgency when Thompson conceived a $2.3 billion bond issue for public works called "Build Illinois."

"When he first initiated that program, he kind of kept it under wraps," Ryan recalled with some wonderment. "There wasn't any kind of big deal about it, and the legislators really didn't realize the magnitude of that program." Inevitably, the news got around. "The list [of legislators' pork-barrel projects] just grew, just grew. This was before the bill passed. So Thompson calls me in and says, 'This thing is out of hand. We just can't afford to do it. I can't make the cuts in this.'"

Rather than anger the legislators with unilateral cuts, Thompson named Ryan to head a five-man team to travel the state and vet the local pork requests. Ryan found one request, Kankakee's $2.5 million for downtown renewal, to be especially worthy.

"Small communities, they just didn't have the tax base to do it [locally]," Ryan said.

> I went back to him after I looked over these projects. I sorted out a few, said, "You know, this is a scam and this I think isn't, but for the most part, Governor, you gotta do them all."
>
> "How the hell do we pay for them?"
>
> "Ain't gonna do it in one year, spread it out over two or three years, hell, do it." So we did.[2]

In time, as governor himself, Ryan would see Thompson's $2.3 billion Build Illinois, raise it $9.7 billion, and call his $12 billion bond program "Illinois FIRST." Public works make up one of the fetishes of the political class. There seems to be no end to the advantages of visible, tangible improvements to the infrastructure. Politicians are happy to get credit for the projects, bond houses are happy to float the bonds, bond attorneys are happy to handle the sales, contractors are happy to get work, trade unions are happy to get jobs, voters are happy to see their neighborhood improved. Everyone is happy. Some of these people are apt to express their gratitude in the form of campaign contributions or at least votes.

State and federal money flowing to a municipality for pork seems almost to be "free." In the end, of course, the government has to tax that money out of the economy or else borrow it from the capital markets. Either way, taxes or debt, the public eventually pays the bill. Public works might generate economic growth and jobs in a locality, but they are offset by the cost of taxes and debt in the aggregate. If pork projects really created jobs, politicians could just keep adding new programs until full employment were achieved. Economists understand this point, but many politicians resist it. Public works are their heroin, their cocaine.

Thompson and Ryan gave their most spectacular tandem performance in winning pork—it was sold as "economic development"—on a warm June night in 1988.

In Chicago, the Cubs represent baseball's National League and the city's North Side; the White Sox, the American League and the South Side. Those teams are not just emblems of geographical and league loyalties but hold something of a mythopoeic status for their respective, cultlike fans.

The White Sox played in a badly decayed Comiskey Park, built in 1910 in the heart of Bridgeport, ancestral home of the Daleys and other mayors. The team owners made noises about moving the team to a more lucrative locale in St. Petersburg, Florida. So in 1986, the General Assembly passed a law approving state subsidies for building a new Comiskey Park. That law was never implemented because Thompson and Chicago mayor Harold Washington kept fighting over who would control the contracts and patronage. In November 1987, Washington died.

Then Thompson and Ryan forced another stadium subsidy law through the legislature with last-minute deals and institutional finagling. Both men regarded the new Comiskey Park (now called U.S. Cellular Field) as a personal triumph. That it might have represented the victory of corporate interests over the public interest apparently did not enter their minds, certainly not their public statements.

"Stopping the clock" is part of the lore of many state legislatures. Often, the lawmakers must conclude a session by a certain time set by law. Various hijinks are employed to stop the clock so that crucial bills might pass before the deadline. Lawmakers have been known to climb a stepladder and literally turn back the hands of a clock on the legislative chamber's wall. Electronic voting and time stamping were supposed to prevent such shenanigans. Illinois had not stopped the clock since the new state constitution took effect in 1972. In handling the stadium subsidies issue, Thompson and Ryan, in collusion with Democrats, not only stopped the clock but also brazenly falsified the time stamp.

The new Sox stadium bill appeared dead on June 30, 1988, just hours before the midnight deadline. For the bill to pass after midnight, it would need an insuperable three-fifths majority. As mentioned, team owners Jerry Reinsdorf and Eddie Einhorn were threatening to take the Sox to Florida if they did not get a new stadium. What was not known was that Thompson himself had induced Reinsdorf and Einhorn to make such a threat as a means of putting pressure on lawmakers.

In a state that chronically underfunds its hospitals and schools, and after Thompson's latest proposed income tax increase failed in a bitter struggle, downstate Democrats and suburban Republicans were in no mood to give a handout to wealthy baseball owners. On the floor of the House, stadium opponents chanted, "Na na na na; hey, hey, hey, goodbye," the Sox fans' anthem, derived from a pop song, sang when an opposing pitcher was yanked, a Sox player hit a home run, and such.

At about 4 P.M., Thompson encountered the chairman of the Illinois Sports Facilities Authority (who later became Thompson's law partner) on the Capitol steps. When the chairman said the bill was dead, Big Jim got mad. He stormed into the office of Senate Republican leader James "Pate" Philip.

"Pate, I don't care whether you're a Sox fan or not. It's now personal. We're one of the few cities to have two Major League teams, and we're not losing one."[3] ("It's now personal" is nearly the ultimate weapon of a political boss, up to presidents.) Philip assented. The Senate passed the bill with the minimum of thirty votes needed. Thompson then personally carried the legislation under the rotunda and into the House. Left on the clock was less than thirty minutes.

Thompson and Ryan now launched a frantic auction for votes. Both men openly finger-pointed, shouted, and grew red in the face on the House floor. Legislators toggled the voting switches on their desks from red to green and back again as deals were made and unmade. Thompson sent his aides to stand by legislators' desks; these "spotters" would point down to a member who might profit from a Thompson visitation.

"I knelt down next to one guy on the House floor," Thompson remembered, "and I said, 'What can I help you with?'"

> He said, "I want to be secretary of state."
> I said, "You want to be *what?*"
> "I want to be secretary of state."
> "No, you can't be secretary of state, Greg Baise is going to be secretary of state" [not, it should be noted, George Ryan].
> "Oh, OK, I'll vote for it."
> I go over to another guy, he said, "The roof on my veterans' home is leaking."
> "It's raining on the veterans?"
> "Yeah."

"Well, we gotta fix that, obviously!"

He said, "OK, I will vote for it."

Next, Thompson approached a downstate Democrat. The voting light on her desk was red, meaning no.

I said, "Why are you red?"

"Oh, did you want me to be green, Governor?"

"Absolutely!"

"OK, I will vote green."

The next morning she was in my office. She said, "I forgot to ask you for something." I said, "Too late, but there is always next year."[4]

Before that representative remembered to ask for something, at five minutes before midnight, Thompson and Ryan still had only fifty-four votes—six votes shy. Midnight came, but House Speaker Michael Madigan held the roll call open. The minority leader, Jim McPike, presided while the Speaker roamed the floor to cut his own deals. Three minutes after the deadline, a suburban Republican cast the deciding, sixtieth vote. McPike immediately banged the gavel, declared the bill passed and the time as 11:59 P.M. Actually, it was 12:03 A.M. and, by law, the bill then needed a three-fifths majority, or seventy-one votes.

Gary LaPaille, then the top aide to the Democratic Speaker, instantly deployed his staffers to snatch up copies of the printout from the electronic voting machine. They dabbed Wite-Out on the time stamp of 12:03 A.M., then wrote in 11:59 P.M. in pen. They neglected, though, to efface the telltale July 1 date.

The deal allowed the state to sell up to $150 million in stadium construction bonds, financed by a lodging tax in Chicago and outright subsidies from the city and state. Among other provisions favorable to the Sox owners, they did not even have to pay rent to the state if seasonal attendance fell below 1.2 million.

Thompson's law office features a photo of his throwing out the first pitch at the new ballpark in 1991. He says to this day that he gets more thanks for the new Sox park than anything else he did as governor. At the time, Speaker Madigan dismissed concerns that the courts might void the bond issue just because the bill was fraudulently passed. "I don't think there is a judge in the nation, especially in Illinois, who would challenge this," he said.[5]

Especially in Illinois.

The 1980s saw blows befall Ryan personally and his hometown economically. Jeanette, one of Ryan's triplets, suffered a three-week coma and severe brain damage after an auto accident in 1983. Donald Udstuen, lobbyist for the state medical society, gave her a clerical job there, and she slowly regained her mental faculties. In 1985, Ryan's appendix was removed at a Kankakee hospital. In February 1989, his mother, also named Jeanette, died at age eighty-three. She was president of Ryan Pharmacies (the family sold the business in 1991). In August 1989, Richard B. Warner, the son of Ryan's friend Lawrence E. Warner, choked to death at age twenty-seven. He had worked in Ryan's 1986 reelection campaign.

Characteristically, Ryan responded to this array of bad news by throwing a political party. Held in Chicago in May 1989, it celebrated his approaching twentieth year in elective office. The guests included Donald Rumsfeld, the former and future secretary of defense; W. Clement Stone, the Chicago insurance magnate and bankroller of former president Nixon's campaigns; and people in the orbit of President George H. W. Bush. Ryan had backed Bush in 1988 over his rival for the Republican nomination, Senator Bob Dole of Kansas. Ryan's brother, Tom, made an appearance. Since being defeated for mayor of Kankakee in 1985, Tom Ryan had held a job as a technical adviser for the state Department of Transportation while he worked full-time for Ryan Pharmacies.

His brother was not the only person George Ryan took care of in Kankakee. The 1980s were hard times for American manufacturing in general and Kankakee in particular. By 1982, the city's unemployment rate was 26 percent, a Depression-era level. The Roper Corporation and A. O. Smith factories turned off their lights. Today, a bronze bench with statues of two sitting children, funded by private donations, sits on the lawn of the Kankakee County Courthouse. A plaque honoring George and Lura Lynn Ryan lies on the ground facing the bench. The George H. Ryan Gymnasium adorns Kankakee Community College. Splash Valley, a water park underwritten by state funds assigned by Ryan, officially is called the George H. and Lura Lynn Ryan Aquatics Center. There is a new county jail and sheriff's office, also built with Governor Ryan's Illinois FIRST money.

For all that, Kankakee falters in the twenty-first-century information-age economy. One reason the town placed last in the 1999 *Places Rated Almanac* was that its illiteracy rate was an appalling 25 percent. Ryan responded traditionally by sending governmental pork barrel home. Whatever good the pork did, it did not modernize the town's economy.

In the 1950s, the new interstate highway bypassed Kankakee to relieve downtown traffic congestion. By the 1980s, vacant commercial and industrial space downtown could hardly be sold or rented even at giveaway prices. In a pattern repeated in many towns across the country, downtown merchants resisted a new shopping mall lest it destroy downtown retail. The mall simply went elsewhere, namely the town of Bradley bordering Kankakee on the north, prompting the Bradley board of trustees to taunt:

> Whereas, the Kankakee Downtown Development Corp., those who now stand to pay the price for their continued disregard of the needs of

their customers, first snickered and chortled over the audacity of a little village that thought it could build a mall, then engaged in a sniping attack by raising petty and insignificant objections hoping to defeat and delay, have suddenly been smitten with the realization that some folks don't listen to them and, as a result, feel they must now resort to power politics, and

Whereas, the City Council of the City of Kankakee has chosen to ignore the rampant unemployment facing its citizens, and the citizens of the entire county, the affect [*sic*] of that unemployment and the critical need for jobs, and rather than fight to help provide work for its people has instead chosen to oppose and object to the construction of a mall . . .[6]

and so forth; the resolution went on to urge passage of a certain transportation bill favorable to the Bradley mall. In the meantime, the Ryan brothers were busy on another matter, getting Tom Ryan public contracts for electronic monitoring devices used for prisoners under home arrest.

By 1990, Thompson did not want George Ryan to run for secretary of state. The governor favored Greg Baise, who had managed his 1986 reelection campaign, for that office. Thompson tried to dissuade Ryan from the race, offering visions of big money in the private sector based on Ryan's corporate contacts. "George and I traveled the state, all over the country, doing this kind of economic development work," Thompson recalled. "He'd go to business meetings, he'd go to the ag [agricultural] meetings, he'd go to the plant openings on the smaller facilities. . . . I told George he could be a very prominent international business consultant . . . but he wasn't buying that. He liked to be in public life." Thompson added wryly, "It's awfully hard to talk people out of running, just as it's hard to talk them into running."[7]

When Ryan's defense attorneys argued years later that he was not motivated by thirst for money, they had a point. At the time, Ryan frankly said his intention was to be governor or maybe a U.S. senator. Lura Lynn said she had not heard of the possibility of the Senate, but the governor's mansion would be nice. Ryan's ambition was so naked that he hired Scott Fawell on the lite gov's payroll, then assigned him to work full-time on Ryan's planned 1990 campaign for secretary of state as a launch pad for the governor's office. That using public funds to advance a personal political campaign was improper, let alone illegal, apparently never troubled either Ryan or Fawell. Eventually, Fawell testified that he could not remember even stepping foot into the lieutenant governor's office during those years. He was out running a campaign all that time.

Many people have suggested that Fawell became like a surrogate son to Ryan, but in fact their relationship was more pragmatic than emotional, at least on

Fawell's part. Born in 1957 at the peak of the baby boom, Fawell came from a generations-old political family in the Republican suburbs west of Chicago. Here are some factors that make his a quintessential Illinois political story:

1. His father, Bruce, retired as a DuPage County judge in 1989 after being reprimanded for performing weddings outside the courthouse and pocketing the fees.
2. His mother, Beverly, retired as a state senator in 2000, whereupon Governor Ryan promptly found her a top job with the state toll highway authority.
3. His uncle Michael Fawell was the public guardian of DuPage County. He was convicted of mail fraud in a 1983 bankruptcy, then of theft and official misconduct in 1985 after looting estates of $17,450, and was disbarred.
4. Another uncle, Tom Fawell, formerly ran the local airport authority.
5. Another uncle, Harris Fawell, served in the U.S. House with distinction for fourteen years. Harris Fawell was Marion Seibel's clout in Ryan's secretary of state's office. Seibel took $82,000 in bribes for truck driver's licenses, passed the money to Ryan's campaign fund, and became one of the first persons to plead guilty in Operation Safe Road.
6. Scott's sister-in-law Blanche Hill Fawell made $125 an hour as a hearing officer for a secretary of state board that arbitrated disputes between car dealers and manufacturers.
7. Scott Fawell married his second wife, Joan Mitnick, just as he went to work for Ryan in 1988. In time, Ryan named Mitnick deputy director of the state lottery at $83,904 a year. Shortly before the couple divorced in 2003, Ryan appointed her to a four-year term in a state financial institutions department post at the same salary.

Fawell never competed for the title of "Mr. Congeniality." He was brusque and hot-tempered and liked to throw his weight around. Nicknamed "Scooter," Fawell grew up in West Chicago and played hockey in high school. About the time he was graduated from North Central College in Naperville, Illinois, his father divorced his mother and married a woman twenty-four years his junior. Scott Fawell took a township job in DuPage County, then worked for the reelection campaign of U.S. senator Charles Percy in 1984. The next year, Fawell took a low-level job with Republican secretary of state Jim Edgar's office before leaving to serve in Governor Thompson's 1986 reelection campaign under Greg Baise. When he signed on with Ryan in 1988, Fawell was running the presidential campaign of Vice President George H. W. Bush in Illinois. Ryan gave Fawell, now serving both Ryan and Bush, a personal services contract for $1,500 a month in taxpayer funds. In short, Ryan and Fawell knew everybody in the Republican Party. They drew criticism from members of both parties for their arrogance and sense of entitlement.

For instance, media reports accused the lieutenant governor and others of using their state police bodyguards as personal valets. In 1988, George and Lura Lynn took a golfing vacation in Scotland, and one trooper recalled handling more than twenty pieces of their luggage. WLS-TV in Chicago videotaped another trooper stepping off a state plane laden with Ryan's coats and bags.

At the 1988 Republican National Convention in New Orleans, Ryan displayed a singular sense of entitlement. Ryan set up a hospitality suite in his hotel—a common outreach for politicians at conventions—and handed out bags of souvenirs and sample products from Illinois. Meanwhile, executives from Quaker Oats Company, a pro-Republican firm headquartered in Chicago, visited the New Orleans convention that nominated Vice President Bush for president. The new Quaker CEO got to know Ryan there. When it came time to check out of the hotel to return to Chicago, Ryan approached the CEO in the lobby to cadge a ride home on Quaker's corporate jet. According to a former Quaker executive, the conversation went something like this:

CEO: Sure, there's room for you, George.
Ryan: Can Lura Lynn come too?
CEO: Well, um, sure.
Ryan: Well, you know I always travel with security.
CEO: Really? Well, I guess we have room for your state troopers.

Ryan and his entourage ended up taking most of the seats on the small jet. They boarded carrying satchels of souvenirs. One Quaker executive had to fly with satchels piled on his lap. Then, as the plane was taxiing to the runway, Ryan leaned over to the CEO and said, Hey, do you think the pilot would mind dropping me off in Kankakee?[8]

Politics is a rough and tumble game, not for the faint of heart. Even so, there was something about George Ryan that seemed always to turn his campaigns personal and nasty. Ryan's move from lieutenant governor to secretary of state would seem on its face to be a routine, lateral transition between secondary, "down-ballot" offices. Actually, the secretary of state's was a much more powerful office. Maneuvers behind Ryan's move left hard feelings in both parties.

Thompson announced in 1989 that he would not run for reelection in 1990. Both Ryan and Secretary of State Edgar wanted to succeed Thompson. Edgar apparently had enough public support to be elected governor, but many county Republican chairmen—the workhorses of the party—backed Ryan for the nomination. Edgar and Ryan made a deal. Edgar would support Ryan for secretary of state; Ryan would back Edgar for governor. That way, the two men would avoid possibly destroying each other in a Republican gubernatorial primary. Perhaps it was a good deal for Edgar and Ryan, but it left Thompson in the cold. Thompson wanted Edgar to be governor but his state transportation chief, Greg Baise, to be secretary of state. Frosty relations between the two governors, Thompson and Edgar, go back at least to this disagreement. At length Baise dropped out of Ryan's race, ran for state treasurer instead, and lost.

The incumbent state treasurer, Jerome Cosentino, was Ryan's Democratic opponent for secretary of state. Theirs was a dirty campaign. Eventually, both men were convicted of corruption charges. Of all things, the candidates' Springfield residences became a campaign issue. Illinois law requires statewide elected officers to maintain a home in the capital—taxpayer-paid. Cosentino rented a house on Lake Springfield for $825 a month. Taxpayers paid $1,075 a month for Ryan's ranch house at 203 Golf Road in the city. Taxes also paid to cut Ryan's grass and shovel his snow.

But the rentals were small potatoes. Cosentino and his wife owned a trucking firm. As state treasurer, Cosentino placed $10 million in state funds in a certain bank. That bank loaned Cosentino's trucking firm $250,000. His trucking company also used an Indiana subsidiary to employ nonunion drivers and evade higher Illinois workers' compensation premiums—still another fallout from Governor Walker's 1975 unemployment and workers' compensation bonanza. Crossing organized labor is not a recommended tactic for Democratic politicians.

Ryan's most serious misdeeds did not emerge for many years. He declared his candidacy for secretary of state in August 1989. Within weeks, he authorized Scott Fawell to hire Fawell's pal Richard Juliano and others to run Ryan's campaign full-time, although taxpayers paid their salaries from the lieutenant governor's office.

Both candidates could appear affable, but they were mutually hostile. Cosentino once invited Ryan to step outside and settle their dispute with fisticuffs. Meanwhile, "Dr. Don" Udstuen was judged to be brusque and malicious enough to stand in for Cosentino when Ryan staged mock campaign debates with his opponent. Also it should be noted that Cosentino, from a Cook County suburb, was personally friendly with Thompson. Perhaps it is not just coincidental that Cosentino made hay of ethical charges against Ryan while Thompson did not strain himself to defend his lieutenant governor against those charges.

Ryan followed the precedent of the nursing home scandal: he did not deny the essential facts, merely an invidious interpretation of them. The General Assembly had created the World Trade Center Association in Chicago to seek to enhance the state's share of U.S. exports—one more response to the shift to a postindustrial economy. Three of Ryan's pals were funneling state World Trade Center funds into companies they privately owned. A television station in Chicago broke that story and also reported that eleven Ryan family members had won state jobs. Further, family members, friends, and former Ryan pharmacy employees worked for the Manteno Veterans Home in Kankakee. Ryan denounced the charges as "twisted and distorted . . . political rhetoric." Then he changed the subject. Cosentino had shown "a pattern of disregard for the law."[9] Next, just days before the election, the *Chicago Sun-Times* revealed that a Springfield businessman had helped to guarantee a personal loan to Cosentino. That same businessman was a Republican boss who already had won sweetheart state financing from Cosentino's office for a hotel project—Republicans cutting deals with Democrats in the Illinois tradition. Cosentino objected that he was suspected of criminality just because he was an Italian American.

Sun-Times editors could not stomach either candidate and declined to make an endorsement. *Chicago Tribune* editors endorsed Ryan while allowing, "Both candidates have some explaining to do about questionable government practices in their current government posts."[10] Ryan defeated Cosentino on November 6, 1990, with 54 percent of the vote. In 1992, Cosentino pleaded guilty to one count of bank fraud and was sentenced to nine months of home confinement.

Ryan named attorney Dan Webb of Winston and Strawn and Don Udstuen of the medical society to guide his transition to the secretary of state's office. A decade earlier, Webb had reviewed that office for incoming secretary of state Jim Edgar and reported it corrupt. Twelve years later, Webb would defend George Ryan against charges that his office was corrupt.

6 These Are My Guys

George Ryan put the group together, and it pleased the members to call themselves the Old Timers Club. They were middle-aged, not old, but all had served in the General Assembly and moved on to better-paying jobs. Their monthly get-togethers over spaghetti *alla como* rang with masculine bonhomie, with the backslapping good cheer of mutual joshing and mock insults and cussing and gossiping. Surely none of the men anticipated how misfortune would strike them. In years to come, many would suffer ill health, financial ruin, criminal prosecutions, or all three.

A novelist or filmmaker working up a treatment of Illinois politics might hesitate to depict this group as inbred and insular and self-regarding as it really was. The backroom deal, the smoke-filled room, and the three-martini lunch are fixtures of American folklore, but the Old Timers Club was the real thing. Even with hindsight, a chronicler is challenged to unravel the skeins of personal connections. Let us start with George Ryan.

During his years as lieutenant governor and his first term as secretary of state, Ryan gathered his former legislative pals at the Como Inn at 546 North Milwaukee Avenue in Chicago. Opened by an Italian immigrant in 1924, the Como developed into three buildings with thirteen dining rooms. It became one of the "stations of the cross" for politicians seeking support in Chicago's polyglot electorate. Italian, Polish, and Irish Democrats staged banquets and fund-raisers there, just as they made sure to visit Jewish voters at Manny's Coffee Shop or African Americans at Army and Lou's soul food place. The Como also hosted Republicans such as Ryan, who was close to many Chicago Democrats. Ryan decreed the custom that each Old Timer pay for all their lunches in turn, and the man who got stuck with the check had the privilege of inviting a guest. Ryan's young aide Scott Fawell and his old friend Larry Warner were frequent diners there, though not members of the club. Both men later were sentenced to prison.

Old Timer Arthur Telcser was never accused of wrongdoing, but his death in 1999—Parkinson's disease claimed the sixty-seven-year-old—visited a particular misfortune on Ryan. Friends speculate that Telcser was the one Ryan mentor who was straight enough and tough-minded enough that, in good health, he might have steered Ryan away from at least some of his cruder scams. No member of Ryan's "kitchen cabinet" could take his place. Telcser was a pharmacist, like

Ryan, and the two had been close since the 1968 Ogilvie campaign for governor. Telcser was one of the last of the Chicago "lakefront liberal" Republicans, booted from office by the Cutback Amendment. In his last term, he was majority leader under Speaker Ryan.

Another deceased Old Timer was Henry Klosak of Cicero. That town on the west flank of Chicago is infamous as the headquarters of Al Capone in the 1920s. Representative Klosak was part of an enduring Cicero Republican machine that matched Kankakee's. Facing the loss of his seat under the Cutback Amendment, Klosak became Cicero town president. He was driven to the Como Inn lunches by Frank Maltese, the Cicero township assessor—a do-nothing job. Maltese was a bookmaker for the mob. He died in 1991, a year before Klosak. Maltese's widow, Betty Loren-Maltese, succeeded Klosak as town president; she went to prison on racketeering charges. The point here is not to smear Ryan with guilt by association because he knew a guy who knew people in the mob. The point is that everyone who counted in Illinois politics knew everyone else.

Bob Blair, whom Ryan had backed for Speaker over Henry Hyde, was an Old Timer, at least until Blair fled to the Dominican Republic to avoid having to split his estate with his ex-wife after their 1990 divorce. Even Don Totten, who had run against Ryan for lieutenant governor, joined the Como Inn parties. Once when it was Totten's turn to pay, he tweaked the group by bringing as his guest a noted investigative reporter, Carol Marin. The buzz around the table was subdued that day. Another old Ogilvie hand was former state senator Arthur "Ron" Swanson of Chicago. Tossed from his seat, Swanson turned to lobbying. He was apt to give Ryan cash for gambling in Las Vegas. Swanson won some state contracts under Ryan, including a do-nothing lobbying position for a major state facility. Eventually, Swanson pleaded guilty to lying to a federal grand jury about that job.

Former representative Roger Stanley of Streamwood, a Chicago suburb, was called "The Hog," initially after a television character, but the nickname came to connote avarice. Secretary of State Ryan gave Stanley a six-week job in his office, which had the effect of more than doubling his state pension (others received similar pension benefactions). Stanley got lots of political direct-mail work from Republicans. He arranged vacations in Costa Rica for his pals, with complimentary fishing trips and free or cut-rate prostitutes (prostitution is legal in that Central American country). Stanley had a secret second family there. He pleaded guilty to corruption charges, cooperated with the government, and was sentenced to twenty-seven months in prison.

Lobbyist Donald Udstuen was called "Dr. Don," partly because he lobbied for the state medical society and partly because he could cure his clients' governmental ailments. He was not an Old Timer but an occasional guest of the club. Udstuen got his start as Governor Ogilvie's patronage chief. He took more than $300,000 in kickbacks on contracts that Ryan issued as secretary of state. In another scene seemingly conjured by a hack novelist, he pocketed $4,000 in cash from Ron Swanson in a men's room. He resigned from the doctors' group with a $4.9 million payout. Soon Udstuen's cooperation with the feds extended to wearing a wire in a phone call with Ryan, although nothing came of that particular incident. He was sentenced to eight months in prison.

Scott Fawell, Larry Warner, Ron Swanson, Roger "The Hog" Stanley, "Dr. Don" Udstuen . . . they all became headline names as Operation Safe Road unfolded. In time, Ryan's supporters raised the argument that he had been betrayed by his friends, that he was just a pharmacist from Kankakee taken advantage of by city slickers. This theory is so implausible that even Ryan's defense lawyer, Dan Webb, disowned it at Ryan's sentencing hearing. Ryan craved the camaraderie and admiration of those men. That he sold his integrity and his reputation so cheaply to a bunch of petty swindlers is another mystery of his life story. If you are going to steal, you might as well steal millions of dollars. In for a dime, in for a dollar. Ryan suffered from "politician's disease," the need to be universally liked. In interviews with me, when certain names would come up, Ryan would ask almost plaintively, "Did he say anything bad about me?" The Old Timers at their raucous luncheons might not have felt part of a "lonely crowd," but presumably some of them came to know real loneliness in prison.

The Como Inn had nothing to do with any mischief hatched by the Old Timers in its dining rooms, yet even the restaurant fell on hard times. It filed for bankruptcy in 1996 and closed in 2001. The founder's sons and grandsons opened other banquet halls in Chicago and a suburb, but the Old Timers are a memory. Other restaurants such as Gene & Georgetti's steakhouse near the Loop were trendy hangouts for politicians and media people. During his trial but before his sentencing, Larry Warner, emotionally and financially broken, would go to Gene & Georgetti's and drink.

Governor Thompson, planning to step down from office but still seeking ways to harass Democrats, wanted to elect a Republican state's attorney in Cook County, the Daley fiefdom. In 1990, he deputed his protégé, the corruption-busting former U.S. attorney Dan Webb, to find a suitable candidate. Webb had performed the same chore in 1986, coming up with Terry Gainer, another former Thompson aide, who got creamed in that election. So the second time around, Webb told Thompson, "The hell with you. Find your own candidate."

Still, the word went out, and a thirty-eight-year-old partner in the gold-plated Chicago law firm of Winston and Strawn walked into Webb's office there one day. Jack O'Malley said, "I hear you're looking for a state's attorney."

Webb said, "You don't know anything about politics."

O'Malley said, "I don't care, I'm interested, and I know I can do it."

Webb noted O'Malley's boyish good looks and squeaky-clean reputation. He called Thompson and said, "I have a candidate for you."

"I want to see him now," said Thompson, who was in his Chicago office. O'Malley did not know where it was. Webb gave him directions.[1]

"Over he came," Thompson said. "Standing at the desk in front of me was a dream candidate. He was tall, young, smart, Irish, he had a good wit, he didn't take himself too seriously. His father was a fireman of rank, he'd been a copper and a city prosecutor for a while. He would have been a perfect Democrat. So I grabbed him."[2]

Thompson called his pal back: "Webb, I love you."[3] O'Malley won an upset election. Soon Thompson joined Webb at Winston and Strawn, whence they later would direct Ryan's legal defense.

In 1992, about a year after Ryan became secretary of state, state's attorney O'Malley paid Ryan a visit. They had arranged a news conference to announce a case against the fraudulent issuance of driver's licenses by the manager of the secretary of state's office in Midlothian, a Cook County suburb (this was years before Operation Safe Road). O'Malley urged developing more criminal cases against secretary of state employees.

"Fuck you, Jack, these are my guys," Ryan replied.[4]

The importance of "my guys" might not be clear to those who believe patronage is merely a fringe benefit for politicians, not their lifeblood. Thompson had his own issues with his "guys." The governor had imposed a hiring freeze in 1980 during one of the state's perennial budget crises. This freeze was a consolidation of power. Thompson personally had to approve filling any state job or any promotion or transfer. Every year, about five thousand employees were exempted from the freeze. The exemptions were checked for their Republican bona fides. Cynthia B. Rutan, a rehabilitation services employee, and other workers complained in court that they were passed over for promotions just because they were Democrats. A federal judge threw out the case.

On June 21, 1990, the U.S. Supreme Court ruled on appeal that party affiliation may not be considered in deciding whom to hire, promote, transfer, or recall from layoffs, except for high-ranking, policy-making officials. The 5–4 *Rutan v. Republican Party of Illinois* ruling effectively outlawed partisan patronage in state governments. Such patronage already was banned in the city of Chicago under so-called Shakman (from *Shakman v. Cook County Democratic Central Committee*) consent decrees. Naturally, politicians found ways to get around these restrictions. In 2006, the U.S. attorney was winning convictions of Chicago city officials accused of fraudulent hiring schemes that evaded *Shakman*.

Thompson still insists that the *Rutan* ruling was an antidemocratic blunder. He notes sardonically that Justice William J. Brennan Jr., who wrote the opinion, "did not get his seat on the Supreme Court by taking a [civil service] quiz." Indeed, Brennan "came out of New Jersey politics," that is, a patronage-ridden system with a history of corruption. "If the governor does not exercise patronage," Thompson says, "somebody else will. It can be the bureaucracy, who will hire their cousins and their nephews and their uncles, or it will be a labor union who will hire their cousins and their uncles and their nephews, but somebody will. And the labor union was not elected and the bureaucracy was not elected. The governor was elected. . . . You either believe in how democracy works or you don't."[5]

The spoils system in American politics goes back at least to the election of 1800, after which President Thomas Jefferson threw former president John Adams's Federalists out of public jobs. Since then the managerial revolution has made the government ever more professionalized, permanent, and non-political. These reforms have not been altogether beneficent. Civil service has developed its own inefficiencies and pathologies. As Governor Stratton's aide once wondered, is murder a sufficient offense to warrant dismissal of a civil servant? What is clear is that Ryan was little deterred by *Rutan* or *Shakman*. He always favored "my guys." To the extent that loyalty to friends is a virtue, Ryan was virtuous.

Dan Webb did many services for Jim Thompson. Back in late 1980, when Thompson named Jim Edgar secretary of state, Edgar wondered just what he was getting into. That office is much larger and more powerful than in most states, functioning in effect as a department of motor vehicles. Webb, at the time Thompson's director of state police, scrutinized the secretary of state's office on Edgar's behalf.

It did not take Webb long to figure the office out. By January 1981, he found that its employees were pressured to sell tickets to their boss's political events. "Since these employees did not operate in a social climate that would enable them to legitimately sell hundred dollar or two-hundred dollar tickets," Webb stated in a memo, "they would accept bribes from people doing business with the secretary of state's office in order to secure money to pay for these tickets."

Further, Webb said, "It appears that there is substantial graft and corruption spread throughout the secretary of state's office." For one thing, "There has never been any selection criteria for the hiring of [secretary of state] investigators. All the current investigators appear to have been hired strickly [*sic*] on a political patronage basis."[6]

Webb was referring to conduct under former secretary of state Alan J. Dixon, the newly elected senator. Dixon denied that his employees were pressured to sell fund-raising tickets. Edgar said he did not recall any such problem as secretary himself. In any case, an official review alleged that bribes were paid for driver's licenses as early as 1981—*twenty-two years* before Ryan was indicted on charges derived from a licenses-for-bribes investigation. Under this simple fact, two familiar defenses raised by Ryan's supporters fail—that he could not be expected to know about illegal conduct in his scattered field offices and that prosecutors were overzealous in pursuing him.

When Ryan was elected secretary of state in 1990, he named Webb to his transition study team. Ryan also appointed a pal from Kankakee, Dean Bauer, as the secretary of state's inspector general to root out internal corruption. Bauer was a walking caricature of a Kankakee pol. He grew up with George and Tom Ryan on the south side of the town. As a lineman for Illinois Bell in the 1950s, he took coffee breaks in the Ryans' drugstore. Bauer followed his father into a job as a Kankakee County sheriff's deputy. Bauer's wife, Monica, was clerk of Kankakee County circuit court. Mayor Tom Ryan named Bauer chief of police in 1970. Bauer was accused of whitewashing a shoplifting investigation of one of his patrolmen. Bauer said a store security guard had cleared the officer. However, the security guard Bauer claimed to have interviewed was deceased. The chief also was criticized for assigning his officers to drive politicians to Chicago airports and for favoring people who bought Ryan fund-raising tickets. Bauer lost his position when Tom Ryan was beaten for mayor in 1985. Before leaving office, Tom Ryan cut Bauer a check for $10,800 in accrued sick time, but the new city attorney said the payment was improper. Bauer's successor as police chief entered the office to find only a desk, chair, and telephone—every personnel file was stripped clean. Bauer went to work for a developer who was a major contributor to George Ryan, then Ryan hired him in 1991.

By 1993, the state's attorney in Lake County, north of Chicago, dragged Inspector General Bauer into an investigation of bribery for licenses at a secretary of state's office in Libertyville. Evidence that the bribes were collected for Ryan's campaign fund was, literally, sitting in an open briefcase.

On the morning of March 9, 1993, authorities raided the Libertyville facility. Later that day, Ryan said at a news conference, "We will let the chips fall where they may. This will not be tolerated."[7] While vowing a crackdown, Ryan portrayed the case as a matter of a few greedy employees selling licenses as phony IDs. Political fund-raising as a motive for taking bribes there was kept covered up for years. State employees were expected to sell or buy tens or hundreds of $100 tickets to Ryan's fund-raising events each spring and fall.

Certain persons served as middlemen for illegal immigrants seeking driver's licenses, needed as identification to get a job. The immigrants paid the middlemen up to $800. Certain state employees provided "courtesy" to the middlemen if they bought Ryan fund-raising tickets. Courtesy meant that they and their clients got to move to the head of the line for expedited processing of the licenses. Fake licenses were issued in as little as five minutes.

James Quinn was the zone manager in charge of Libertyville and four other licensing facilities. Quinn was issued as much as $30,000 worth of fund-raising tickets at a time. He told investigators he had to sell the tickets to keep his job.

During the raid, agents found in Quinn's office written driver's test materials and laminates used for producing licenses—unusual items in a zone manager's custody. Agents also found an open attaché case on a credenza in the office. Inside the case was a manila envelope containing about $2,500 in cash and sixty-four tickets for Ryan's spring fund-raiser. Handwritten on the envelope were ticket sales records. Inspector General Bauer took the briefcase as evidence. On a wall of Quinn's office was a framed photograph of him and Ryan at a political golf outing. Bauer took that, too. The briefcase and picture soon disappeared and were never found.[8]

In little more than a year, 927 people received fake licenses at Libertyville. Seven people were convicted in the case, including a secretary of state's employee. Quinn was not charged with a crime but was fired for failing to check license applicants' Social Security numbers.

In time, Ryan boasted that he had broken up fourteen operations across the state that illegally sold driver's licenses. The scams involved outsiders selling fake licenses to immigrants and underage drinkers, he said. As for the Libertyville raid, he called it a textbook case where his agents cooperated with local law enforcement officials. In 1994, Ryan was reelected secretary of state without much strain.

7 The One Guy Left in This Business

During the presidency of Jimmy Carter, the United States deregulated the airline, railroad, and trucking industries. During the presidency of George H. W. Bush, Communist states in Moscow and Eastern Europe collapsed. These seemingly unrelated events oddly conjoined to figure in the eventual prosecution of George Ryan in Illinois.

Republican president Gerald Ford had wanted to deregulate transportation, but his Democratic successor, Carter, actually did so. Congress, pressed by Carter, restored market forces to airlines in 1978 and to railroads and trucking in 1980. Although airlines and railroads wanted to be deregulated, truckers bitterly fought it.

Truckers had been insulated against competition since the Motor Carrier Act of 1935 during the New Deal. The federal government controlled entry into the industry, routes served, and rates charged. In effect there was a trucking cartel, allowed to fix rates under immunity from antitrust laws. Two powerful institutions—the trucking lobby (the American Trucking Associations) and organized labor (the International Brotherhood of Teamsters)—profited from this arrangement and did not wish to change it. That it took a Democratic president to uphold the Republican principles of free markets and open competition is a mostly unnoticed irony. The primary sponsor of Carter's trucking deregulation bill, by the way, was Senator Edward M. Kennedy of Massachusetts.

Independent truckers and trucking firms, at last able to get into the business and compete on rates, consequently created a freewheeling, brutal industry. Trucking evolved from a stable, controlled system to an unstable, uncontrolled one. Truck driving became a job of long hours, low pay, and skirted safety regulations. Indeed, trucks were the new "sweatshops on wheels," one scholar concluded. Between 1977 and 1995, annual earnings for drivers, adjusted for inflation, dropped 30 percent. By the late 1990s, the median long-haul driver was working sixty-five hours a week (even though the legal limit was sixty hours) and driving 117,000 miles a year.[1]

While the government deregulated the economy of trucking with one hand, it imposed new restrictions on drivers with the other. In January 1992, all motor carriers were required to conduct drug tests of prospective employees, then randomly or for reasonable cause once they were on the job. In April 1992, all truckers had to carry a state-issued Commercial Driver's License (CDL) appropriate to the equipment driven and loads hauled. At the state level, laws against drunken driving were steadily made tougher.

The upshot of "sweatshop" wages and stricter regulations on drivers was, predictably, a shortage of drivers. Then, after Communism fell, Eastern Europeans were free to migrate to America and seek work. And so it came to pass that people like the Reverend Grouu Tzonkov appeared on the scene.

Tzonkov left Bulgaria in 1990 for Dearborn, Michigan. Spurning welfare, he worked as a dishwasher and hotel receptionist, saving enough money to open his own fast-food restaurant. Tzonkov also was an ordained priest.

On the Northwest Side of Chicago, the St. Sophia Bulgarian Orthodox Church was looking for a new priest. Its former priest had been dismissed for the alleged sexual harassment of a parishioner's wife. Seeking a go-getter and a consensus-builder, church trustees called Tzonkov in Dearborn. Tzonkov accepted the position on one condition—that he be permitted to run a sideline business of his own. The business he had in mind was trucking. With some reluctance, the trustees agreed. In 1994, Tzonkov moved with his wife and teenage son into an apartment above the church on North Lawndale Avenue.

In 1997, Illinois banned the use of translators in driver's license facilities after discovering that many of the interpreters were helping applicants cheat. Tzonkov was undeterred. From scratch that year he founded Americans Truck Company, also known as Bul Am Trucking, and soon built it into a seven-figure firm. A small subculture grew up of Eastern European men in their thirties and forties who lived in cheap apartments near Tzonkov's church. He referred many of them to a driving school in Florida, where translators still were used. Some students paid bribes to get their Florida licenses, then returned to Illinois and exchanged them for valid Illinois licenses. When Illinois secretary of state agents caught on to this scam, they sardonically referred to these applicants as "suntan CDLs" because, in fact, they lacked the suntans that actual residents of Florida normally bear. Anyway, Tzonkov contracted with a major carrier, Watkins Motor Lines, to provide drivers.

All big trucking firms had trucks sitting idle for lack of drivers. Bulgarians, Yugoslavs, Serbs, and other Eastern Europeans were pouring into Chicago (along with Latin American and Asian immigrants) and were willing to work cheap. Many of them spoke little or no English and could hardly drive. Nonetheless, they managed to obtain Illinois CDLs.

When secretary of state agents demanded bribes for greasing licenses, these immigrant workers seldom reacted with shock. They had grown up in Communist nations where corruption and deceit were the norm. Illinois, in that respect, must have reminded them of home. Some of their bribe money lined the agents' pockets; much of it battened the campaign fund of the secretary of state. The drivers just paid the bribes, got their licenses, and went out on the road. Many were incompetent; some caused accidents, sometimes fatally.

Tzonkov said he was unaware of any bribery scheme. The Illinois-Florida fraud connection became a dimension of Operation Safe Road, but Tzonkov was never charged with wrongdoing. Still, personal travails seemed to smudge the lives of everyone who stepped too close, however unwittingly, to Ryan's scandals. In 2004, the St. Sophia Bulgarian Orthodox Church fired Tzonkov for spending too much time on his trucking business at the expense of his pastoral duties.

The situation that Tzonkov exploited, trucking deregulation and a fresh supply of immigrant drivers, was developing when George Ryan first ran for secretary of state in 1990. Any cop will tell you that any crime has two elements, opportunity and motive. The state of the trucking industry and the means of its regulation provided the opportunity for widespread bribery. The motive, greed, was a fixture of Illinois politics.

Dan Willis was an elated young man. He had recently graduated from Maranatha Baptist Bible College, gotten married, and moved into a new apartment in Watertown, Wisconsin. His parents and six of his eight siblings were coming up from Chicago to celebrate birthdays. Dan would turn twenty-three the next day; his brother Ben would become a teenager four days later.

The Reverend Duane "Scott" Willis and his wife, Janet, were evangelical Christians who homeschooled their children and voted Republican. Scott had entered the ministry in 1983 after teaching elementary school. In 1990, he became pastor of Parkwood Baptist Church, which had only a few dozen members in the heavily Catholic Mount Greenwood neighborhood at the southwest corner of Chicago. The pastorate thrived under the Willises.

They voted early on Election Day, November 8, 1994. Then they loaded Ben, age twelve; Joe, eleven; Sam, nine; Hank, six; Elizabeth, three; and Peter, six weeks, into their Plymouth Grand Voyager. They headed north to visit Dan in Wisconsin.

That same morning, Ricardo Guzman left a freight yard at Western Avenue and Sixteenth Street in Chicago. The gate inspector, frustrated when Guzman could not understand his instructions, had to find another driver to translate in Spanish. Born in Mexico in 1965, Guzman lived in Humboldt Park, a Mexican neighborhood of Chicago, and worked for the Mendoza Trucking Company.

Gonzalo Mendoza's girlfriend was Marion Seibel, manager of the secretary of state office in McCook, Illinois. Beginning in 1991, Seibel took bribes to fix CDLs and sent the money to Ryan's campaign fund. Mendoza was a middleman who bought bribed licenses for about eighty of his drivers. So it happened that Ricardo Guzman obtained CDL number G255–7366–5213 in November 1992.

Guzman could not speak English, but probably he could not have passed a legitimate driving test in any language. From 1986 to 1997, his record included eight tickets and six accidents.

By 10:30 A.M. on November 8, Guzman, driving an eighteen-wheel semi-trailer on Interstate 94 north to Fond du Lac, Wisconsin, was near West Layton Avenue in Milwaukee. The Willises' Grand Voyager was right behind. A forty-two-pound mud flap/taillight assembly dangled from the truck. Other drivers tried to warn Guzman over CB radio, but he did not respond. He testified later that the radio was not working that day. However, one trucker was so alarmed that he pulled alongside Guzman, blew an air horn, waved, and gestured frantically to the rear. Guzman did not respond. He testified later that he did not want to pull over for fear that a nearby police car would follow and perhaps find some defect on the trailer.

A weld failed; the chunk of metal fell to the pavement and pierced the Willises' gas tank, which exploded. Scott and Janet, who had been high school sweethearts, managed to unbuckle their seat belts and flee the flames, suffering severe burns. The only child to make it out of the van was Ben. By chance, one of the first motorists who stopped to help was an acquaintance—his brother's girlfriend was the daughter of Scott Willis's best friend. He yelled to Ben to stop, drop, and roll, then grabbed him and yanked him to the ground, where Ben started rolling. He died the next day. As Janet was being placed in an ambulance after watching her children burn to death, she kept repeating to herself the opening verse of the Thirty-fourth Psalm: "I will bless the Lord at all times: his praise shall continually be in my mouth."

Four days later, back in Illinois, Russell Sonneveld, one of Inspector General Dean Bauer's investigators, started looking into the accident. Sonneveld knew about allegations that Seibel was selling licenses for bribes at McCook. Within three days, Sonneveld had enough evidence to ask Bauer for permission to open a case on Guzman and to travel to Wisconsin to interview authorities there.

Instead, Bauer demanded that Sonneveld give him all his related documents and to leave the case to Wisconsin authorities. Perhaps not at that moment, but on at least six different occasions, Bauer told Sonneveld: "We don't want to do anything to embarrass George Ryan."[2] It was Bauer who had removed the briefcase and cash during the 1993 Libertyville raid.

The day after hearing from Sonneveld, Bauer called Willie Thompson, deputy director of the secretary of state's police force. When Bauer mentioned the Willis tragedy, which had been splashed over the news for a week, Thompson considered the call so important that he interrupted it to ask his secretary to take shorthand notes. Guzman allegedly got his CDL illegally, Bauer said, and so he was launching an "active" investigation of the matter. Thompson wrote a memorandum summarizing the call and sent a copy to Bauer. Eventually, federal investigators subpoenaed all of Bauer's documents related to Operation Safe Road, but Bauer did not provide the Willie Thompson memo. When he finally pleaded guilty to a single count of obstructing justice, it involved telling his secretary to deep-six that memo.

Bauer perhaps had reason to be disappointed with Sonneveld's investigative eagerness, for Sonneveld had gotten his job through his friendship with Ryan's daughter Nancy. In 1995, Bauer in effect fired Sonneveld by assigning him to inspect auto parts at a salvage yard. "You fucked the wrong guy," Sonneveld told him, and later gave evidence to the government in Operation Safe Road.[3]

Seibel, the McCook supervisor, and Mendoza, the trucking company owner, both pleaded guilty to racketeering conspiracy and were sentenced to eighteen months in prison.

During a civil lawsuit brought by the Willises, Bauer invoked the Fifth Amendment protection against self-incrimination six times. Guzman likewise took the Fifth. Guzman was not charged with a crime in the Willis accident and the question of his licensure was never adjudicated, but that is not the end of his story. He surrendered his CDL in 1999 rather than take another driving test as ordered by a new secretary of state. In 2002, Guzman was convicted of stealing a lawn mower, tools, and bicycles from garages in Chicago; he was deported to Mexico the next year.

In 1999, the Willises were awarded $100 million from various defendants in a settlement of their lawsuit. Their lawyer, Joseph A. Power Jr., a powerful figure in the Democratic Party, said, "Only one person has not owned up to his responsibility and that is George Ryan." The recently elected governor said, "This case has been investigated thoroughly and, unfortunately, Mr. Power continues to make claims he knows are false."[4]

After a few months, Scott Willis preached his final service at Parkwood Baptist Church. "It's time to get away and cry now," he explained. "I don't want to sound morbid, but we really haven't had that opportunity."[5] He and Janet visited Jerusalem, moved to the Printers Row neighborhood near Chicago's Loop, then returned home to Tennessee. "People would remark about our great faith and we would say, 'No, it's a little faith but we have a great God,'" Scott said.[6] While Janet recited the first verse of the Thirty-fourth Psalm the day of the accident, Scott took special comfort from the third verse: "O magnify the Lord with me, and let us exalt his name together." Verses from that psalm adorn a portrait of the six deceased children in the Willis home; they also are etched on the gravestones of Benjamin, Joseph, Samuel, Hank, Elizabeth, and Peter Willis.

Ryan's Democratic opponent for reelection in 1994 was Patrick Quinn, the state treasurer and father of the 1980 Cutback Amendment. Quinn was a reformer, but the race was no less bitter on either side because of that. Ryan attacked

Quinn for accepting donations from entities that benefited from a loan program that Quinn administered as treasurer. Quinn retorted that the purchase of $1.2 million in TV ads by Ryan's office to push an organ donor registry in Ryan's office—prominently featuring Ryan himself—was a political abuse of public funds. A Democratic effort to halt those ads failed after legislators realized it might threaten their own taxpayer-paid newsletters. The *Chicago Sun-Times* reported that taxpayers paid $12,065 over five years to cut the grass and shovel the snow at Ryan's Springfield home. Ryan protested indignantly that taxpayers would not want to see an unkempt lawn at his place. Quinn reacted typically. He called a news conference to brandish hedge clippers, garden tools, and an advertisement for lawn mowers. Quinn said he would cut Ryan's grass himself if that was what it took to save taxpayers money. Ryan struck back, charging that in 1993 Quinn had flown 14,892 miles on state aircraft for political purposes. All of these incidents happened before the end of June. The election was in November. And so it went.

The November 8 elections were a Republican triumph nationally, as the party captured control of Congress for the first time since 1954, and in Illinois. Students of the Daley dynasty would not be surprised to learn that Chicago mayor Richard M. Daley backed Ryan over Quinn. Daley claimed that he was praising Ryan's performance as secretary of state and state librarian, not endorsing him for reelection. Nobody believed that and nobody was expected to. Even so, Ryan did not take his reelection for granted. Dean Bauer ordered Russell Sonneveld and another aide to conduct an electronic sweep for bugs at Ryan's campaign office. They did so with state equipment on state time. No bugs were found.

After taking postelection vacations, Ryan and his staff considered their goals for a second term. Chief of Staff Scott Fawell wrote Ryan a seventeen-page memo on December 14, not missing the opportunity to preen a bit. "Obviously I believe, as I think you do, that the political operation is if not the best in the state then damn close," Fawell said. Still, he warned, the "operation needs to be kept together to allow you to be in a position for any future plans to run for higher office."[7]

Ominously for Dean Bauer, Fawell was not sure Bauer was the best man for the job. Apparently, Bauer's mere scuttling of the Libertyville and Guzman investigations was insufficient. "Another tough one for you personally I know," Fawell said. "I know Dean's health is not good but this place needs help. My suggestion is we move Dean and get rid of [Chief Deputy Joseph] Jech [who was fired] and start over. Dean could go to [secretary of state's police] in a Deputy or Chief Deputy title (if we can move Will Thompson) and let's get someone in there who won't screw our friends, won't ask about FR [fund-raising] tickets, and who will run a no nonsense shop. Someone tough has to go in there and get the investigators to no longer free lance as they see fit. This department has always been problems. Need to clean house in my opinion."

"Let's get someone in there who won't screw our friends, won't ask about FR tickets" was such an incriminating passage that prosecutors highlighted it in the corruption trials of Fawell and Ryan both. In terms of understanding the career of George Ryan, though, and the nature of machine politics, another of Fawell's statements was perhaps more profound: "You have a great reputation for being the one guy left in this business who takes care of people who have helped you."

8 They Thought It Was Too Political

George Ryan accomplished some tremendous things for the public good. Quite apart from his releasing everyone from Illinois death row, his policies undoubtedly saved some lives.

Early in his first term as secretary of state, Ryan went home one weekend, picked up the *Kankakee Daily Journal,* and saw that a boy named Jeremy Jenesco needed a liver transplant to survive. The operation—if an organ ever became available—would cost $300,000. The next weekend, Ryan returned and learned that neighbors had held a bake sale for the boy, raising a few hundred dollars.

"I said, 'Jesus, a kid's life is at stake,'" Ryan recalled. "I got six kids. What if I was in that position, what the hell would I do, where would you get the money to save your kid's life?" Back in Springfield, Ryan told his staff to devise a program for state funding of organ transplants. "It isn't long before they're back and they say, 'We can't do this program.'"[1]

The Regional Organ Bank of Illinois, comprising the lung, heart, kidney, and other associations, warned that state funding could trigger medical rationing. Suppose the state fund is down to its last $300,000 and three children need transplants. Who decides? Or how would the fund be replenished? Would every transplant require a legislative appropriation? (President Clinton encountered similar rationing issues in trying to enact national health care.)

If, typically, Ryan had not foreseen the roadblocks of such practical details, he knew how to get around them. He coupled the organ donation issue with, of all things, library improvements. (One of the secretary of state's titles is state librarian; Ryan took that role seriously.) Absent a state transplant fund, Ryan figured, the best policy was to increase the number of organ donors. First, starting in January 1993, he required all applicants for driver's licenses to sign an "anatomical gift" option on the back of the license. Drivers also could join a central registry for organ donors.

Next, Ryan announced a Live and Learn program. "Live" alluded to organ donor awareness, "learn" to libraries. "We increased some fees, I don't even remember what the hell, and we saved the libraries," Ryan said years later. In July 1993, Governor Edgar signed the Live and Learn bill into law. It increased vehicle title fees from five to thirteen dollars and plate transfer fees from two to twelve dollars. Probably only Ryan, not Edgar, could have persuaded the legislature to approve such steep new fees on consumers. The bill raised $33 million—$19 million for libraries, the rest for organ donor promotion and other Ryan initiatives.

Soon the state was paying to put Ryan's face on television in donor-awareness ads. When his election opponent Patrick Quinn and even the *Chicago Tribune* scolded Ryan for self-promotion, he cried foul. "Unlike some who are quick to criticize," he huffed in a letter to the *Tribune*, "I have met many of these people [needing transplants] and their families, and I have been deeply moved by their courage and resolve. No matter what the cost, personal or political, I cannot sit idle. . . . People can second-guess our approach, or attack me for making a personal appeal for a few seconds at the end of each ad," Ryan maintained, going on at considerable length.[2]

Quinn and the *Tribune* did not know it, but Ryan was just getting started. Within a year, 2.5 million drivers signed up to donate their organs at death. The number of transplant operations in Illinois increased about 11 percent—unfortunately, demand went up 30 percent. Next, all 137 driver's license facilities in the state featured posters with photographs and statements from area residents whose lives were saved by organ or tissue donations. By 1998, Ryan was running for governor with a new media campaign.

Movie patrons saw an ad before the feature film showing a young boy playing in a field. His mother's voice is heard saying she was planning the boy's funeral. The camera cuts to her as she recalls the moment when doctors brought her the news: "We have a heart." Next on-screen is Ryan with the boy—an authentic Illinois transplant recipient—on his lap. "I'm George Ryan. To be an organ donor, sign the back of your driver's license and tell your family."[3] The state spent more than a million dollars for such ads.

Ryan said later the program attracted free media coverage. "I think we probably paid for some, too. Matter of fact, we did, we put ads on television. They are since banned. I started that and they banned it because they thought it was too political." (Ryan alluded to the State Officials and Employees Ethics Act of 2003.)

What happened to Jeremy Jenesco, the Kankakee boy whose plight sparked Ryan's concern? "He ended up never having to need a transplant," Ryan said. "I just talked to him about two or three months ago. He's a young man now, he's working someplace, going to school, but he's still got a little problem, he's a sickly kind of guy."

In August 1994, Governor Edgar signed Ryan's "zero tolerance" bill suspending the driver's license of any teenager with even a trace of alcohol in his or her blood. Seemingly a victory, the bill actually represented defeat or at best half a loaf, for Ryan had failed once more to enact "point-oh-eight." He strived annually to reduce the legal test for drunken driving from a blood alcohol content of 0.10 percent to 0.08 percent. Besides his usual buttonholing tactics, he filled a wing of the Capitol, where legislators passed each day, with pictures of drunken driving victims.

Ryan proceeded to tighten the DUI laws—limiting a drunken or drug-impaired driver to but one court supervision in his lifetime, barring lawsuits against doctors who give prosecutors the results of blood tests of crash victims—but point-oh-eight continued to elude him. Finally, after six years, Governor Edgar signed the point-oh-eight bill in July 1997. The alcoholic beverage industry remained opposed to the measure. What had changed? Ryan made a deal.

Despite the struggles of Mothers Against Drunk Driving and other advocates, point-oh-eight always ran into an insuperable wall in the person of James "Pate" Philip, Republican leader of the Senate. Ryan called on Philip to let him know he was going to run for governor in 1998 and that Philip would not want to have an enemy in the governor's office. ("It's personal now"—again, the politician's equivalent of a neutron bomb.) Ryan said, "Pate understood the politics of it, besides the fact that it ought to be done—and Pate understood that—and then he helped me pass the bill." Illinois thus became the fifteenth state, and the first in the Midwest, to enact the point-oh-eight standard. "Good bill today, probably saved a lot of lives," Ryan said.

Al Ronan was a state representative from suburban Chicago, a member of Chicago ward boss Richard Mell's machine (Mell is the father-in-law of Governor Blagojevich). The two had a falling out, and Mell dumped Ronan from his seat in 1992. So Ronan became a lobbyist. He once handed out envelopes filled with campaign contributions just off the House floor. Even for Illinois, that was considered bad form.

The reform group Common Cause joined hands with—of all people—Ryan to pass tougher lobbying restrictions. Fawell admitted later that Ryan embraced this cause to blunt an expected election challenge from reformer Pat Quinn.

The twenty-year-old state lobbying law was easy to evade. For instance, corporations could hire out-of-state lobbyists on contract and thereby not have to register them as Illinois lobbyists and disclose their activities. Governor Edgar signed the new lobbyist disclosure law in August 1993. "Where our past law has proven almost worthless," Ryan said, "we are now providing a window into the activities of lobbyists in Illinois."[4] Of course the new law contained loopholes as well. Even so, Ryan might have come to regret providing such a window, for his relations with lobbyists clouded the rest of his career.

As for Ronan, he patched things up with Mell and steadily attained power. Under Governor Ryan, his firm, Ronan Potts LLC, improperly obtained sealed-bid information from Scott Fawell and passed it on to a client, who used it to win an $11.5 million state contract. Ronan and Fawell were pals, making golfing trips to Palm Springs, California, together. In February 2004, Ronan Potts was indicted on mail and wire fraud charges tied to the rigged contract. The firm paid a $350,000 fine, forfeited $67,000 in fees, and accepted two years' probation.

Ryan, though, never betrayed the slightest embarrassment over disclosures under the new lobbying law. For a Christmas present in 2000, the Illinois Asphalt Pavement Association gave Lura Lynn Ryan a fruit basket costing $217. Pate Philip's wife got a basket costing only $127. By this lobby's calculation, therefore, the governor appeared to be 71 percent more powerful than the Senate president. If either Ryan or Philip noted this discrepancy, he might have wondered at the reckoning.

Organ donations, point-oh-eight, lobbyists' disclosures—these were Ryan's "good government" causes, yet he never was considered a good-government, reform candidate. His problem was that he never stopped being George Ryan. Comguard is a case in point. As with many Ryan activities, it takes some patience to sort out the facts, and whether the facts add up to criminality is arguable.

Tom Ryan was out of a job after his defeat for reelection as Kankakee mayor in 1985. Within a month, he landed a $40,000 position as a technical adviser for the Illinois Department of Transportation. Actually, he worked full time for Ryan Pharmacies. To avoid embarrassing his brother's 1990 campaign, Tom Ryan resigned from IDOT. Ryan Pharmacies soon was sold, and Tom went into the business of marketing electronic detection devices for home-bound felons. He was president of and an investor in the Home Incarceration Program of Illinois, which was a subcontractor of the Cook County jail. At that time, the Cook County sheriff was a Republican (later ousted from office in a corruption scandal). Then Tom bought one-fourth of a Kankakee firm, Comguard, Incorporated. Governor Edgar's Department of Corrections hired Comguard to monitor up to 200 inmates for $180,000 a year in 1993. Comguard was the second lowest of eight bidders and wrested the contract from PMI McLaughlin of Arlington, Texas, which had served Illinois since 1989.

Comguard had financial problems, so Secretary of State George Ryan managed to expedite the state's payments. In 1993, the Kankakee County board of supervisors gave Comguard a $145,000 business loan. That was just the start of loans that were not repaid in full, never repaid, or concealed from lobbyists' disclosure statements. George Ryan's friend Larry Warner, lobbyist nonpareil, was behind most of the transactions. Ryan's lawyer Jeremy Margolis was hired as a liaison between Edgar's Department of Corrections and Comguard. Margolis would figure prominently in later Ryan scandals.

Warner made two loans to Comguard of $50,000 and $95,000. He used a Kankakee lawyer, Richard Ackman, and a local retired industrialist, Harry Lockman, to front for the loans to hide his own involvement. In 1997, the county board placed a $106,595 lien on Comguard. Next, Tom Ryan retired the loan with $95,000—the county waived the interest charges. The county board president asked Tom whether he had George Ryan to thank for paying off the politically embarrassing loan. Tom just smiled and winked.

Actually, it was Lockman who paid the $95,000. He did so anonymously through a trust bearing Ackman's name. "It was a business deal I offered to a friend I have known for 40 years," Lockman explained later. "Tom Ryan is a decent, honorable man who made a bad business decision. That happens to all of us."[5] Comguard made payments through the trust to Ackman, who then forwarded them to Lockman, who in turn sent them to Warner. Soon, Warner bought the $95,000 loan from Lockman. Eventually, Warner got his $95,000 principal back, but no interest, and of his earlier $50,000 loan, only $8,300 was ever collected. Nonetheless, when Comguard's contract with the state expired in 1997, the Edgar administration extended it for five years. By that time, Comguard had laid off employees, subcontracted the monitoring back to PMI McLaughlin, and supplied only the electronic bracelets and other equipment.

Tom Ryan said he was just an investor and referred questions to Comguard's president, Michael Reeves. Reeves was the brother-in-law of L. Patrick Power, the Kankakee County Republican chairman and former state's attorney. Reeves was under indictment at the time for mail fraud in an unrelated business scam.

At length, Tom Ryan sold most of his share of Comguard to an Israeli company. Two days after receiving the money in December 1999, Tom Ryan's wife sent a $3,500 check to George Ryan, writing "gift" on the check. George Ryan did not report the gift on his state Statement of Economic Interests. A few months later, a federal grand jury started looking into the Comguard matter. George Ryan was represented by Margolis's Chicago law firm, Altheimer and Gray. Probably Ryan never dreamed of how Altheimer and Gray's alleged misconduct would affect his life. Nor did he dream of how Warner's clout would help take him down.

Tom Ryan to George Ryan to the Kankakee County board to Larry Warner to Richard Ackman to Larry Lockman and back to Warner, then back to the brothers Ryan, with Margolis in the mix, the transactions not fully disclosed as required by law—perhaps the U.S. Department of Justice should not be faulted for taking all of seven years to investigate the Ryan and Warner dealings. In any case, Warner now walks on stage as a major player in the Ryan drama.

9 Some Comic Book Character Called "The Fixer"

More than once while Lawrence E. Warner was growing up, his parents were evicted from their apartment for failure to pay the rent. While in high school, Warner worked as an errand boy for one of the apartment buildings housing rich people on Chicago's Lake Shore Drive. By the time he was a young man, Warner already had amassed more wealth than had many of those Lake Shore Drive tenants.

Supporting his divorced parents and an unmarried aunt, he dropped out of college. He married young, fathered a daughter and a son, and then his wife died of a brain aneurism at the age of thirty-nine. Warner remarried, only to suffer another family tragedy. His daughter, Laura, phoned him one night in 1989 from the apartment of his son, Richard. Warner and his new wife, Cindy, rushed to the apartment, where paramedics tried and failed to revive Richard, who had choked to death at age twenty-seven.

Warner threw himself back into his work, which was prodigious. He had a role as an investor or officer in more than eighty corporations. His major businesses, run from offices on North Western Avenue in Chicago, were a fire insurance adjustment firm, a construction maintenance and supervision firm, and two consulting companies. He knew everybody who counted in Illinois politics and finance, and everybody knew him. His closest friend was George Ryan.

The night Ryan was elected secretary of state in 1990, Warner remarked, "George has got to have somebody in there who will say no to people."[1] It was more the other way around—somebody should have said no to Warner. He brazenly worked out of Ryan's suite of offices in the Capitol and flatly announced to staffers that he would handle state leases. As early as April 1991, he paid a visit to James Covert, Ryan's chief of vehicle services. Twice, Covert called Ryan to complain that Warner was clouting contracts.[2] Ryan shrugged it off. "Larry is my friend," he said, "just a businessman trying to do business," and ordered Covert to resume taking Warner's calls.[3] Unfortunately for Ryan but luckily for the feds, Covert kept detailed diaries.

Ryan and Warner had met during Governor Ogilvie's administration through Art Telcser, a respected Chicago Republican legislator. Telcser, Ryan, Warner, Donald Udstuen, and Alan A. Drazek formed a kind of boys'-night-out fraternity. Udstuen had been Ogilvie's patronage chief; Drazek was Ogilvie's personnel director. Ryan, Warner, Udstuen, and Drazek all would be indicted and convicted. Of this quartet, Warner was the neat, quiet, publicity-shy one. Drazek, also a low-key sort, was in business with, among others, Roger "The Hog" Stanley. "Dr. Don" Udstuen was the personification of a cigar-chomping, smooth-talking lobbyist (though the cigar often was unlit). And George Ryan—well, he was the unofficial president of the Old Timers Club.

Prosecutors accused Warner of illegally making $3.4 million from clouted leases and contracts over nine years under Ryan.[4] Warner's business dealings are impossibly entangled, a magpie's nest of connections and concealments. Perhaps the general operation of the scams might be illustrated by a simple, trivial matter—the awarding of low-digit "vanity" license plates.

It would take some doing to exaggerate the importance some people attached to vanity plates as cachets of clout. Warner himself drove a Mercedes-Benz with a license plate bearing only the letter *O*, a gift from Secretary of State Ryan. Even James Covert, the vehicle services chief, had a vanity plate—just the letter *C*. Jim Edgar had awarded it first to Covert's father, a major Edgar contributor. As for Ryan, he had *R*.

Anthony De Santis, a wealthy businessman, offered Ryan a campaign contribution of $2,000. They were on Lake Michigan aboard the *Blue Moon*, a yacht owned by racing impresario and Republican boss Richard Duchossois, during a Ryan fund-raiser in August 1997. Problem was, donations exceeding $500 had to be reported on disclosure forms. De Santis did not want his name listed thereon. He had friends in both parties, he explained. De Santis's reluctance exemplified how campaign financial reforms that limit contributions and require disclosures can benefit incumbents. Many contributors are not eager to displease incumbents, or other members of the incumbents' party, by appearing on their challengers' disclosure forms.

Ryan had a solution. He told De Santis to write four checks for $500 each to Ryan, Lura Lynn, and Ryan's son and daughter-in-law. After the checks were deposited in September, Ryan's secretary called De Santis and offered, as a thank you, a license plate with the low digit 217. De Santis accepted it. As it happened, that number had become available only because a family that had held it for fifty years let it lapse. The family actually sued (unsuccessfully) to recover the plate. That is how seriously some people took this matter.

Warner became in effect the broker of these coveted plates. At times he would enter Scott Fawell's office to ask for a computer check of whether a certain number was already assigned. If not, Warner gave that number to a friend or contributor. He did this so often that he kept a "kitty" in the drawer of one of Ryan's secretaries to pay the eleven-dollar processing fees. That unfortunate secretary sometimes felt the wrath of Ryan as he demanded to know how Warner learned that a number had become available before he did. Over eight years,

Ryan approved at least seventy-three low-digit plates at Warner's request. There would have been more except that Ryan's predecessor Edgar already had given out most of the low numbers.

Petty, but not illegal? In fact, the plates were an item in count two of the federal case against Ryan and Warner. Ryan did not declare any of the De Santis money either as gifts or campaign contributions on forms required by the state. After learning that the feds had discovered the De Santis checks, Ryan amended his Statement of Economic Interests to reflect those "gifts" from De Santis. As for Warner, the feds said his role as de facto plate broker inured to his personal and financial benefit.

Turning now to serious money—Warner was involved in three secretary of state building leases and at least five major secretary of state contracts with a complex scheme of influence peddling. Warner gave some of the money to Don Udstuen. Alan Drazek laundered some of Warner's payments to Udstuen, keeping a portion for himself.

Before these schemes are examined in some detail, a closer look at Warner's personal relationship with Ryan and his family might better illuminate how the gears meshed, how the matrix of favors and coercions aligned.

Ryan's son, George H. Ryan Jr., called "Homer," fumbled for a career. There was a craze for cigars during the 1990s, and Homer opened the Cigar Czar shop in Bourbonnais, near Kankakee. He asked his father's associates, including Fawell, for $1,500 loans for the business. Fawell did not esteem young Ryan and refused. Warner, though, put at least $6,000 into the store. George Ryan's campaign fund bought $3,200 worth of cigars there in one year. Even so, the store foundered. Homer now sells insurance from that office, and his former walk-in humidor houses his impressive collection of sports memorabilia. Warner bought some of his companies' insurance from Homer.

Ryan's daughter Lynda was divorced with three children. Warner sent a construction crew to build a room in her basement for a home-based business. He billed her for $11,000 and in effect wrote off $8,326 of it. The next year, he in effect wrote off $1,040 in flood damage at George Ryan's Chicago apartment. Also, Warner paid most of the bill for roof repairs at Ryan's Kankakee home.

Lynda married her second husband, Michael Fairman, on New Year's Eve of 1995. Misfortune visited the marriage—Fairman was a drinker and a gambler who declared bankruptcy in 1997. The bankruptcy happened even after Fairman received a $5,000 loan, never collected, from Warner, along with $55,000 from Ryan's campaign organization, for which he did no work. Fairman was ticketed thirty-four times and arrested twice for drunken driving between 1993 and 2004. The second DUI would have caused revocation of his license under a crackdown that Ryan had championed. However, the first DUI either was expunged from or never entered into state records while Ryan was secretary of state. Lynda Fairman herself pleaded guilty to drunken driving in 2004. Her blood alcohol level exceeded point-oh-eight.

In 1997, Ryan's daughter Jeanette married James Schneider, a secretary of state employee since the Jim Edgar days. Nine months before the wedding, Schneider got an 11 percent raise under Ryan, and three months later, he received a 10 percent raise. By the time Ryan left office, his son-in-law's salary had nearly doubled. At Jeanette's wedding reception at the Kankakee Country Club, Warner signed a blank check to pay for the band; Ryan filled out the amount, $3,185. The band leader had played with Survivor, the group with the hit "Eye of the Tiger." (The country club's bill, $10,000, was paid by Citizens for Ryan.)

So a wealthy businessman did favors for Ryan and Ryan's children—so what? That is what friends are for. Or so Warner's defense attorneys made the case. The Justice Department countered that Ryan steered lucrative state contracts to Warner in exchange for cash, gifts, and favors in violation of the laws. The feds never charged that Ryan extracted bribe X in exchange for action Y. It was not that simple.

The jury that tried Ryan and Warner listened to months of mind-numbing testimony about the intricacies of their dealings. Three contracts will be reviewed as specimens, parts for the whole.

It is 1991. Honeywell has the contract to run the secretary of state's computers. They are inadequate, out of date. After Ryan is elected, his transition team says the computers must be upgraded. Honeywell makes its pitch to do so to Ryan, Warner, Udstuen, and others. Warner and Udstuen tell Honeywell that if the company wants the contract, they have to be hired as lobbyists. Their fee: $250,000. Honeywell's representative reports this demand to his superiors, who say, come on, try to reduce that amount.

The Honeywell representative soon sees Ryan and Warner riding a golf cart at a Ryan fund-raiser, then later that day spots Warner drinking alone at the bar. The man from Honeywell asks for another meeting regarding the computer contract. When the meeting occurs, Warner and Udstuen suddenly are burdened with ethical concerns. They were part of Ryan's transition team that recommended a computer upgrade and so they really should not, appearance of impropriety and all that, be involved with the computer upgrade contract. The Honeywell representative does not appreciate this ethical nicety. Warner and Udstuen then suggest that he go see Ron Swanson, Ryan's pal.

Swanson in turn tells the man from Honeywell that he could get him the contract; however, his fee is $750,000. The Honeywell representative freaks. Swanson then indicates that the company could pay a million dollars over four years. To Honeywell, this is no better. At the time, Honeywell already retained two other lobbyists in Springfield. The representative tells this story to one of his lobbyists, Robert Cook, a pal of Ryan's. Cook is shocked and goes to see Ryan, who says he knew nothing about this and would ask Udstuen about it. Ryan later calls Cook back and says that Udstuen's story is that Honeywell sought *them* out and that he is relieved that Warner and Udstuen did nothing wrong. Cook concludes he can't trust Ryan and drops further contact with him.

During this time, a Springfield Republican powerhouse named Robert Kjellander calls Udstuen. Kjellander, formerly Governor Thompson's patronage chief, lobbies for International Business Machines, a much bigger firm than Honeywell. Kjellander tells Udstuen that, because Scott Fawell detests him, IBM needs to hire another lobbyist to seek the computer contract. Udstuen suggests Larry Warner, which Kjellander thinks is a great idea. In fact, the idea is so exciting that Udstuen calls Fawell about it. As for the Honeywell representative, he is screwed.

Meanwhile, Ryan needs to hire somebody to supervise the computer upgrade. Kjellander calls Frank Cavallero and offers him the job. Cavallero soon has lunch with Warner and Udstuen. Look, Warner and Udstuen say, let's go with IBM, not Honeywell. Cavallero agrees; he is a tech guy and knows this stuff. After Cavallero's interview with Ryan, Ryan is indecisive and tells Fawell he is not sure Cavallero would be "his guy." Fawell points out that Ryan was the one who told Larry and Don to find him a guy; what do you want? So Ryan hires Cavallero.

Then two men from IBM come down from Minnesota and have lunch with Warner in Chicago. They hire Warner, who would get 3.5 percent of IBM's net revenues from any subsequent secretary of state business.

Cavallero meets with Fawell, then meets again with Fawell and Udstuen. Everyone wants IBM. But Ryan's office needs political cover against a sole-source contract. So Udstuen calls the secretary of state's general counsel and describes the emergency. The general counsel agrees. IBM and Honeywell are the only bidders on the sole-source emergency contract. Ryan's selection committee recommends IBM. Ryan balks at first at the $28.5 million price tag, but then he stands up, walks across the room, lights a cigar, and dismisses the meeting. Ryan thinks, though, that he has an airtight defense against any allegation of contract-rigging: IBM was the better supplier, and his official review committee recommended it.

IBM pays Warner $991,000. Under Warner's contract, he cannot hire subcontractors. Even so, Warner gives a third of the IBM money to Udstuen via Drazek. IBM's contract with Warner expires in late 1994. Trouble is, Ryan in his good-government posture has gotten the Lobbyist Registration Act of 1994 passed. IBM tells Warner that, under this law, he must register as an IBM lobbyist. Warner refuses and suggests writing a new contract under which he would subcontract with Kjellander's firm, thereby evading his own registration. IBM says, "No way." Talks ensue. IBM then tells Warner that the company will pay him $2,700 a month in addition to the 3.5 percent commission, but only if he duly registers. Warner finally agrees: "I am now prepared to register as your Lobbiest [*sic*]."[5] A new four-year contract is signed; it makes no mention of Udstuen and Drazek. A few times a year, Drazek goes to see Udstuen in his Chicago office, hands over cash.

Every year, Illinois motorists must obtain a colored sticker to affix to their vehicle license plates, denoting current registration. American Decal Manufacturing (ADM) made a metallic security mark for these stickers and had sold the stickers to Illinois since 1986. The security mark prevented counterfeiting. ADM won the secretary of state contract without hiring a lobbyist.

In the spring of 1991, ADM president Thomas O'Brien gets a call from Warner, whom he does not know. Warner tells O'Brien that ADM's chief competitor, Minnesota Mining and Manufacturing (3M), had hired Jim Thompson as its Illinois lobbyist—something like telling a White Sox manager that the Yankees have hired Babe Ruth. Warner is disingenuous: 3M had long retained two members of Thompson's law firm as lobbyists but never approached them about the stickers contract.

Warner warns O'Brien that "Big Jim" will get the security mark requirement deleted from the bid specifications, thereby opening the door for 3M to bid. When the two men meet for lunch, Warner says he is close to Ryan and can keep the specs as they are, beating Big Jim, for $2,000 a month. Sure enough, when the new specs come out, they have not changed. In July 1991, O'Brien agrees to pay Warner $2,000 a month until November 1992 and $3,000 a month after that. Warner insists on one small change in the agreement: he is a consultant, he says, not a lobbyist.

In August 1991, Warner comes back with more news. For an extra fee of $67,000, he can take from 3M the contract to produce the laminated security strips placed on vehicle titles (not the stickers on the plates). ADM previously had not sought this business, but O'Brien pays Warner the $67,000. Warner then tells James Covert, the secretary of state vehicle services chief, to keep doing business with ADM and not to do business with 3M, because 3M had refused to hire Warner as a lobbyist. Warner to ADM: You have to pay me enough to keep me from defecting to IBM. Warner to Covert: Spurn IBM because they won't hire me.

Pretty soon, Warner asks Covert to stall the specs for a new title security strips contract. Warner and Udstuen meet with Covert and advise him, "Do not give American Decal blatant advantage" in writing new specs. Covert underlines "blatant" in his notes, understanding them to mean that he shouldn't make it obvious the new specs are tailored for ADM. 3M invites Covert to tour its plant in Minnesota. When Ryan hears of the trip, he cautions Covert against "getting too close to 3M."[6] ADM gets the new security strips contract.

Meanwhile, Warner keeps calling O'Brien to demand timely payments of his monthly fee. Once he tells O'Brien that 3M had offered to pay him $8,000 a month to lobby for them, which is untrue. Then ADM is sold. The new owner wants to know exactly what Warner does for ADM. Warner refuses to explain, telling O'Brien:

> I just received your message wherein you requested that I send a letter to you describing the scope of services I provided since representing American Decal. . . . I know that I have made you aware of my frustrations in getting paid by your company, and as of now, you are six months delinquent in paying me. Quite frankly, I don't understand your requesting this information from me, inasmuch as if anybody is aware of the services I have provided your company, you should be aware. And, therefore, if you want an essay on what I have done for American Decal, I suggest you write it, because I'm not going to. I will expect payment in full by Monday, September 14th [1992]. If this is not met, I'm through and there will be no more conversations.[7]

O'Brien leaves ADM. Warner goes to see the new ADM president, John Koepke, and demands $3,000 a month.

An internal secretary of state committee recommends dropping the metallic security mark from the stickers, thus inviting other bidders with different security devices. Covert agrees and opens the bidding. When Koepke finds out, he calls Warner, who calls Covert at home on a Saturday morning and chews him out. Next thing Covert knows, he gets a call from Ryan: Why the hell were the specs changed? Covert replies that he is trying to protect Ryan with a fair competitive bidding process. Ryan calls a meeting with Fawell and others. The result? The metallic security mark is put back in the specs.

ADM salesman Mike Kelly attends a Ryan fund-raiser and sees Warner smoking a cigar outside by himself. Warner tells Kelly he gives cheap cigars to most people but keeps good cigars for important people; he then offers Kelly an expensive cigar. Warner tells him he could get anybody at the secretary of state's office fired but finds it easier just to stroke them, give them small gifts.

ADM is sold again. Warner meets the interim ADM vice president and demands $5,000 a month to keep the stickers contract for the company. ADM refuses and continues paying $3,000. Then new executives come on board. Warner calls the new president, who has never heard of him. Warner says he had quit as ADM lobbyist because his $5,000 fee was rejected. Warner gets the higher fee. Yet another new president takes over, and then the company is sold yet again. Warner demands a payment of $20,000 plus $8,000 a month. He also wants a written contract so that if ADM goes bankrupt, he would be on the books as a creditor. Otherwise, he will go to 3M. ADM stalls and offers Warner an upfront payment of $5,000. Warner quits. The next year, 1999, ADM loses the stickers contract to a Detroit-based company made up of former ADM officials who had hired Warner. The computers, plate stickers, and title laminates are just three of the contracts Warner clouted.

The Justice Department indicted Warner, Udstuen, and Drazek on May 21, 2002. Warner hired Edward M. Genson, one of the top criminal defense lawyers in the nation. Most of Warner's business already had fallen away, but he still spent many nights in his office until late, seemingly dazed and depressed. Genson put tens of thousands of pages of case-related documents on a computer hard drive and gave it to Warner. Night after night, sometimes all night long, Warner read the contents of that hard drive over and over.

Warner went to a psychiatrist for depression. He was in his mid-sixties with rapidly failing health. By the time of his trial, he was taking Lipitor for high cholesterol, Flomax for an enlarged prostate, Effexor for depression, and two powerful medicines, Digoxin and Amiodarone, for an irregular heartbeat. While taking these drugs, Warner was drinking heavily as well. Once during the trial, he fell, hurt his face, and was taken to a hospital emergency room. Warner's ordeal was difficult for his wife, Cindy, too. After he was convicted, she collapsed in her house and was incoherent when medical personnel arrived. She was treated at a hospital.

Sure, Larry is a tough, hard-nosed businessman, one of Warner's attorneys told the jury, but he is kind and generous to friends and even to strangers when he hears of their troubles. "Larry Warner is a real live human being and not some comic book character called The Fixer."[8] The lawyer did not ask such people as James Covert and Thomas O'Brien, but that is exactly how they might have described him.

House Speaker George Ryan's campaign poster for lieutenant governor is displayed at one of the Ryan family's pharmacies in Kankakee. Photo by Perry C. Riddle; as published in the *Chicago Sun-Times*. Reprinted with permission.

"Six grown men at Disney World"—(*standing, from left*) lobbyist Lawrence E. Warner, Ryan's chief of staff Scott Fawell, insurance executive Richard Parillo; (*seated, from left*) Cook County Republican chairman Manny Hoffman, Secretary of State George Ryan, Chicago Bulls executive Joseph O'Neil—was government exhibit 01–051 in *U.S. vs. Warner and Ryan.* Courtesy of the U.S. Attorney's Office, Northern District of Illinois.

Congressman Glenn Poshard, the Democratic nominee for governor in 1998, shows copies of checks and fund-raising tickets, suggesting that Secretary of State Ryan's office sold licenses and other favors for cash. Photo by Scott Stewart; as published in the *Chicago Sun-Times*. Reprinted with permission.

Republican governor Ryan and Democratic mayor Richard M. Daley of Chicago collaborated on renovation of Soldier Field, expansion of O'Hare International Airport, and other "pork barrel" projects. Photo by John H. White; as published in the *Chicago Sun-Times*. Reprinted with permission.

Jeremy Margolis, attorney for Citizens for Ryan, attempted to deflect Operation Safe Road charges against Ryan and his friends. Here he discusses a casino proposal favored by Governor Ryan. Photo by John Sall; as published in the *Chicago Sun-Times*. Reprinted with permission.

Dean Bauer (*left*), former inspector general for former Secretary of State Ryan, was the first of Ryan's major associates to be indicted and to plead guilty in Operation Safe Road. His attorney, Edward M. Genson, accompanies him to a federal court appearance. Photo by Perry C. Riddle; as published in the *Chicago Sun-Times*. Reprinted with permission.

Businessman Harry Klein accepted thousand-dollar checks from Ryan for weekly vacations at his Jamaican estate, then gave Ryan one thousand dollars in cash back for each check. Ryan was convicted of lying to federal agents about these transactions. Photo by Scott Stewart; as published in the *Chicago Sun-Times*. Reprinted with permission.

Lobbyist Donald "Dr. Don" Udstuen pleaded guilty to one count of tax fraud conspiracy and testified against Ryan. Photo by John J. Kim; as published in the *Chicago Sun-Times*. Reprinted with permission.

Political consultant Roger "The Hog" Stanley pleaded guilty to one count of mail fraud and one count of money laundering and cooper-ated in the investigation of Ryan. Photo by Al Podgorski; as published in the *Chicago Sun-Times*. Reprinted with permission.

Arthur "Ron" Swanson (*left*), here with his friend Sandra McAvoy, George
Ryan, Mrs. Ryan, and New York Yankees owner George Steinbrenner,
pleaded guilty to one count of perjury but declined to testify against Ryan.
Government Exhibit 16–082, U.S. vs. Warner and Ryan; courtesy of the U.S.
Attorney's Office, Northern District of Illinois.

Governor Ryan named his protégé Scott Fawell to run the mammoth
McCormick Place convention center in Chicago. Here, Ryan listens to Fawell
after signing a bill to fund a major expansion of the facility. Photo by Jim Frost;
as published in the *Chicago Sun-Times*. Reprinted with permission.

Sisters Gertrude Burts and Emma Burts, who each lost three children in an arson fire set by a death row inmate, comfort each other during a clemency hearing on capital cases. Three months later, Governor Ryan issued a blanket commutation. Photo by John H. White; as published in the *Chicago Sun-Times*. Reprinted with permission.

The governor and Lura Lynn Ryan appear contented, even serene, on the night when Democrat Rod Blagojevich was elected as Ryan's successor, ending twenty-two years of Republican control of the governorship and Ryan's thirty-two years in public office. Photo by Richard A. Chapman; as published in the *Chicago Sun-Times*. Reprinted with permission.

U.S. attorney Patrick J. Fitzgerald (*left*) and his assistant Patrick M. Collins, the lead prosecutor in Operation Safe Road, announce Ryan's indictment on eighteen counts of corruption on December 17, 2003. Photo by Richard A. Chapman; as published in the *Chicago Sun-Times*. Reprinted with permission.

"The best trial lawyer in America" and a protégé of former governor James R. Thompson, Dan K. Webb prosecuted crooked judges as a U.S. attorney and was the criminal defense lawyer for former governor Ryan. Photo by Jim Frost; as published in the *Chicago Sun-Times*. Reprinted with permission.

Andrea Coutretsis, Scott Fawell's aide and girlfriend, helped persuade the imprisoned Fawell to "flip" for the government and testify against Ryan. Photo by Jean Lachat; as published in the *Chicago Sun-Times*. Reprinted with permission.

Judge Rebecca R. Pallmeyer faced many difficult rulings on allegations of juror misconduct in the trial of Ryan and Warner. Photo by Jean Lachat; as published in the *Chicago Sun-Times*. Reprinted with permission.

Lawrence E. Warner, Lura Lynn Ryan, and George Ryan leave the federal courthouse in Chicago after Judge Pallmeyer sentenced both men to prison on September 6, 2006. Photo by Scott Stewart; as published in the *Chicago Sun-Times*. Reprinted with permission.

Former governor James R. Thompson, whose law firm defended Ryan for free, waits to testify in an unrelated legal matter shortly after Ryan was sentenced to prison. Photo by Brian Jackson; as published in the *Chicago Sun-Times*. Reprinted with permission.

10 Boy, Those Guys Are Good

Harry Klein was a portly man who once owned twenty-five currency exchanges in Illinois. Currency exchanges function as banks for people too poor to have regular checking accounts. Customers usually go to a currency exchange to cash their payroll, government, or insurance checks, but they can also buy money orders, pay utility bills, register their cars, buy city and state vehicle stickers, even (a service seldom offered in Chicago) buy hunting licenses. Currency exchanges are lucrative, and Klein co-owned a villa in Jamaica he called Seven Seas. The villa came with seven servants and offered four bedrooms, four baths, and tennis courts on three and a half acres. Klein usually charged $1,000 a week to rent it, but his pal George Ryan stayed there for free.

Ryan had no idea how the way he finagled these free Jamaican vacations would trouble his later years. His deceit in the matter angered federal investigators and, apparently, offended his jurors. Ryan wrote Klein checks for $1,000 a week. Klein deposited the checks. Then Klein gave the money back to Ryan in cash. Ryan thus had a fake paper record showing he had paid.

Manny Hoffman, the Cook County Republican chairman, introduced Ryan to Klein. Soon, George and Lura Lynn Ryan and Manny and Judy Hoffman were on their way to the Seven Seas in January 1993. Ryan liked the place so much that he called Scott Fawell, who was vacationing in Hawaii, to rave about it. Back in Illinois, Ryan said Fawell had to join them next time. Fawell did so and did the same checks-for-cash-back fandango with Klein, then dropped it as pointless after a few years. He thereby angered Ryan's lawyer, Jeremy Margolis, who insisted on the check-writing arrangement. Ryan persisted until 2002, writing $13,500 in checks and pocketing the same amount in cash. Ryan and Fawell also enjoyed November visits to Klein's place in Palm Springs, California. One time they chartered a plane there on a whim and took off to Las Vegas for a day's gambling junket.

Klein's hospitality was repaid after a fashion. Ryan gave him a low-digit license plate. He paid for cable TV at the villa. Meanwhile, currency exchanges were seeking a raise in the state-regulated fees they charged customers. Klein mentioned this policy proposal to Ryan. And so it came to pass. Actually, currency exchanges probably could have won a fee hike without Klein's help—the industry had not had an increase in ten years.[1] Under Ryan, the state also leased one of Klein's buildings for $10,000 a month—nearly tripling his revenue from previous tenants—but that arrangement was harder won.

Returning from his January 1997 visit to Jamaica, Ryan told Fawell and another aide, R. Michael Chamness, to see about renting property from Klein. A building Klein controlled in South Holland in suburban Cook County might be used as a driver's license facility. Ryan told Chamness that Klein was a dear friend, gave him Klein's phone number, and cautioned that when the lease was worked out, Ryan personally wanted to give Klein the good news. The secretary of state's office canceled a lease in Lake Calumet, another Cook County suburb, deciding to move to South Holland instead. Soon, Chamness, Fawell, and Klein attended a Chicago Bulls basketball game. Klein thanked Chamness for having leased the South Holland property.

The next day, Ryan called Chamness in a rage. "He said, 'I thought I told you I wanted to be the one to tell Mr. Klein I had a deal,'" Chamness testified. "He told me that if I couldn't follow instructions, he would find someone who could."[2] Chamness protested that he had not told Klein it was a done deal, that there were problems with the site. It was a modest, one-story, mostly vacant brick building, hard to reach from a frontage road off Interstate 94. The parking lot was too small for trucks to maneuver well in CDL tests. Klein wanted the state to pay the renovation costs, Klein wanted the state to pay the property taxes, Klein wanted the lease to drop the standard termination clause. Ryan told Chamness to bend things Klein's way. When the lease was finally ready, Ryan signed it personally—typically he used an autopen for routine documents. For the price, $25 a square foot, the state could have rented luxury office space in the Loop.

Ryan also struck real estate deals with Arthur "Ron" Swanson, the Springfield lobbyist who had sought a fee of $750,000 from Honeywell for the secretary of state's computer contract that ultimately went to IBM. Swanson, a former state senator, was good to Ryan, and Ryan was good to him. Swanson, like Larry Warner, openly conducted his lobbying business from an anteroom to Ryan's Capitol office. In perhaps an even larger display of status and clout, Swanson had a free parking spot on the Capitol grounds.

Swanson hosted the Ryans at his time-share condominium in Cancun; Homer Ryan hosted Swanson at the young Ryan's condo in Lake Tahoe, Nevada. Swanson paid for a Disney World trip for Ryan's daughter Julie and her family. He gave George and Lura Lynn a Lladro porcelain figurine, a Limoges porcelain box, a St. John's dress, Cuban cigars, golf bags, and cuff links. He gave cash gifts to six of Ryan's aides. In addition, Swanson made a curious practice of withdrawing large sums of cash from his accounts on or just before Ryan's birthday, February 24.

Swanson was the rental agent for Lincoln Towers, an office complex across from the Capitol in Springfield. Ryan told Fawell to rent secretary of state space there. Swanson's price far exceeded the norm, so the always resourceful Fawell added to the square footage areas usually omitted, such as hallways. In that way, the price per square foot appeared more reasonable. When Ryan stepped down as governor in January 2003, he still was trying to get the state to buy Lincoln Towers outright. The transaction would have provided Swanson a commission of $1.7 million.

Wisconsin Energy Corporation, based in Milwaukee, was looking for business—and hence a lobbyist—in Illinois. An investor in the firm asked Don Udstuen to recommend a lobbyist, so Udstuen talked with Ryan. The man they recommended was Swanson. After Wisconsin Energy hired Swanson in 1999, Swanson gave Udstuen $4,000 in cash in a men's room in Lino's, a restaurant in Chicago's trendy River North area. Swanson assured Udstuen that he was taking care of Ryan as well—"You know I always take care of George."[3]

Economically distressed small towns in Illinois competed avidly to host a new maximum-security prison. Governor Ryan and his aides in February 2001 chose Grayville, population 1,800, in the southeastern corner of the state. Ryan strolled from his office, saw Swanson, and told him of the Grayville selection, although it would not be publicly announced for weeks. Swanson speedily got Grayville to hire him as a lobbyist for the prison project for $50,000. Sure enough, Ryan vindicated the town's payment to Swanson by declaring it the winner in May. Grayville, though, still does not have a prison. Ryan's successor, Governor Blagojevich, canceled the project after the state already had spent millions of dollars.

Shortly after becoming governor, Ryan named Fawell as CEO of the Metropolitan Pier and Exposition Authority ("McPier"), which runs Chicago's huge Navy Pier and McCormick Place facilities. Ryan told Fawell to hire Swanson as a lobbyist for a McPier expansion project. Problem was, McPier already had a lobbyist, a gold-plated Chicago law firm. Never mind, Ryan said; hire Swanson. He was paid $180,000 for little or no work.

Besides McPier, another major public authority favored by Ryan and his pals was Metra, the commuter railway for the Chicago region. Udstuen sat on the Metra board. Roger "The Hog" Stanley was associated with five companies that received $4 million of Metra contracts. Stanley kicked back $130,000 to Udstuen. Under the Metra contracts, Stanley was required to subcontract a certain amount to businesses controlled by minorities or women. He did so to a firm owned by his wife.

A tall, loud chain-smoker with a white toupee that looked more like a helmet, Stanley had been a state representative from the Chicago suburb of Streamwood.

In 1997, he worked for Ryan's secretary of state's office for six weeks. Those six weeks increased his annual state pension from $23,800 to $55,253. At the time, former legislators could draw 85 percent of their final government salary, regardless of length of service, starting on their fifty-fifth birthday.

Stanley's Universal Statistical Services (Unistat) provided direct-mail surveys and brochures, legislators' newsletters, lists of registered voters, and related services, mostly for Republican clients. He won the contract to publicize Ryan's organ donor program, although, typically, it was hidden under another corporate name. He paid the managers of various political campaigns, including Fawell, to steer business to Unistat. Stanley's business partner was Alan Drazek, who laundered money for Warner and Udstuen through a company of his own.

Also, Stanley was a partner in a Costa Rican travel agency that provided prostitution services on the side. Stanley gave Fawell free or discounted vacations in Costa Rica as well as in Door County, Wisconsin, and Lake Ontario, Canada. Fawell had arranged for Stanley's six-week, no-show job to boost his pension. Unistat and other Stanley ventures won more than $3 million in state contracts, many of them without competitive bidding.

Klein, Swanson, and Stanley were, so to speak, understudies to the masters Warner, Udstuen, and Fawell. As the feds were trying to untangle all their malversations, a friend called Warner to warn that federal agents had approached him about a certain contract that Warner was trying to clout. "Boy," said Warner, "those guys are good."[4] That was about the time—April 2002—when Udstuen became the first of these men to "flip," to cooperate with the government in exchange for leniency.

With all this smoke, how is it that voters did not notice that it arose from flames in Ryan's office? After all, voters could hardly complain that they were never informed of allegations that Ryan was unethical. Aside from the 1982 nursing home scandal, allegations of Ryan's strong-arm fund-raising tactics surfaced as early as November 11, 1993. WMAQ-TV, the NBC affiliate in Chicago, launched a three-part series that day on the results of a joint investigation with the Better Government Association. Anonymous car dealers said they felt coerced to give funds to secretary of state agents for fear of retaliation. In eight years as lieutenant governor, Ryan had raised $26,200 from auto dealers. In two and a half years as secretary of state, he increased that number eightfold. Ryan issued the first of many denials that his employees were forced to sell fund-raising tickets on the job. In response to the reports, he also directed that secretary of state inspectors could not raise campaign funds on or off state time. Maybe some people took this edict seriously.

The next spring, WMAQ and the BGA struck again. Despite Ryan's new policy, they caught on camera a secretary of state inspector selling tickets to an auto body shop owner. Other secretary of state employees, disguised on camera, described heavy pressures to sell tickets. Ryan's allies accused WMAQ and the BGA of grandstanding on behalf of Patrick Quinn, Ryan's election opponent. Ryan made another gesture of reform, saying he had forbidden secretary of state workers from soliciting donations from businesses they regulated.

For all that, much of Ryan's politicking remained concealed. Bruce Clark, who was married to Ryan's niece Kathy, ran for the state House in 1992. Fawell obligingly named a secretary of state employee to run Clark's campaign on state time. That transgression made even a secretary of state official nervous. In a meeting with Ryan and Fawell, he suggested taking Clark's manager off the state payroll in the final weeks before the election. Fawell refused.

Fawell's mother, state senator Beverly Fawell, faced a contested primary in 1994. Fawell told his six top aides to make the senator's campaign their top priority. Senator Fawell won the March primary, after which Fawell's gang turned to reelecting Ryan in November. A few workers actually were transferred from the secretary of state payroll to Citizens for Ryan (CFR), the campaign fund, but Fawell and others ran the campaign on state time.

Safely reelected, Ryan dismantled the secretary of state inspector general's office. All investigators were transferred or fired—as Fawell commented, "You can't trust those fucks anyway"—but Dean Bauer was allowed to keep the title of inspector general.[5] Meanwhile, the BGA found that several trucking schools were scamming CDLs for out-of-state truckers at the secretary of state's Elk Grove Village facility. As many as 154 Eastern European immigrants, many of whom did not speak English, had claimed the same Illinois motel as their residence. Rather than run to the media with this story, the BGA presented its evidence to Ryan's aides. An investigation was promised and promptly dropped.

Ryan turned his attention to the race for the 1996 Republican presidential nomination. Early on, Texas senator W. Philip Gramm raised the most money. Ryan agreed to host a Gramm fund-raiser in March 1995 but did not commit to endorse him. "If he bombs and doesn't make the grade, I'll be with Bob Dole," Ryan calculated.[6] However, Governor Edgar was the Illinois chairman for Dole, the Kansas senator and eventual nominee. Endorsing Dole thus would give Ryan no added clout in the Dole campaign or among Illinois Republicans. The Gramm campaign, though, would let Ryan run the show. Also, it presented Ryan an added attraction—he might make some money from it.

Ryan endorsed Gramm and kept secret the profits he made from chairing the Gramm campaign in Illinois. He asked Udstuen for advice on how to launder the money. Udstuen suggested using Drazek's company, American Management Resources (AMR). The Gramm campaign paid AMR, which then paid Ryan, Fawell, and Fawell's aide Richard Juliano. Ryan directed his cut of the money to his daughters: Lynda, newly married to an alcoholic gambler, Michael

Fairman, received $5,950; Nancy, $1,725; Julie and Joanne, $1,000 each. Testifying under immunity, one or more of the daughters said they might have done a nominal amount of work for the money. AMR's payments to Ryan, Fawell, and Juliano, exceeding $33,000, naturally did not appear on Gramm's federal election reports. Gramm was a good fund-raiser but a weak candidate. He had such little support in Illinois that Ryan's staffers called the Gramm campaign the "Gramm pain."

With Gramm's campaign dead by February 1996, Ryan turned to the November elections for the Illinois House. He made a deal with Republican Speaker Lee A. Daniels to assign secretary of state and Citizens for Ryan coordinators to Daniels's targeted districts. Fawell said the secretary of state/CFR coordinators had been volunteers for Ryan's 1994 reelection but that they should be paid for their efforts this time around. Their payments were laundered through Roger Stanley's Unistat. (Ten years later, Michael Tristano, Daniels's former chief of staff, pleaded guilty to assigning legislative staffers to do campaign work on state time, effectively having cost the state $200,000.)

By 1997, Ryan was planning to run for governor, and Larry Warner offered to sponsor an event to raise $100,000. Warner himself put up $25,000, but the checks were not in his name or in the names of his major businesses. Thus, he did not appear on campaign financial reports. The fund-raiser was held at Lino's, the restaurant where Swanson would hand over $4,000 to Udstuen in a men's room.

While Warner was organizing this fund-raiser, a secretary of state employee, Laurie Roff, in Pontiac, Illinois, kept telling her supervisor that licenses were being sold for bribes. The supervisor, Kathy Clark, pooh-poohed the idea but duly reported Roff's allegations to secretary of state investigators. Clark is Ryan's niece, the daughter of his sister Kathleen Dean. Roff was so frustrated by secretary of state inaction that finally she blew the whistle to the media. On February 10, 1998, WLS-TV, the ABC affiliate in Chicago, broadcast Roff's allegations. Her identity was disguised with her face in shadow and voice distorted.

The next morning, Ryan called Roff. How he learned her identity was never explained. Quickly she was summoned to a meeting with Kathy Clark, Inspector General Dean Bauer, Mike Chamness, and others. An investigation was promised and promptly dropped. Bauer complained that the WLS report had compromised his own investigation, but that was untrue.

As governor, Jim Thompson had built an ultramodern, seventeen-floor state office building in Chicago's Loop. The building was named the Thompson Center in his honor in 1993. From the fifth floor, the secretary of state's suite, Fawell ran the Ryan campaigns. To manage the Thompson Center office, Ryan had named Glen Bower, a former state's attorney from southern Illinois. Bower was disturbed by all the empty desks of secretary of state employees who were off doing campaign work. He took special note of the empty desks of Andrea Coutretsis Prokos, Fawell's aide and mistress, and her sister, Tina Lundberg. Fawell did not appreciate Bower's pointing out these absences to him. Bower went to Ryan. Ryan told Fawell to work it out with Bower.

Prokos invited Bower to a meeting with Fawell—not in the Thompson Center but in the campaign office across the street—in February 1998. The proximity made it easy for secretary of state staffers to haul reams of paper and other supplies from the Thompson Center. Fawell told Bower, among other things, that the multimillion-dollar Citizens for Ryan could not afford to pay all the campaign workers' salaries. (Perhaps Fawell had a point—CFR paid Ryan's son-in-law Michael Fairman $55,000 to do nothing; such disbursements added up.) Bower observed that just down Dearborn Street, in the federal courthouse, Chicago aldermen were being prosecuted for ghost payrolling in the Operation Haunted Hall investigation. Fawell replied that he, not Bower, would decide who was on the campaign payroll and for what percentage of the time. Bower did not again complain to Ryan.

But if Ryan and Fawell thought that squelching Roff and Bower contained the damage, they were dreaming. Whistle-blowers and investigators would continue to torment them for the next eight years and more. Not the least of their worries was that in December 1995, Joseph Power had filed a wrongful deaths lawsuit on behalf of the Reverend Scott Willis and his wife. Power was aptly named; he was a major Democratic Party figure and top-drawer litigator. The deaths of six Willis children also had provoked the BGA to investigate Ryan's fund-raising methods. For Ryan even to consider running for governor in these straits, he should be credited with audacity or blamed for ethical blindness. Or maybe he should just be considered an Illinois pol.

11 We Looked Thirty-two Ways for That

Governor Jim Edgar easily could have been elected to a third term in 1998. Edgar was nerdy and low-key, which led many to underestimate him, but he was the most popular politician in Illinois. He was broadly praised for steering the state through a recession in the early 1990s without a tax increase or a budgetary meltdown. And like Governor Ogilvie, Edgar had a reputation as being incorruptible.

The Edgar administration was hardly scandal-free, though. Edgar named Robert Hickman, former mayor of Edgar's hometown of Charleston in east central Illinois and one of his biggest fund-raisers, to head the state toll highway authority. Hickman was convicted in a real estate scam in 1997. Later that year, the former owner of Management Services of Illinois (MSI) was convicted of bilking the state out of $7 million in a computer services contract. Testifying at the federal trial, Edgar said he did not remember details of a dinner at which MSI officials pledged $40,000 to his 1994 campaign.

Ryan hoped that Edgar would heed GOP party leaders' pleas that he run for the U.S. Senate in 1998, in which case Ryan would run for governor. If Edgar ran for reelection instead, then Ryan would seek reelection as secretary of state. On August 20, 1997, four days after the MSI verdict, Edgar surprisingly announced his retirement from politics, leaving the dais with tears in his eyes. He insisted that the MSI scandal had nothing to do with his stepping down—"I decided I'm not going to let how the media plays an issue determine what I'm going to do the next five years."[1] Edgar also had health concerns, having undergone heart bypass surgery in 1994. Maybe, too, he was just tired of the job. Senate Republican leader Pate Philip seemed to have even more fun thwarting Edgar than he did thwarting governors Thompson or Ryan.

Jack O'Malley, the Cook County state's attorney and Thompson's protégé, wanted to run for governor and so did other Republicans, but Ryan managed to clear the field. Ryan declared his candidacy on September 2, 1997, making a traditional eight-city "flyaround" of multiple press conferences. He also took the precaution of getting $24,222 of now-tainted MSI money out of his $2.6 million CFR, transferring that sum to the state school fund. That same month, Anthony De Santis wrote the Ryan family four $500 checks to avoid disclosure laws, and Harry Lockman arranged to pay off the Comguard loan anonymously. Having quelled possible ethical issues, Ryan on the political front decided to balance his ticket with a pro-choice female for lieutenant governor. At Udstuen's urging, he selected state representative Corrine Wood of Lake County—but their relationship in office would not be a happy one. On March 17, 1998, Ryan won the Republican primary against a fringe right-wing candidate.

Glenn Poshard, a congressman from deep southern Illinois, won a four-way Democratic primary. Ryan's race against Poshard was a typical Illinois brawl, with charges of poison-pen tactics and dirty tricks on both sides. Both men also had to run in effect a second race against disgruntled members of their own party—Chicago-area liberals in Poshard's case, the Christian right in Ryan's. Unfortunately for Ryan, he also was running a third race, a shadow one against whistle-blowers and investigators. Ryan might have thought he had silenced Russell Sonneveld, who tried to investigate the Guzman-Willis accident in November 1994, and Laurie Roff, who appeared on television in February 1998. Really, though, the whistle-blowers and investigators were just getting started.

Tammy Sue Raynor was a typical secretary of state patronage employee. She lived in Cicero and was clouted into her job by Charles J. Slezak, a Republican boss in that suburb on the west flank of Chicago. Raynor started as an $18,000-a-year counter clerk in 1991 at the secretary of state's station in McCook, a village of 250 people in western Cook County. As CDL testing facilities go, McCook was among the grimiest, both figuratively and literally—little more than cinder blocks and asphalt. Hardly had Raynor started on the job when a truck driver walked up to her counter and frankly asked, "I'm here for a test. Who do I pay?"[2] Later, as a license examiner herself for both the written and road tests, Raynor observed cheating even more blatant. It was she who coined the epithet "suntan CDLs" for truckers with fraudulent licenses from Florida.

Yet she did not see the half of it. McCook was where Gonzalo Mendoza bribed his girlfriend Marion Seibel for a CDL for Ricardo Guzman in 1992. Still, the operations sometimes were more sophisticated than crude licenses-for-bribes might suggest. Like characters in a spy thriller, some conspirators spoke in code. In Melrose Park, another secretary of state facility in western Cook County, the manager, the assistant manager, and a retired secretary of state worker often chatted on the phone about recipes and sewing. The FBI decoded their talks thus: the "recipe book" was the bribery scheme, "eggs" were bribe payments, "hemlines" were the amounts ("two and a half inches" equaled $250), African American truckers were "black dresses," and white truckers were "white dresses."[3] (The code was revealed in a court document unsealed two days after Ryan was elected governor.)

At McCook, Raynor voiced her concerns to her sponsor, Charles Slezak, who had two pieces of advice: look the other way and shut up. Then Raynor found a kindred spirit in Tony Berlin, another patronage worker at McCook. Berlin noticed that a trucker knocked down four traffic cones while maneuvering his rig—hit even one, you are supposed to flunk—but that man got his CDL. In November 1993, Berlin started keeping a log of the "specials" he observed—what Libertyville called "courtesy," McCook called "specials." In cryptic notes, Berlin recorded truckers' names, license numbers, the state workers involved, the payoff amounts, and the use of state trucks for fixed road tests.

Before long, the project obsessed Raynor and Berlin; they both started documenting the corruption at hand. They met after work to compare notes and exchange information. Raynor, feeling bad about neglecting her husband and daughter, even dropped her hobby of competitive country-and-western dancing.

CDL applicants kept Raynor and Berlin busy. One trucker proclaimed to Raynor the injustice of paying a $700 bribe and not receiving a permit to haul hazardous material. No fair, he said; the man next to him had to pay only $500. She also noticed that many foreign-speaking truckers did not know English. After they somehow passed their tests, she would say something like "Go sit over there" or "Go pay the cashier," and they did not understand. In August 1996, Raynor told her story to Inspector General Dean Bauer, who assigned an investigator to work with her. The next May, Raynor helped set up a sting operation against a bribe in progress. The sting worked, but Bauer refused to press criminal charges. (A later sting failed when the agent's cover secretly was blown from "downtown"—that is, secretary of state offices in Chicago.) In December, Raynor was abruptly transferred out of McCook. The alleged cause was insubordination. Berlin, though not transferred, was harassed—ordered, for example, to pick up trash in the parking lot. The day of Raynor's transfer, she and Berlin talked over their options and decided to call Joseph Power, the attorney for the Willises in their wrongful deaths case. In retrospect, their visit with Power, perhaps as much as any other event, sealed George Ryan's fate.

Out of desperation, Raynor also turned to—of all people—Lura Lynn Ryan. Raynor spent days writing a letter detailing the corruption she had witnessed and the official resistance she had met. The Ryans were to attend a charity banquet in Addison in western Cook County on February 7, 1998. Raynor's mother, Dorothy Allen, had Republican connections. Allen attended the banquet along with her lifelong friend Milly Slezak, the widow of Charles Slezak. Allen went to the table where the Ryans were dining and handed her daughter's letter to Lura Lynn. Both Ryans later said they had no memory of the incident, but the letter had swift repercussions for Raynor. Bauer and his aide Mike Chamness told her, from now on, deal directly with Bauer alone, nobody else.

Meanwhile, Raynor was protesting her transfer from McCook through her union. Chamness wrote the union's attorney: "Ms. Raynor's allegations that she was transferred because she would not participate in the illegal issuance of commercial driver's licenses is [*sic*] ludicrous."[4] Then, Raynor gave a sworn deposition in the Willis case in January 1998. Two months later, deposition in hand, she sat down with federal investigators. Chamness allegedly offered to transfer her back to McCook on condition that she provide a copy of her deposition; she refused. Chamness later denied asking for the deposition and noted that she was transferred back to McCook anyway.

Power leaked Raynor's and Berlin's stories to WLS-TV news, which had aired whistle-blower Laurie Roff on February 10. The station interviewed Raynor and Berlin for three hours and on April 7 broadcast nine and a half minutes of their allegations with their identities concealed. Asked to comment, Ryan, although he secretly had ordered the retesting of forty-two truckers at McCook, denied that anyone had provided solid evidence of wrongdoing there or anywhere else in the secretary of state complex. He kept denying it for the next six years.

Ryan could be affable and jolly in private; in public, although he had a powerful baritone voice, he often sounded flat and tired. His opponent Glenn Poshard was tightly wound in private, yet could be fiery on the stump. Aside from personal differences, the Democratic nominee was more conservative than Ryan on the issues of abortion, gun control, gay rights, and environmental protections. Poshard had defeated three liberals in the primary, but Chicago-area liberals figured, well, he had to hang right to please his downstate base. Once he was the statewide candidate for the November election, they were certain he would lurch to the left by Memorial Day. That did not happen. OK, then, by the Fourth of July. Labor Day? But Poshard meant what he said and stuck to it.

Regarding abortion, Poshard was pro-life down the line. Ryan took the standard Republican pro-life position while allowing exceptions for rape, incest, or to save the life of the mother. Scott Fawell and Roger Stanley put out the word to pro-life activists that they should back Ryan over Poshard. Terry Cosgrove, head of Personal PAC, a pro-choice lobby, set up a meeting of Ryan, Fawell, and a few pro-choice folks.

Vicki Stella's story was heartbreaking. A mother of three from the Chicago suburb of Naperville, she was thirty-two weeks into her fourth pregnancy when ultrasound tests produced dire news. Her son had nine major anomalies, including no brain—a "neural tube defect" that did not show up in an earlier amniocentesis. Both her physician husband and her gynecologist recommended an intact dilation and evacuation (D&E), or what pro-life advocates call a partial-birth abortion. This procedure, a particularly grisly one, is an inflammatory issue in the abortion debate. In other words, Cosgrove and Stella were not presenting Ryan with an easy case.

"I'm a diabetic," Stella said. "Other procedures would not have been what I needed. I don't heal as well as other people, so other procedures were not the answer. I could have gone on and maybe tried to give birth to a child that would not live." ("Other procedures" could have been a cesarean section or induced labor.) However, Stella had some happy news as well. She got pregnant again and delivered a healthy boy, Nicholas, in June 1996. Indeed, Stella had brought the toddler along to meet Ryan.

Ryan started weeping. Fawell erupted in anger: "Cosgrove, you asshole, you blindsided me with this!"

Ryan turned and said, "Scott, I'm pro-choice."

"No, you're not!"

"Yes, I am!"

And so on.[5]

Of course this encounter was kept secret. However, Roger Stanley soon was preparing mailings to Chicago-area liberals condemning Poshard's hardcore pro-life stand.

The obverse of liberal Democrats thinking they might prefer Ryan was that conservative Republicans thought they might prefer Poshard, a conservative Democrat. The Christian right wing grew so restive with rumors that Ryan was not true-blue that a meeting was set up with about thirty right-wing leaders headed by U.S. representative Henry Hyde. To understand the mood of the Christian right, recall that they had spent twenty-two years under moderate Republican governors—Thompson and Edgar—who more or less openly disdained them. Ryan was supposed to be a real conservative, but they did not fully trust him.

Thomas F. Roeser, a conservative activist and writer, helped to arrange the Hyde meeting. Roeser's son worked for Ryan, and Roeser also supported him. The meeting did not go well. "Single-issue people, they can really put you through the paces," Roeser said, "and he [Ryan] was bobbing and weaving, and finally at the very end, he couldn't do anything more; he indicated that Hyde's seat was a hostage because there was going to be redistricting."[6] That is, Hyde, revered by the Christian right, could be gerrymandered out of his seat by a Democratic governor after the 2000 census. Therefore, Hyde and his fans were stuck with Ryan. The meeting broke up with hard feelings all around.

"I talked to Henry afterward," Roeser continued. "I'm not at liberty to tell you what Hyde said. [Hyde told me he did not remember this incident.] At the same time, I was talking to Cosgrove and I knew the fix was in; I knew he [Ryan] was a goddamn liar. So I didn't vote for him; I voted for Poshard. I was always happy I did."

Ryan said he did not remember Vicki Stella, Terry Cosgrove, or the meeting Roeser referenced. He said, "I was a pro-life person, I ran as a pro-life person. . . . Where they got mad at me was after I got to be governor; [it] wasn't during the campaign, as I recall. . . . I don't know how many of these lunatics you know. But there are a lot of them. I'm talking about the real right-wing nuts. They're just terrible to deal with in a lot of cases, but in this case they came to me and said, look, there is no case that a woman's health could be at risk and an abortion can help her. I said, I don't believe that, I've been in the health care field all my life and I just don't believe that. They said, there might be a case where you might have to have an abortion to save a life, but her overall health, no."[7] Whereupon the General Assembly passed a bill forbidding state Medicaid payments for abortions when the mother's mere health was in peril. Although Ryan had promised during the campaign to sign such a bill, he vetoed it, further embittering social conservatives. One ramification is that when Ryan got into trouble on criminal charges, he had no base of hardcore conservative Republican support.

As early as April 10, 1998, Poshard demanded that the state police investigate allegations of licenses for bribes in Ryan's secretary of state's office. Two weeks later, the state police shut down its probe because, after all, Ryan had announced that he was appointing former state police director Jeremy Margolis to conduct a thorough, independent review. If a good tactical decision in the thick of a campaign, hiring Margolis was a strategic disaster for Ryan. Margolis's "investigation" was ridiculous, and his legal representation of CFR caused untold problems for Ryan down the road. (Margolis was never charged with a crime. The U.S. attorney's office declined to comment on whether Margolis ever was a subject of Operation Safe Road.)

Margolis discredited whistle-blower Tony Berlin as having a "lengthy arrest record." Actually, Berlin had been arrested just once for driving under the influence. Margolis dismissed charges against Ryan as political. "This is campaign time. Six-hundred-dollar bribes which you [reporters] wouldn't normally report are big news now."[8] In Illinois, a mere $600 for a mere CDL was chicken feed.

Ryan announced the hiring of Margolis on official secretary of state stationery. However, he later agreed to have CFR, not the state, pay Margolis. Margolis billed CFR $115,650. Federal attorneys said that at least $170,000 in license bribe money flowed to CFR. In effect, then, 68 percent of $170,000 in bribery went to Margolis to investigate it.

Aside from Margolis, Ryan made another fateful decision during the 1998 campaign, although he had no way of knowing it then. Carol Moseley Braun of Illinois was the first female African American U.S. senator. Because of a spat with Moseley Braun, Senator Phil Gramm of Texas for several months had put a secret hold on appointing new federal judges in Illinois. The feud escalated to threats to bring to a halt the work of all Senate committees. Ryan called Gramm, the crisis was solved, the hold lifted. That cleared the way for Senate confirmation of Judge Rebecca Pallmeyer of Wilmette, Illinois, who eventually would preside over Ryan's trial.

In June 1998, a messenger delivered a strange package to Poshard's campaign office in Chicago. Photocopies of more than $80,000 worth of checks to Ryan's campaign had been leaked. All the check stubs had the initials *MCC–MS* for "McCook–Marion Seibel." Poshard's informant told him that the checks included Gonzalo Mendoza's bribe for Ricardo Guzman's license. Poshard's campaign went nuts trying to decide what to do with this explosive information that was officially still sealed in court. Then a gaffe by Ryan's campaign in August gave Poshard another opportunity to demand an investigation.

A campaign strategy memo was mistakenly faxed from Ryan's state office—not the campaign office—to WILL, the public radio station in Champaign. The fourteen-page memo outlined plans for Progressives in Politics, a Ryan front organization, to harass Poshard for his record on gay rights. Also discussed was the use of the secretary of state's office to politick among gun-control advocates, labor unions, veterans' organizations, pharmacists, and senior citizens. This report surfaced shortly after the *Chicago Sun-Times* disclosed that Ryan's office had charged taxpayers $143,000 to mail refrigerator magnets bearing Ryan's name to half a million senior citizens. The state police promised to look into Ryan's alleged use of state resources for his campaign.

Diane Ford, general counsel for the secretary of state, went to see Earl Hernandez, state police deputy commander, in Springfield. "Her exact words were, 'The secretary isn't very happy about the way you're doing this,'" Hernandez recalled.[9] (When Ryan was elected, Hernandez, knowing Ryan's reputation for vindictiveness, had little hope of keeping his job, and so he quit to become chief of police in Platteville, Wisconsin.) Before the end of August, Dean Bauer and Jeremy Margolis sent Poshard's campaign certified letters stating that their investigations had found no criminal activity. A similar letter arrived in September from state police—state employees were not being drafted to work in Ryan's campaign. (Actually, state police compiled a thousand-page report. Less than two years later, they were about to comply with FBI requests to give them their report when the ever-at-hand Margolis suddenly claimed to represent the state police and temporarily thwarted the FBI.)

Poshard paid a visit to the Reverend and Mrs. Willis, who shared supper with him and then showed videotapes of the six children who had died in Wisconsin. It was perfectly ordinary family stuff—ballgames, recitals, holidays—yet all the more affecting for that. Poshard thought he had never endured anything more emotionally wrenching. He asked, and the Willises granted, permission to use a photo of their burned-out Plymouth Grand Voyager in a campaign ad.

The first TV spot ran in early October. Over a gruesome black-and-white photo of the Willis van, a narrator intoned, "Citing concerns for our safety, the FBI is arresting Ryan employees. Unsafe truckers are on our roads. A family has paid a terrible price. Six children are dead. His office riddled with corruption and George Ryan wants to be governor?"[10]

The reaction was scathing. The *Chicago Tribune* editorialized, "George Ryan hardly deserves a pass over allegations of license-selling in his office. But blame him for those deaths? This is about as cruel as politics can get."[11] Such a comment from a Republican-leaning editorial page might be expected, but even Paul Simon, the retired senator regarded as the conscience of Democratic liberalism, said, "It goes too far. I'm voting for Glenn. But restraint has to be used. You go beyond a certain point and ads like that boomerang."[12] Poshard pulled the ad, which had been planned for a ten-day run. Four years later, Poshard said, "When major Democratic leaders said, 'You've gone too far, this isn't true,' you could just feel the air come right out of our campaign."[13]

But at the time, Ryan was worried about the air coming out of his campaign. He attacked attorney Joseph Power:

I don't know if you realize how much money he's given to the Democratic committee and to the Friends of [Speaker] Mike Madigan, but about $350,000. [The actual number was $329,000.] Now all of a sudden he has an interest in a crash that happened in Wisconsin. He could end up possibly profiting from it. I don't think he cares about that client, in my personal opinion. I think his concern is more about who's going to be the governor and the next speaker of the House. . . .

Like I said about this Willis case, the truck driver, they're trying to claim he had an illegal license. He doesn't have an illegal license. We looked 32 ways for that and haven't found any way he has an illegal license.[14]

At a prayer breakfast, Scott Willis approached Ryan face to face for the first time since his children were killed. Ryan immediately started berating Power. "I'd say he lit into him," Willis recalled. "I was astonished by that reaction."[15]

12 Fat Friday and Fab Five

George Ryan's family, on their way to his victory party in a hotel ballroom on the night he was elected governor, got stuck in an elevator. To develop this incident as a metaphor for his term in office would be facile. Suffice it to say the ballroom crowd was puzzled, then annoyed, when the band played "When the Saints Go Marching In" twice, then again, then again and again. George and Lura Lynn were ready to take the stage and claim victory at midnight, but about twenty relatives and staffers were stuck in an elevator car between floors. Rescue workers used "Jaws of Life" to cut a three-foot opening so the passengers could crawl onto the third floor. First the adults boosted the children out, then they stood on a plastic tub—handed in by hotel staff—to hoist themselves up. Ryan made his victory speech at 12:40 A.M.

Glenn Poshard, outspent by better than 2–1, still held Ryan to 51 percent of the vote. Ryan raised $15 million and, after giving lavishly to other politicians and enjoying personal perks such as paying for Lura Lynn's mother's caretaker, still had $2 million left over. Poshard raised less than $6 million. Ryan won by 119,903 votes out of 3,308,295 cast. Ryan, Lura Lynn, Scott Fawell, and others promptly left for two weeks at Harry Klein's place in Jamaica.

Poshard was much lesser known throughout the state and started far behind. His campaign got a boost when FBI agents and postal inspectors raided the secretary of state's office in Melrose Park on September 3. Ryan absurdly claimed that he was "proud of the fact that we brought it to the forefront" when it was entirely a federal operation.[1] A postal inspector, posing as a CDL applicant, met with a retired secretary of state agent at her home. She took $600 from him and sent him to Melrose Park. There, an assistant manager told him to answer only three or four questions on each of five written tests. The supervisor filled in the rest, using the same red ink as the applicant (supervisors' legitimate marks were in black ink). In another sting, an undercover FBI man was steered to the manager, who ran the same fill-in-the-blanks scam. The three women were arrested and charged with extortion. On September 14, federal agents announced two more arrests, charging a driving school instructor and the owner of a truck repair shop with paying bribes for licenses at Melrose Park.

On October 6, the first formal indictments were released, "Operation Safe Road" was revealed, and the U.S. attorney made a comment that, many Democrats bitterly complained, gave the election to Ryan. For the first time, the feds stated flatly that much of the bribe money ended up in Ryan's campaign. However, "Mr. Ryan is not a subject of the investigation," U.S. attorney Scott Lassar said. Lassar had been appointed by Bill Clinton, a Democratic president. There was much speculation, unflattering to Lassar, about why a Democratic prosecutor would let a big-time Republican politician off the hook.

Some of the bitterness might have stemmed from confusion over legal jargon. Although Lassar said Ryan was not a "subject," the *Chicago Tribune* sub-head-line read, "Candidate Not a Target of Probe." Thereafter, Lassar often was mis-quoted as saying Ryan was not a "target." Prosecutors are interested generally in what a *subject* did, but a *target* is in their crosshairs as a probable defendant. Thus, Lassar at that early stage was misinterpreted to mean that Ryan was not and would not be a defendant.

Far from wanting to meddle in an election, Lassar's motive might have been the opposite—to try to take the election calendar out of Operation Safe Road. Republicans accused him of bias for announcing the charges so close to an election (which he did); Democrats objected that he was keeping key evidence sealed until after the election (which he also did). He probably wished the election would just go away.[2]

In any case, if few were aware of the oceanic extent of the corruption at the time, consider what already had been placed on the record by Election Day, November 3, 1998:

November 11–13, 1993—WMAQ-TV and the BGA report fund-raising abuses by Ryan's secretary of state's office.

March 23 and April 19–20, 1994—WMAQ-TV and the BGA further report that secretary of state employees were forced to sell Ryan fund-raising tickets and faced reprisals if they did not.

February 10, 1998—WLS-TV airs allegations by disguised secretary of state whistle-blower Laurie Roff.

April 7, 1998—WLS-TV airs allegations by disguised secretary of state whistle-blowers Tammy Raynor and Tony Berlin.

August 21, 1998—A misdirected fax from the Ryan campaign reveals plans to use secretary of state resources for political advantage.

September 3, 1998—A federal raid at the Melrose Park secretary of state facility results in three arrests.

September 14, 1998—Federal agents charge a driving school instructor and the owner of a truck repair shop with offering bribes for licenses at Melrose Park.

October 6, 1998—Official disclosure of Operation Safe Road investigation charges for the first time that licenses-for-bribes money went to Ryan's campaign fund.

October 7, 1998—Ryan denies knowledge of licenses for bribes and that Ricardo Guzman illegally got a trucker's license.

October 10, 1998—Proceedings in the Willis case reveal that Dean Bauer squelched Russell Sonneveld's investigation of the 1994 Guzman-Willis accident.

Reviewing such a catalog of allegations, one might wonder how a politician under such pressure could hope to win an election, even in Illinois. Ryan responded in part by attacking Poshard's ethics, as he had done against Jerome Cosentino when they had both run for secretary of state. Poshard had pledged not to accept funds from PACs (political action committees, or interest-group lobbies), and Ryan charged that he sneakily found ways to get around his own rule. (In fact, many races across the country have shown that spurning PAC money does not help a candidate's electoral chances much, if at all.)

Meanwhile, Fawell and Bauer remained active. Immediately after the Melrose Park raid, Citizens for Ryan bought an industrial-capacity shredder. On September 8, Fawell ordered the destruction of all campaign-related documents from the Chicago secretary of state's office. That night, as many as twelve bags of shredded documents were thrown in the trash bin. On September 30, Fawell ordered the destruction of documents in the Homewood secretary of state's office—these records related to the 1996 Illinois House races. Fawell and others also used computer "wiping" equipment to delete campaign-related files from secretary of state computers.

Eight days after the election, two of the women arrested in the Melrose Park raid pleaded guilty. Three days later, on California Highway 99 near Fresno, Adem Salihovic lost control of his truck in dense fog. Salihovic, a Bosnian who spoke little English, had paid $800 to get his Illinois CDL at Melrose Park that June. A car smashed into his overturned truck. The resulting chain reaction wrecked seventy-four cars stretching over a mile. Two people were killed and fifty-one others injured. The Melrose Park connection was not revealed for more than a year.

Incredibly, the Ryan family got stuck in an elevator again during Ryan's inauguration ceremonies. George, Lura Lynn, and nine others were trapped for ninety minutes at the Springfield Hilton before a hook-and-ladder from the local fire department rescued them. They climbed a stepladder to emerge from several feet below the mezzanine floor level. That evening, they attended a formal inaugural reception costing $1,000 per person and featuring the singer Ray Charles.

Ryan took office on January 11, 1999, in happy times, the apex of the national dot-com boom. Whereas Edgar had inherited a billion-dollar state deficit from Thompson, Edgar passed on more than a billion-dollar surplus to Ryan. At age sixty-five, Ryan was Illinois's oldest governor, but he obviously relished the job he had sought for decades, gleefully passing spending bills through the General Assembly. Republican representative Douglas L. Hoeft of Elgin commented after the first, especially lavish session, "We adjourn tonight because there aren't any more rich . . . white guys to service."[3] Hoeft referred to what became known as "Fat Friday," May 21, 1999:

- On this date, the legislature saw Ryan sign into law a bill favoring William Wirtz, a major liquor distributor and the owner of the Chicago Black-hawks hockey team. Wirtz had given $40,000 to CFR and $10,000 to the House Republican leader. Wirtz's liquor business was in danger of losing two of its key suppliers. The new law virtually locked suppliers into their current contracts with distributors. (This law was ruled unconstitutional in 2002.)
- Ryan also signed a similar bill protecting the distributorship interests of Harry Crisp, a downstate soft-drink bottler. Crisp had given $13,500 to CFR and $16,500 to the House Republican leader.
- The legislature passed through the House a bill thought to guarantee the construction of a new state-franchised casino in Rosemont, next to Chicago's O'Hare International Airport. (Ryan had campaigned against putting casinos in Cook County.) The mayor of Rosemont, Donald E. Stephens, was a Republican powerhouse. Certain Rosemont casino revenues and tax breaks would go to Arlington International Racecourse, owned by Republican powerhouse Richard Duchossois. The Senate passed the Stephens/Duchossois bill the next week. (For various reasons, including allegations of mob ties, the Rosemont casino was not built.)
- Above all, the legislature passed Ryan's sweeping, $12 billion Illinois FIRST bond issue, the largest borrowing program in Illinois history.[4] It would be financed by raising 140 taxes and fees, primarily the vehicle license plate fee, which went from $48 to $78, and various taxes on alcoholic beverages. (Ryan had campaigned on a promise not to raise taxes.) "They're talking about the Fab Five down here," said Republican senator Steven Rauschenberger of Elgin, referring to Wirtz, Crisp, Stephens, Duchossois, and Springfield Republican boss William F. Cellini.[5]

Ryan had called the "Four Tops," the Democratic and Republican leaders of the House and Senate, into a conference room behind the governor's office to propose to them $12 billion in public works. "The drool was running out of their mouths," Ryan remembered sardonically. Pate Philip, the Senate president, objected that $12 billion was too much; maybe he could go as high as $10 billion, but not twelve. This stance was almost a parody of ritualistic male combat: two old bulls facing off, snorting, and stamping the ground. Philip's implied message was, You will get what we give you, Governor, no more. Ryan slammed shut his briefing book and said, "It's either $12 billion or nothing; if you guys don't want to be for $12 billion, then there will be no $12 billion." He then walked out of the room.[6] And so $12 billion came to pass—however, Philip did force Ryan to dump a certain state Republican chairman.

Ryan also proposed an annual state budget of $41 billion. One evening he hosted a reception at the governor's mansion with U.S. senator Peter Fitzgerald (whom Ryan despised). State senator Rauschenberger, a budget expert, was approaching to shake hands with Fitzgerald. Ryan said, "That son of a bitch didn't have a good thing to say about my budget. He doesn't need to be here."[7] Rauschenberger, overhearing the comment, merely waved to Fitzgerald and departed. Thereafter, Rauschenberger's district was not blessed with Illinois FIRST boodle.

If he punished some Republicans, Ryan rewarded many Democrats. To co-chair the Illinois FIRST task force he named Ed Bedore, budget chief for Chicago mayor Richard M. Daley. Thus, Chicago was assured its share of the pork. The Republican co-chair was businessman John Glennon, who had helped Governor Thompson spend money on the earlier Build Illinois projects.

For all his early success and celebration, there seemed something gloomy hidden in Ryan, something under the usual crankiness. Before Ryan took office, Glennon offered congratulations and was surprised to find him subdued. Ryan predicted that he would not have an easy or a happy term. The CDL scandals seemingly would never stop. Why, the BGA had just filed suit in federal court alleging that Ryan's fund-raising abuses had violated voters' civil rights. Jim Thompson was defending against the BGA suit and probably would get Ryan off, but still. "This issue will not hit you personally," Glennon ventured hopefully. "Right?" Ryan just shrugged.[8] (Glennon was indicted in 2005 in an unrelated kickback scheme.)

Ryan was feeling merrier in late May when he revived the traditional party at the governor's mansion marking the end of the legislative session. Thompson had started the practice and Edgar, a teetotaler, continued it for a couple of years, serving apple cider. People stopped coming, so Edgar stopped throwing the party. Now, Ryan and Thompson worked the crowd at the beer wagon as though it were the 1980s again. Served up with the beer was barbecued pork.

Death haunted Ryan in the early months of 1999, perhaps explaining some of his occasional glumness. The year began with what was practically a death in Ryan's own family. Scott Fawell's brother Steven died of liver cancer at age forty-five.

Less than two weeks later, Ryan and Lura Lynn were watching television news at the mansion and saw Anthony Porter released from death row. Ryan recalled, "They tell the story about the journalism students from Northwestern

University being the ones who had really freed the guy, not the system, not the courts, fifteen years on death row, appeal after appeal, level after level of bullshit government, and they can't find anything wrong with this case and they're ready to execute the guy." He turned to Lura Lynn and said, "How the hell would that happen in America? Fifteen years of his life for a crime he didn't commit? Jesus, how does that happen?"[9]

On March 15, an Amtrak train smashed into a truck at a rail crossing in Bourbonnais, near Kankakee. Eleven people died and 122 were injured. The driver, John Stokes, had an Illinois CDL. Over thirty years he had been involved in nine accidents and convicted thirteen times of traffic infractions. There was no allegation that he obtained his CDL through bribery.

Two days later, Ryan had to decide whether the state should kill Andrew Kokoraleis. He had been convicted as part of a satanic cult that killed and mutilated women. At first, Ryan refused to sign the warrant of execution, wondering whether "bullshit government" was at work. "I stopped it and I studied the whole case, talked to everybody I could, learned as much as I could. In the end I said, 'That's a bad guy. Kill him.' And I regret it to this day."[10]

However, he did not heed calls to appoint a commission to study capital punishment or to declare a moratorium on executions. The courts and the attorney general's office already were reviewing Illinois capital cases. Illinois Supreme Court justice James Heiple deplored the "hand-wringing" and "bandwagon psychology" behind these reviews merely because eleven men had been exonerated after being sentenced to death. (Two years earlier, Thompson had saved Heiple from impeachment. Heiple had flashed his court badge and otherwise used his clout to get out of speeding tickets. He agreed to step down as chief justice at once and to retire from the court completely in 2000.)

Ryan named Scott Fawell to head the McPier authority at $195,000 a year—more than the governor made. Both men knew Fawell was under investigation. Jeremy Margolis called Fawell to his office and introduced him to a man he had never met. That is your attorney for Operation Safe Road, Margolis said. The deal was, CFR would pay defense bills only if Margolis chose the lawyers. The implied message: your legal bills will be covered, but only if you don't give the feds what they want. Hush money, in short. Fawell refused, saying he would retain his own attorney if needed. Like some others in Ryan's inner circle, Fawell distrusted Margolis.

Meanwhile, Ryan named Fawell's wife, Joan, assistant director of the state lottery. Fawell's chief of staff and mistress was Andrea Coutretsis Prokos. She was still living with her husband, Dean Prokos, who also worked for the lottery.

The Prokoses had boxes of documents relating to the Ryan campaign stashed in the basement of their home in Hawthorn Woods north of Chicago. Fawell wanted the incriminating papers destroyed.

It was the day before Halloween, 1999. The Prokoses hauled the boxes to the nearby home of Dean Prokos's sister, Frances Katris, and brother-in-law, Ernie Katris. Andrea started going through the items to identify which ones she wanted destroyed first. Documents, office supplies, and computer disks were tossed together in disorder. Andrea told Ernie that this material could get lots of people, up to George Ryan, in lots of trouble. Ernie had a shredder in an office in his basement, so they started shredding documents. The job was tedious, and Andrea said they really needed a crisscross shredder, which Ernie did not have.

They decided to try to burn the documents over a barbecue grill in the backyard. Fat file folders stuffed with papers did not burn well, even as Ernie kept squirting lighter fluid on the charcoal. It was a windy day, and ashes and smoke blew over the yard, inviting neighbors' curiosity. Back to the Katrises' basement went the boxes. At this point they came across a computer Zip drive and disk. Andrea proposed pounding it with a hammer, but her husband, Dean, wanted to keep it, to hold incriminating evidence as insurance against harassment from Ryan's people or the government's. "Get rid of it!" she said. "I won't roll over on these people!"

As a compromise, Ernie Katris kept the disk with the understanding he would destroy it later. Meanwhile, Andrea asked Ernie to take some of the remaining boxes out with the garbage each week, but not too many at once, lest they attract attention.

Eventually, Dean Prokos learned of his wife's affair with Fawell. She got a restraining order against her husband. The couple divorced in 2001. On the day Fawell was indicted in 2002, he and Andrea were on vacation together. Six days later, Joan Fawell filed for divorce from Scott.

Dean Prokos was cooperating with the FBI and asked Ernie Katris for the Zip drive. They handed it over to the government after securing immunity from prosecution.[11]

Fawell, the Prokoses, and the Katrises had an urgent motivation for their Halloween barbecue. On September 28, 1999, Gonzalo Mendoza had pleaded guilty to racketeering conspiracy, admitting that he had bribed officials to issue more than eighty fraudulent trucker's licenses—including one for Ricardo Guzman.

Meanwhile, Glenn Poshard had become vice chancellor of Southern Illinois University. Poshard always had refused to comment when reporters called him about Operation Safe Road developments. But once Mendoza had pleaded guilty, Poshard told a Chicago reporter that "I thought it verified that what we were saying during the campaign was the truth."

Soon, Hazel Loucks, Ryan's deputy governor for education, spoke at Poshard's campus. "She pulled me aside and told me that I was not to open my mouth about George Ryan anymore," Poshard recalled in 2003. "Now this is the deputy governor of Illinois lacing me down." Loucks said she had been in a meeting with Ryan and his chief of staff, and Ryan "went straight through the ceiling when he read my comments. She intimated to me that if I said anything else, it could threaten future projects at SIU and even a project that I helped secure for John A. Logan College [in Carterville, Illinois]. It was just one more time that I had been told not to say anything, not to open my mouth. I would never jeopardize this university, so I have kept quiet all the time I've been here."[12] Poshard made these remarks to the *Southern Illinoisan* only after he had decided to retire from the university (although he later became the university's president).

If asked at the time, Ryan probably would have said he knew nothing about Loucks's visit with Poshard, or the Fawell-Prokos affair, or the Prokos-Katris destruction of evidence. He was busy being governor. George Ryan, of all people, was planning to visit Cuba, of all places.

13 Castro Set It Up

When George Ryan received an honorary degree from the University of Havana on October 27, 1999, Fidel Castro, seated in the front row, rose and led a standing ovation. The antecedents of this improbable event were in the Illinois gubernatorial campaign.

Many liberal Democrats could not accept their party's conservative nominee, Glenn Poshard, and made friends with Ryan. Edgar Lopez, a Democratic state representative from Chicago, even had Ryan speak at a fund-raiser for his own campaign. Afterward, Lopez and a colleague talked with Ryan in Ryan's campaign van and asked whether, as governor, he might want to visit Cuba.

"God, it never entered my mind, never even gave it a thought. Why the hell would I want to do that?"

Because, they said, it would be good for Illinois business and agriculture if trade could be resumed with Cuba, under embargo by the United States since 1962. Ryan said he would consider the matter and then forgot about it until after the election.[1]

Fernando Remirez, a Cuban envoy in Washington, wanted to visit Illinois but could not leave the capital without a formal invitation—America had severed diplomatic relations with Cuba in 1960. At Edgar Lopez's urging, Ryan arranged a state dinner in Springfield for Remirez in 1999, and the State Department approved. "The Cold War is over," Remirez said. "Cuba is a market of 11 million people, who are familiarized with American products."[2] At the dinner, Remirez extended Ryan an official invitation to Cuba. He would be the first U.S. governor to go there since Castro took power in 1959.

Visiting a Communist dictatorship was diplomatically a ticklish affair, and Ryan was, after all, not a diplomat. The State Department officially frowned on his trip, but Ryan always believed that President Clinton secretly favored it. Anyway, the federal government allowed only humanitarian missions to Cuba, so Ryan put together donations of medicines from drug companies based in Illinois, plus some school supplies, clothing, and such.

The Four Tops—senators Emil Jones Jr. and Pate Philip and representatives Michael Madigan and Lee A. Daniels—had been at the Remirez dinner, and Ryan invited them to go along. "They all said yes, they wanted to go, they were kind of excited. Go down and have a cigar with Castro, all that bullshit." But the next day, Philip called back: "'I'm not going to Cuba with that goddamned

Communist bastard; what are you doing associating with that guy?' Oh, God, he went nuts. Some of his right-wing friends got a hold of him." Ryan also invited U.S. House Speaker Dennis Hastert of Yorkville, Illinois. Hastert said he wanted to go but dared not offend Cuban exiles in south Florida. Hastert needed their congressmen's votes. "The Cuban delegation can kill anything I try to pass," he explained.[3]

The plane carrying Ryan and an entourage of about ninety people landed in Havana on October 23. Fernando Remirez planned to greet the plane with "The Star-Spangled Banner" and children waving American flags, but the State Department squelched that, lest Castro use the scene for propaganda. Ryan was met by Cuban National Assembly president Ricardo Alarcon. The delegation's buses to a Havana hotel passed billboards bearing messages such as "Yankee Embargo = Genocide Against Cuba."

Ryan's initial foray into international diplomacy was inauspicious. The Illinois delegation was cheered as they pulled up to the Parque Central Hotel. Ryan worked the crowd like the politician he was. Later, he told Alarcon, "I thought they were voters and I went to shake their hands. Maybe someday they can be voters, Mr. President," he joshed. At once the room fell silent. Foreign journalists were ushered out of the room.[4]

As yet, Castro had not agreed to meet with Ryan, and the joke that fell flat was not thought to be encouraging. But Ryan was not about to allow Republican critics charge that he kowtowed to Castro (critics of the trip had included Governors Jeb Bush of Florida and George W. Bush of Texas). Ryan openly met with eight Cuban dissidents who faced a real threat of jail for criticizing Castro. Bluntly, Ryan later said, "Basically, that's the problem with Cuba, Fidel Castro. The people here are warm and gracious and wonderful and good. But 40 years of heavy communist rule under Castro has left its mark."[5]

For his part, Castro was not about to let an opportunity to try to reopen trade with America pass. On October 26, he invited Ryan and his party to the presidential palace at 6:30 P.M., served a dinner of lamb and potatoes at 11 P.M., and spent most of the time until 12:30 A.M. talking. He noted how easy it would be to ship grain down the Mississippi River to New Orleans and thence to Cuba, mentioning that the Mississippi begins in Illinois. No, said the Illinoisans, the river actually originates in Minnesota. Castro then consulted an atlas but did not admit his mistake.

Ryan made two requests. The first was that Castro free four human rights activists jailed since 1997. This was denied. The second was that Raudel Medina Alfonso, a seven-year-old boy with a rare liver ailment, be allowed to seek treatment in the United States. This was granted. The boy and his mother accompanied Ryan on his flight home on October 27.

Castro, then seventy-three years old and struggling to save his rule after the collapse of the Soviet Union had ended that bloc's foreign aid, held a rare news conference. "Gov. Ryan has made a very good impression here," he said, praising Ryan's "very rational, very articulate" support for lifting the American embargo.[6] The Clinton administration officially urged other governors not to follow Ryan's example, lest they show support for Communist oppression.

However, other governors made that very trip. The next February, Ryan and Lura Lynn spent a night in the White House and discussed Cuba and the death penalty with Clinton. Before leaving office, Clinton eased the embargo to allow selling food and fiber to Cuba on a cash-only basis. Governors who went to Havana to negotiate such deals included Dave Heineman of Nebraska, Kathleen Blanco of Louisiana, John Hoeven of North Dakota, and Jesse Ventura of Minnesota. If Ryan had ignored the capital punishment issue, he still would be a footnote in history for going to Cuba.

Ryan flew to South Africa on May 24, 2000, to open an Illinois trade office. Monica Faith Stewart, a former state representative from Chicago, had moved to the newly freed nation and opened a restaurant in Cape Town. In Stewart, Ryan had a natural choice to head the state's trade office. Also, the U.S. secretary of commerce was Bill Daley, brother of the mayor of Chicago. Both Daleys were helpful.

Ryan and his wife, Emil Jones—the African American president of the Illinois Senate—and his wife, and a few others met in Johannesburg with the liberator of the nation, Nelson Mandela. Now eighty-one years old and retired as president, Mandela had led the country out of apartheid in 1994. He had been released from prison in 1990 after twenty-seven years.

"They beat the hell out of him, and this great man kept telling us how honored he was to meet us!" Ryan marveled. "I couldn't believe how I felt. Yes, I got teary. Who wouldn't?"

Mandela charmed Lura Lynn by asking how long it took her to say yes when George proposed. "Not long," she said.

"Castro was a dictator; Mandela was a liberator," Ryan reflected. "When I met with Castro, he was strident and kept talking politics. Mandela talked in human terms. Castro kept talking about how many calories his people eat each day. Mandela talked about the education of his people and the HIV-AIDS epidemic that is decimating them."[7]

Mandela signed his autobiography, *Long Walk to Freedom,* for Lura Lynn. After about thirty minutes, Mandela escorted the party to his front porch for a group photo. Ryan grabbed his arm to help him down some steps, but Mandela said his knees could not take it. Mandela also had to stand in the shade, out of the sunlight, because his eyes had been damaged by years of mining limestone without eye protection while imprisoned on Robben Island at Cape Town. A few days later, Ryan and his party visited what had been Mandela's cell on Robben Island. On the flight home, Ryan read Lura Lynn's copy of *Long Walk to Freedom*.

Not known at the time was how the Mandela meeting had been arranged in the first place. Mandela was aged and retired and would see only heads of state, not mere governors. But Ryan wanted to meet him, especially after talking with President Clinton. During the impeachment of Clinton over the Monica Lewinsky scandal, "Mandela called him," Ryan said. "He said, 'You know, you can either hate the rest of your life all the people that are trying to do these things to you, or you can forget it and move on with your life. . . . When I got the word that I was going to be released, I was a pretty bitter guy, had a lot of hate in my heart. I argued with myself from the cell to the gate about whether I was going to carry that bitterness with me the rest of my life or whether I was going to forget about it and move on. So not until I got to the gate did I realize that the smart, . . . best thing for me to do was forget it, don't carry it out of here.' He told Clinton, 'That is what I suggest you do.'"

When the South African government declined Ryan's request to meet Mandela, one of Ryan's aides called Fernando Remirez in Cuba. "Let me see what I can do," Remirez said. "He went to Castro and they called Mandela. We got a call back, [and] that's how I got in to see Mandela," Ryan said. "Castro set it up."[8]

Ryan's foreign triumphs did not halt the grinding gears of Operation Safe Road. George and Lura Lynn greeted the new millennium at Ryan's Navy Pier Gala 2000 in Chicago. Each guest received a specially commissioned Beanie Baby. Lura Lynn wore the red St. John's knit suit she had worn to the inaugural. George and singer Harry Belafonte started counting off the ritual "ten—nine—eight—," but before they got further the city's fireworks over Lake Michigan drowned them out.

Just three days later, Marion Seibel was sentenced to eighteen months in prison—the stiffest sentence in Operation Safe Road to date. The former secretary of state manager at McCook, she had pleaded guilty to a racketeering charge and told the court she had traded licenses for bribes from fear of jeopardizing her career if she failed to sell Ryan's tickets. As the year went on, it seemed that every week, somebody was getting indicted, pleading guilty, or being sentenced. Gonzalo Mendoza, accused of obtaining Ricardo Guzman's fake license (although that accusation was not adjudicated), received a prison term of eighteen months on February 25.

The biggest fish caught that year was Dean Bauer, indicted on February 1. He was charged with concealing evidence from the 1993 Libertyville raid, shutting down an investigation of the 1994 Guzman accident, suppressing whistle-blower

Tammy Raynor's allegations, blocking three other cases, and shredding documents. Bauer also was accused of mail fraud, obstruction of justice, and lying to federal agents. The charges were so broad and deep that the political class gossiped about whether Bauer would "flip"—make a deal with the feds for leniency in exchange for providing evidence to take down the governor. Bauer did not betray his friend and patron. In ill health, Bauer pleaded guilty on January 17, 2001, to a single count of obstruction of justice and acknowledged that the government could prove other misconduct at trial. Bauer was sentenced to 366 days in prison and a $10,000 fine.

Yet neither the sentencing of Seibel and Mendoza nor the indictment of Bauer was the worst news for George Ryan in 2000. Perhaps the worst thing that happened to him that year, though he had no idea of its peril at the time, was that the FBI interviewed him and he lied by omission. On January 5, the FBI questioned Ryan in the Safe Road case for the first time. He insisted that he paid Harry Klein $1,000 for every week that he stayed at his Jamaican estate. Indeed, he had the canceled checks to prove it, and he would have his attorney—Jeremy Margolis—send over photocopies of them. In August 2002, Klein's testimony before the grand jury confirmed that the checks were a scam. Klein always gave Ryan the same amount back in cash. It would be hard to exaggerate how much this revelation hurt Ryan's prospects. Scott Lassar, still the U.S. attorney in 2000, had said in 1998 that Ryan was not a subject of the investigation. After the Klein matter, the feds figured that a man so venal and petty about Jamaican vacations would be dishonest about almost anything. This minor incident hardened prosecutors' attitudes toward Ryan from then on. From that point, charges that the feds were "out to get" Ryan might have had some substance. For that matter, the Klein affair hardened attitudes for Ryan's defense as well. Ryan's side thought the feds were making a mountain out of a molehill.

Shortly after that original FBI interview, Ryan wrote U.S. transportation secretary Rodney E. Slater requesting his agency's help in reviewing the Illinois CDL program. Accordingly, the Federal Motor Carrier Safety Administration held hearings in June 2000. "The problems in the Illinois system are an outrage," Ryan testified. "The individuals in the driver's facilities betrayed the public's trust in concert with corrupt driving school operators and other middlemen. Operation Safe Road has done an outstanding job while ferreting out this corruption. In Illinois, unfortunately, this culture of corruption has been a sad fact of life for decades, vexing every secretary of state who has held that office." Ryan seemed untroubled by the illogic of his public statements: (a) I knew nothing about corruption in my secretary of state field offices, and (b) everybody has always known that secretary of state field offices are corrupt. Instead, Ryan offered a new explanation for such corruption—new, tougher federal regulation of CDLs in 1992 invited it. "These standards, while they have a laudable goal of raising the competency level of drivers, may have had the unexpected and unintended consequence of giving rise to corrupt individuals looking to use fraud and bribery to get around the tougher standard."[9] (Ryan's theory about the unintended consequences of anticorruption reforms actually has a long pedigree. As the political scientist Carl J. Friedrich has observed, "Corruption is kept functional by the efforts to get rid of it."[10])

And yet neither the Seibel, Mendoza, and Bauer cases, nor the January 5 FBI interview, nor the embarrassment of the federal CDL hearings, was necessarily the worst thing to happen to Ryan in 2000. The most baleful event that year might have been, perversely, the election of a Republican president, George W. Bush, because it led to the appointment of new U.S. attorneys.

U.S. senator Peter Fitzgerald of Illinois was a Republican. U.S. attorneys are nominated by the president and confirmed by the Senate, but by tradition, they are selected in each state by the senior senator of the president's party. Thus, Fitzgerald went looking for a new U.S. attorney to replace Lassar in the northern district of Illinois. The resulting uproar nearly wrecked the Illinois Republican Party.

An inflexible right-winger and a political lone wolf, Fitzgerald was a state senator and a wealthy banker who had financed his own U.S. Senate campaign in 1998. The Democratic and Republican establishments detested him alike. Thomas F. Roeser, a friend and supporter, said, "This guy was a rich kid who, from the time he was born, thought that people were trying to ingratiate themselves to get something out of him. He's sort of like a Baptist minister in a bawdy house, doesn't understand politics at all."[11]

Fitzgerald had the idea that a U.S. attorney from outside Illinois would be more independent than the usual run of U.S. attorneys in Illinois in uprooting systemic corruption. This idea horrified some people. U.S. House Speaker Dennis Hastert, for one, tried to block Fitzgerald—a breach of protocol, as the House normally does not encroach on Senate prerogatives. (Hastert did manage to appoint a U.S. attorney of his own, Rodger Heaton, in the central district of Illinois. Heaton was friendly with state Republican bosses and Ryan pals William Cellini and Robert Kjellander.)

To replace Lassar, Ryan favored Edward E. McNally, a law partner of Jeremy Margolis's. Ryan took the route of recommending McNally to the elder President Bush, for whom McNally had once worked. (Eventually, McNally was named interim U.S. attorney in the southern district of Illinois and unintentionally hurt Ryan by testifying in Ryan's defense while under an ethical cloud of his own.)

The new President Bush named as attorney general John Ashcroft, former senator from Missouri. Fitzgerald, who had known Ashcroft in the Senate, told him of his plan to pick a rackets-busting U.S. attorney from outside Illinois. "They are going to scream like stuck pigs when I do this," he prophesied.

Before long, Karl Rove, the president's political strategist, called Fitzgerald. Rove had done the direct mail for Fitzgerald's 1998 campaign. "We are not appointing anybody from out of state," Rove told him. "We'll let you pick anybody you want as long as that person is from Chicago." But, Fitzgerald objected, all the applicants from Chicago had political connections.

Fitzgerald called FBI director Louis Freeh and asked, "Who is the best assistant U.S. attorney in the country?" Freeh said, "Patrick Fitzgerald in the southern district of New York" (no kin to the senator). So the senator's chief of staff called Patrick Fitzgerald, who dismissed the call as a joke. Himself a notorious practical joker, "Pat had never been involved in party politics, and he thought this was a trick that somebody was playing on him."

But Peter Fitzgerald talked Patrick Fitzgerald into seeking the position. Part of the senator's suasion was a story from the Al Capone era. The senator had read Richard Norton Smith's *The Colonel,* a biography of the late *Chicago Tribune* publisher Robert R. McCormick. Shortly after President Herbert Hoover was elected in 1928, McCormick called on him to plead for federal help in removing the gangster Capone, who controlled the local police, the state's attorney, and maybe even the U.S. attorney. That passage, Senator Fitzgerald said, gave him the notion of "bringing a new sheriff into town."

Senator Fitzgerald shrewdly preempted opposition by announcing his selection of attorney Fitzgerald on a Sunday, Mother's Day, May 13, 2001—without even first notifying the White House. The senator later said, half-jokingly, that the press was always against him after that because he screwed up senior reporters' Mother's Day by calling such an important news conference. (Reporters disliked him anyway.) The next day, the *Chicago Tribune* praised the choice. The publicity effectively prevented Rove from interfering. For the record, the White House said Bush would not reject a nominee for U.S. attorney just on the ground of state residency. Much later, Rove told the senator, "That Fitzgerald appointment got great headlines for you, but it ticked off the base."[12] If so, Rove's use of the term *base* in this context meant wealthy Republican donors, not the Christian right.

The Senate confirmed Patrick J. Fitzgerald unanimously. He had just won a major victory in *U.S. v. Osama bin Laden et al.,* convicting all four defendants charged in the 1998 terrorist bombings of U.S. embassies in Nairobi and Dar es Salaam. A Brooklyn native and only forty years old, Fitzgerald had been an assistant U.S. attorney in New York for thirteen years, leading the organized crime/terrorism unit. In Chicago he batted one thousand, winning convictions and guilty pleas with no acquittals in more than a hundred cases of political corruption at the city, county, state, and federal levels. Not until March 2007 was a single one of his cases (unrelated to Operation Safe Road) reversed on appeal. Illinois had never seen anything like it, not even Jim Thompson's rampage in the early 1970s.

As for Senator Fitzgerald, he stepped down in 2004 after serving one term. He had angered Speaker Hastert and the rest of the Illinois delegation by appointing Patrick Fitzgerald, then angered them even more by blocking federal pork intended to expand Chicago's O'Hare International Airport and build a new Lincoln museum in Springfield—pet projects of Mayor Daley and Governor Ryan. Illinois pundits were aghast—how could our own U.S. senator oppose our own pork? Unthinkable, indefensible. Still, merely by putting U.S. attorney Fitzgerald in office, Peter Fitzgerald left a larger legacy than did many senators who served much longer. The workaholic prosecutor forced a turnover of political networks. He did not invent Operation Safe Road, but he as much as anyone sealed George Ryan's fate.

14 The World Series of All

Steve Manning was a corrupt Chicago cop, part of an illegal car-insurance scheme. He was sentenced to death for the 1990 killing of a trucking firm owner. The Illinois Supreme Court reversed the conviction in 1998 because improper hearsay evidence from the victim's widow had been used against Manning. The *Chicago Tribune* had revealed misconduct in Manning's prosecution as part of a January 1999 series examining reversals in Illinois capital cases. Cook County prosecutors started to retry Manning anyway, then, on January 18, 2000, dropped the charges. Their main evidence, tapes from a notorious jailhouse snitch, also was ruled out of bounds. The abandonment of the murder case against Manning was significant in a scorecard sense. He was the thirteenth Illinois death row inmate to be cleared, versus twelve executed.

Two weeks later, on January 31, 2000, Ryan declared a moratorium on executions in Illinois. He insisted, then and later, that at that time he still strongly supported capital punishment—he merely intended to repair its machinery. Illinois thus became the first state to halt capital punishment to study it. Nationally, there had been ninety-eight executions in 1999, the most in any year since 1951. Over the preceding twenty-five years, eighty-six death row inmates had been exonerated—Illinois, with thirteen, had the most of any state.

Disturbing as these statistics might be, they did not force Ryan's decision. He made the decision the moment that Attorney General Jim Ryan (no kin to the governor) called that day, January 31, to schedule the next execution date. The attorney general said several death row inmates had lost their final appeals, and it was time to schedule their deaths. "You might want to hold off on that," the governor said. "I might have something to say."[1] At once, he called a news conference to announce a moratorium. Governor Ryan explained later, "I knew I couldn't make myself live through what I'd experienced with Kokoraleis. I just couldn't do it again."[2] Over the next several years, there would be elaborate speculations about Ryan's motives in this issue. However, Ryan's immediate motive was not complex but simple: it was Jim Ryan's phone call. No way; can't do it.

There were two immediate public reactions. The first, suspicion that Ryan was just dodging heat from Operation Safe Road, was denied by his press secretary even before the moratorium was formally announced. Critics noted that the *Chicago Tribune* had reported on January 27 that Dean Bauer expected to be indicted soon—news presumably leaked by the U.S. attorney's office (still under Scott Lassar). On January 30, the *Chicago Sun-Times* disclosed evidence that Ryan had known about a theft of $2,683 from a secretary of state office in 1993. Ryan's timing suggested he was trying to blunt bad publicity. Actually, things were going so badly for Ryan, he could hardly select a date when there was *not* negative publicity.

The other reaction was worldwide applause from death penalty opponents. In Rome, lights burned at the Coliseum to honor Ryan's decision. This reaction surprised the governor, hardly the archetype of a criminal justice reformer. "I am a Republican pharmacist from Kankakee. All of a sudden I've got gays and lesbians by my side. African-Americans. Senators from Italy, groups from around the world."[3]

Ryan next issued Executive Order Number 4 on May 4, 2000, to create the Governor's Commission on Capital Punishment. When Ryan announced the commission, his lawyer Jeremy Margolis was standing nearby but out of camera range. As a prosecutor, Margolis had tried a murder case in 1984 and sought the death penalty. On appeal, the Illinois Supreme Court denounced Margolis for committing "the most flagrant example of improper, prejudicial cross-examination to come before this court in the many cases involving death penalties."[4] The case of that convict, Hector Reuben Sanchez, remained on hold under Ryan's moratorium.

Ryan named fourteen members to his commission. They included Scott Turow, a celebrity author of legal thrillers, former federal prosecutor, and Ryan defender. "What I see is the scandalizing of a man who in his time in the governor's office has been good government incarnate," Turow said.[5] Such sentiments led to the charge that Ryan had stacked the commission with people opposed to the death penalty. Ryan felt this criticism was especially unfair. "You know," he said, "they took a vote at their first meeting to say who was in favor of the death penalty and who was opposed to it. And the majority were in favor of the death penalty. . . . At the end, when they completed their deliberations, two years later, they took another vote and the majority of them were against the death penalty."[6]

For the record, then, Ryan remained a proponent of the death penalty, and the commission was just supposed to study the issue and make recommendations. However, there are indications that Ryan already was swinging to the other side. During a trade mission to Mexico City in September 2000, he told President Ernesto Zedillo that he might never bring back the death penalty. (The Mexican government forbade capital punishment and was highly sensitive about Mexican nationals on death rows in the United States.) In June 2001, Timothy McVeigh, guilty of the 1995 terrorist bombing in Oklahoma City, was put to death. McVeigh "gave up his appeal, he made no claim of innocence, he showed no remorse, and he made no plea of forgiveness," Ryan noted. Even so, after watching news accounts of the execution, "I got a sick feeling in my stomach about the whole process of what we go through."[7]

Of course the commission studied the thirteen cases of exoneration, but the members also decided to look into all pending cases of the 165 men and women then on death row in Illinois. Reopening those cases led in October 2002 to televised hearings on clemency appeals that shocked the state as family members of murder victims wept and accosted defense attorneys and relatives of the killers. Again, Ryan was accused of staging a public horror show to take the spotlight off Operation Safe Road. Of this charge, he is innocent: Ryan's administration had sought written testimony. "We didn't want to have public hearings, call them in to testify, because we thought that was not fair to them to go through all that again. And the prosecutors insisted that we have public hearings with testimony because they wanted the six o'clock news and the ten o'clock news, with the tears and the agony. They insisted on public hearings and they got them. And it was brutal as hell. I had it piped into my office; I listened to every word."[8]

Those hearings dominated Ryan's final months in office in 2002, along with the questions of whether he would issue a blanket commutation and when he would be indicted. Whatever Ryan's ultimate motives in finally issuing that commutation, he had reason to be skeptical of what prosecutors said and did. Further, the charge that Ryan crusaded against the death penalty to build a wall of popularity against the sheriff's posse must answer why, if it was so popular, no other governor followed suit.[9] Those questions were secondary, though, when Ryan first imposed the moratorium. The most pressing question for the political class was whether he would run for reelection in 2002.

Rather in a biblical sense, the fat years of the Internet revolution were followed by lean years after the dot-com collapse that began in March 2000. On June 30, 2002, the state ended the fiscal year with a general fund balance of exactly nine cents. Ryan was compelled to cut spending and lay off public employees—painful for any politician.

Nevertheless, the bipartisan Illinois establishment labored mightily to increase spending on favored projects. Many hundreds of millions of dollars were found somehow to expand a convention center and football stadium in Chicago, entice Boeing to Chicago from Seattle, enlarge Chicago's O'Hare International Airport or build a new metropolitan airport, and build a new Lincoln presidential library in Springfield. In these endeavors, Ryan displayed his usual mastery in making deals.

Boeing built jet airliners in Seattle. The company planned to leave its factories there but move its corporate headquarters. Dallas, Denver, and Chicago were considered. On April 19, 2001, more than a hundred Illinois Praetorians gathered in the Arthur Rubloff Room of the Art Institute of Chicago to wine and dine Boeing executives, offering mixed greens with shrimp and Vermont goat cheese, grilled filet of beef, Yukon Gold potatoes, spring vegetables, and crème brûlée with vanilla wafers in the shape of airplanes, as a string trio from the Chicago Symphony Orchestra played. The state's top industrialists, lawyers, politicians, newspaper publishers, and cultural leaders asked Boeing, in effect, How much do you want?

In media reports, Ryan said the city and state offered tax breaks and incentives amounting to $50 million, then backed off and said the package was worth no more than $5 million. In the end, the total was $60 million over twenty years. Boeing executives flew out of Seattle on May 9, filing three flight plans to Dallas, Denver, and Chicago to maintain secrecy. While airborne, chairman Philip Condit called Ryan, and senior vice president John Warner called Mayor Daley. The Chicago selection was announced when the plane landed at Midway Airport. The celebratory dinner was held the next evening at a Charlie Trotter's, an ultrachic restaurant in Chicago. This time the menu included roasted yellow beet terrine complemented by Veuve Clicquot Brut 1995; salad of Alaskan Dungeness and golden spider crab with Geoduc clams and Beluga caviar, accompanied by Pinot Gris "Clos Windsbuhl" Domaine Zind-Humbrecht 1998; steamed halibut with tofu, soy beans, and braised pig tail along with Leeuwin Chardonnay Margaret River 1999, and so on through another entrée and desserts.

"The mayor and I put the frosting on the cake and took all the credit and waved all the flags," Ryan recalled with a chuckle. "That's how it's supposed to work." Right—a Republican governor and a Democratic mayor making deals in the venerable Illinois tradition. "You know what my theory was, Jim? Look, the guy is the mayor, the biggest city in the state. Now why in the hell do I want to fight with him? Why wouldn't I want to get along with him?"[10]

The Boeing incentives were approved by the General Assembly on May 31 along with another Ryan-Daley deal, an $800 million expansion of the McCormick Place exposition center. Ryan brokered the last-minute deal—the sticking point was the allocation of cigarette taxes and a thirteen-year extension of city taxes on lodging, restaurants, and airport transportation services. "Everybody said it was dead, but it kept coming back," said Scott Fawell, CEO of McPier.[11] In three years, Ryan had increased state spending more than Governor Edgar had in eight. A grateful Daley supported Ryan for reelection, stopping just short, as he usually did for the sake of protocol, of an outright endorsement.

These were heady times for Daley. Even before the Boeing and McPier agreements, Ryan had muscled $587 million through the legislature to remodel Soldier Field, home of the Chicago Bears. The Illinois Sports Facilities Authority would issue $387 million in bonds, with the other $200 million split between the Bears and the National Football League. Ryan joked that his price for the stadium improvement was to see improvement in the Bears' play (which did not happen for several years). Preservationists and aesthetes objected that the new stadium plan looked like a flying saucer placed atop a classical temple, but they failed to stop the project in court.

If Ryan had a Democratic friend in Daley, he had a Republican enemy in Senator Peter Fitzgerald. Detractors said Fitzgerald was naive, and perhaps he was—he thought he could stop a scandal in Illinois before it happened. Ryan and Lura Lynn had set up a foundation to build a $120 million Abraham Lincoln Presidential Library and Museum in Springfield. Fitzgerald believed that Ryan's campaign donors would clout no-bid contracts to build it and Ryan's cronies would get patronage jobs to run it. Carrying charts and a thick notebook, Fitzgerald entered the Senate floor on October 4, 2000, and filibustered to block $10 million in federal aid for the project unless federal bidding rules were followed. (October 4 was a sad day for Ryan in other respects. His adopted sister, Nancy Ferguson, died, and a Cook County judge threw out a Ryan gun-control law.) Fitzgerald spent hours reading newspaper accounts of decades of Illinois political scandals. Senators on both sides of the aisle were irritated and threatened to invoke cloture to shut Fitzgerald up, so he stopped. He did get a bone from Senate majority leader Trent Lott, a clause in legislation requiring competitive bidding, but everybody knew the House under Speaker Dennis Hastert would kill it.

Fitzgerald had cause for concern. Besides Lura Lynn, the foundation's other directors were Julie Cellini, chair of the state's historic preservation board and wife of Springfield developer and boss William F. Cellini, and Pamela Daniels, wife of Illinois House Republican leader Lee Daniels. Ryan intended to name his chief of staff, William Newtson, to head the Lincoln center. Ground was broken in February 2001, but by the time the library got built, Ryan had lost so much clout he could not put Newtson in the job, whereupon Newtson said he never even wanted it.

Ryan also faltered at first on the airport issue. Daley wanted to lay more runways at O'Hare. Republicans who ran the northwestern suburbs that suffered from O'Hare noise pollution favored building a new airport far south of the city at Peotone. Ryan had fudged the issue during the campaign, saying he would back Daley's plan when the nearby suburbs agreed to it, which meant never. As governor he sought a megadeal to satisfy everyone—expand O'Hare, build Peotone as well, and meanwhile keep open Meigs Field, the lakeside downtown Chicago airstrip that Daley wanted to close. In November 2001, the deal fell apart as Ryan and Daley bickered over a mere $3 million. Daley insisted that state subsidies for Meigs come from the general fund. But that fund was bare. If it could not provide the money, then Daley could go ahead and shut Meigs down. (Daley was a bit nutty on the subject of Meigs. He eventually closed it in 2003 by secretly ordering bulldozers to tear up the runway in the dead of night.)

Lo and behold, just a week after the Ryan-Daley deal collapsed, they sealed a new one. Meigs could be closed after 2005 if the General Assembly so approved. As long as it remained open, Meigs would be subsidized by United and American airlines operations at O'Hare, not by Illinois taxpayers. Meanwhile, Daley could build new O'Hare runways, razing hundreds of suburban homes. Also, Daley would join Ryan in lobbying for federal funds for a Peotone airport, thirty miles from Chicago. Daley figured the airlines would never go for it anyway, so that part of the deal was moonshine. After hours of negotiations, breaking a decades-long stalemate, the governor and mayor emerged from city hall late at night and praised each other. "We've done a lot of projects together," Ryan said. "We've done McCormick Place, we've done Illinois FIRST, we did Soldier Field, we've done Boeing, we did Ford, we did Solo Cup [two other new plants]. And now the World Series of all."[12]

But they had not counted on Peter Fitzgerald. He stalled the deal in the Senate, infuriating everybody except the residents of the suburbs surrounding O'Hare and their politicians. Joined by Representative Henry Hyde, he demanded that the inspector general of the U.S. Department of Transportation investigate whether Daley's estimated costs, construction schedule, and funding sources for enlarging O'Hare were realistic and credible. In July 2005, after Ryan had left office, the inspector general concluded that they were not. The overall project is still in doubt.

Conservatives condemned Ryan for breaking campaign promises about O'Hare runways, late-term abortions, tax increases, a Cook County casino, and gun-control laws. For all that, Ryan had such a successful record as a builder and doer that by the normal rules of politics, he should have been sailing to reelection. He needed to make a decision by the fall of 2001. On July 20, 2001, Alex McLeczynsky, the first Operation Safe Road defendant to go to trial instead of pleading guilty, was sentenced to thirty months in prison for bribing secretary of state officials for his driving students' CDLs.

There came a time when George Ryan, Dan Webb, Jim Thompson, and Jeremy Margolis actually failed to make a deal go down. It seems they misplayed a sure hand. Many reasons were cited for the failure, but one reason was simply that Ryan was steadily losing clout under the federal hammering.

One of the deals on "Fat Friday," May 21, 1999, was a law written to give certain investors a license for a new casino in Rosemont, near O'Hare International Airport. Technically, the license would be granted by a five-member Illinois Gaming Board. Following Margolis's recommendations, Ryan appointed

Gregory C. Jones to the board and named Sergio Acosta as the board administrator. Jones, as an assistant U.S. attorney, had declined to prosecute Ryan in the nursing home scandal of 1982. Margolis was an attorney for a consortium of seventy-one suburbs that were to share in Rosemont's taxes from the new casino. Margolis was effectively naming officials of a state board whose decisions would make or lose money for his clients.

The license was intended for Emerald Casino, Incorporated. The major owners were Donald Flynn, who had made a fortune with Blockbuster video rentals and a waste management firm, and his son, Kevin. Many of the fifty-nine other investors were well connected. The law required minority and female investors; two of them were Connie Payton, the widow of Chicago Bears star Walter Payton, and Chaz Ebert, wife of film critic Roger Ebert. These women were not examples of the disadvantaged and dispossessed.

The casino deal looked so certain that developers for Emerald broke ground in October 1999 even before the gaming board considered the matter. The next January, board chairman Robert Vickrey, although an advocate for Emerald, resigned under pressure from Ryan, and Jones moved up to be chairman. A year later, on January 30, 2001, the gaming board shocked the state. It voted 4–1 not only to deny Emerald a Rosemont license but also to revoke the inactive license it held in East Dubuque, Illinois. The board's investigators said some investors had lied to them and others had ties to organized crime figures. For instance, the construction company used by Emerald was owned by the sister-in-law of mobster John DiFronzo. "It was wonderful to see people who thought they had a sure thing get screwed," marveled the Reverend Tom Grey, an antigambling activist. "How did it happen? This is the land of the deal!"[13]

The board's vote provoked much excited commentary about the one time that Illinois clout collapsed before launching a big gravy boat. Again, the merely personal should not be overlooked. The Flynns and other investors offended the board and its staff. In a larger view, Jones and his board members did what they were supposed to do—make a policy decision after an honest review of the facts. No wonder the state was shocked.

Acting late on a Friday afternoon so as to attract minimum publicity, Ryan dumped two board members who had voted against Emerald. He replaced them with people who had business relationships with Emerald investors. New board member Elzie Higginbottom also was Mayor Daley's chief fund-raiser in the black business community. Eventually, Ryan dumped Jones as well, who also had voted against Emerald, and made Higginbottom chairman.

Other figures were hard at work as well. Rosemont mayor Donald E. Stephens, a Republican boss, had been pushing for a casino in his town ever since Governor Thompson signed the first casino bill in 1990. Stephens hired Dan Webb to represent Rosemont before the gaming board. As U.S. attorney in the

1980s, Webb had indicted Stephens twice, one for tax fraud and once for kickbacks on a land deal. Stephens was acquitted both times. Thompson, Webb's law partner at Winston and Strawn, was by this time a lobbyist for racing impresario Richard Duchossois. The original deal had given Duchossois and the racing industry a cut of the Emerald profits. Stephens and Duchossois were behind Ryan's removal of Jones.

And yet all the king's horses and all the king's men could not put Emerald back together again. Emerald was the only one of ten state casino licenses in flux. The firm promptly appealed the board's decision, keeping the issue tied up in courts and the license away from anybody else for years. Meanwhile, the state was missing out on hundreds of millions of dollars in tax revenues that a new casino would generate. In May 2007, the state appellate court ruled against Emerald, but the firm said it would not give up.

Michael "Mickey" Segal was a Chicago insurance magnate and political fixer. In June 2001, Segal, Don Udstuen, and Ron Swanson joined Ryan in New York Yankees owner George Steinbrenner's stadium skybox for a $3,000-a-person fund-raiser. It hardly mattered. Sometime during the early months of 2001, Ryan became unelectable, no matter how much money Citizens for Ryan raised. Segal, Udstuen, Swanson, and Ryan all were under criminal investigation. (Segal was indicted in 2002 and sentenced in 2005 to ten years in prison for looting $30 million from his insurance company.)

Should Ryan run? He got some advice from Dan Rostenkowski, the Chicago Democratic powerhouse who ran the U.S. House Ways and Means Committee for many years before pleading guilty to mail fraud in 1995. (After losing his congressional seat in 1994, "Rosty" set up a consulting office in Segal's shop.) "I went through what reporters and investigative reporters do to you," he told Ryan. "Rerun old stories and keep throwing hash at you. You won't want to go home and see your wife in pain. So if you run, I'll be your campaign manager. That's how highly I think of you. But the pain you'll have to go through isn't worth it."[14]

As Ryan pondered his future in the governor's mansion on the morning of August 8, a storm blew a limb from a big old oak onto the porch roof outside his window. Ryan said he was not superstitious enough to take this event as an omen. Still, there was little doubt about his decision. That afternoon, he took his wife, six children, and fourteen grandchildren to stand with him on the steps of the Kankakee County courthouse. As if to build suspense, the courthouse was decked out in full campaign-rally mode with banners, bunting, balloons, and free hot dogs and soda. Ryan reviewed his achievements—and then attacked his party's right wing. "I worry for the Republican Party—the party of Lincoln under whose banner I have proudly served all of my life. If we're to be successful, we need to listen more and shout less. We need to moderate our positions."[15] At once, political observers knew Ryan would declare he was stepping down—you can't run for reelection against your own party's base.

That same day, Citizens for Ryan spent $35,000 to buy a van from a Chicago Ford dealer. Ryan was not running again, but he had no intention of disappearing from politics, no matter that CFR was under federal scrutiny (or, as Mayor Daley said in addressing one of his own scandals, being "scrootined.")

Ryan took his family to dinner at the Kankakee Country Club that night. The only guests not family members were the Reverend Ignatius D. McDermott ("Father Mac") and former judge Sheila Murphy from Chicago. Ryan had seated them in the front row at the courthouse. Both worked closely with Ryan in providing services to alcoholics and drug addicts.

Ryan once had an alcoholic aide. He secretly arranged a bed for him at a rehabilitation clinic, then, riding an elevator in the Capitol, stopped the cab between floors. "Look," Ryan told the aide, "when these elevator doors open, two guys will meet us. You can either lose your job, and soon enough your life, or you can go off with those two guys into rehab." So he did.[16]

Such unsung charity from Ryan cemented Father Mac's and Murphy's friendship with him. Murphy had a curious history with Ryan. Back during the Equal Rights Amendment struggle in the early 1980s, she was the defense attorney for an ERA activist accused of bribing a legislator. Ryan testified for the prosecution—"George was an astute politician; he had the jury in the palm of his hand," Murphy recalled, and she thought he "was the devil himself."[17] (Her client was convicted of a lesser charge.) As for Father Mac, Ryan got state funding for his Haymarket House rehab clinic. When McDermott died in 2005, shortly before Ryan was to go on trial, he teared up at his funeral. Murphy, who also attended that funeral, grew to esteem Ryan so highly that after he was convicted, she organized a letter-writing campaign asking the sentencing judge for mercy. Ryan's advocacy for addicts is yet another aspect of the paradox of his character. Unlike his actions in the death penalty issue, that aspect is largely unrecognized. He did not trumpet it.

Four weeks after that dinner at the Kankakee Country Club, U.S. attorney Patrick Fitzgerald was sworn into office.

15 If Those Students Had Taken Chemistry

As if to revive past glory, Ryan went back to Cuba in 2002. Castro's government asked Ryan's office for medical assistance after Cuba was devastated by a hurricane. Agribusiness giant Archer Daniels Midland of Decatur, Illinois, already had shipped grain to Cuba—the first such shipment since 1962—in response to the same hurricane. Ryan assembled a few Illinois drug companies and flew to Havana on another "humanitarian" mission in January.

During their first meeting, Castro was a stern lecturer; the second time, he was relaxed and joking. As usual, the dinner lasted five hours, and Castro talked most of the time. Between glasses of Chilean wine and Asian buffalo milk, Castro teased Ryan by saying, "One day a governor of the United States will have a statue here. Or the name of a medical school. There are many ways we can pay homage."[1] Rubbing it in, he added, "So, dear governor, can we exchange Cuban cigars for Illinois white corn, which makes great tortillas?"[2] On the first trip, Ryan gave Castro a bust of Lincoln. This time, he gave him an album of photos of the 1999 trip and invited Castro to Springfield for the opening of the Lincoln Library. However, President Bush's State Department was no friendlier to Castro than President Clinton's had been, and the Illinois visit never happened.

In a speech at a doctors' convention in Varadero, Ryan said, "While we in the United States have turned the other cheek with numerous nations that once confronted our ideals of peace and freedom, we have not offered that same courtesy to the Cuban people."[3] Ryan also visited a cancer hospital to deliver medical supplies donated by the Illinois firms.

Whatever good spirits Ryan might have derived from the Cuba trip were short-lived. On April 2, the feds indicted Scott Fawell, his aide Richard A. Juliano, and the Citizens for Ryan campaign committee. It was the first time a campaign fund ever had been accused of racketeering.

The question now was when, not whether, Ryan would be indicted. *Chicago Sun-Times* political columnist Steve Neal reflected the turning of the tide. Neal generally had supported Ryan, even stated flatly that Ryan "didn't know what was going on" in the corrupt secretary of state field offices.[4] Now Neal wrote, "There is blood on the highways because of governmental corruption. . . . Ryan's strategists allowed our highways to become killing zones. . . . [They] allowed incompetent drivers to obtain what became licenses to kill."[5] By and large, Ryan had enjoyed good relations with Chicago pundits—*Tribune* political writer Rick Pearson's wife had worked for Ryan in the state library—but no more. The political class read "blood on the highways" and knew that Ryan was doomed.

Juliano soon flipped, pleaded guilty to mail fraud, and cooperated with the government. Ryan and Fawell did not know that Udstuen had flipped too. Sitting in a federal office, Udstuen secretly taped a call from Ryan on April 30.

"Ah, shit," Udstuen said, "I've got some problems with the stuff I did with Larry [Warner] and Ron [Swanson], and you know I've got tax problems because of it."

"Yeah," Ryan said, "well, I just called to tell you that, you know, don't let it all get you down. It's easy to say, but nobody's been through more of this shit than I have the last four years. It's been a fucking nightmare."[6]

Hardly incriminating statements from either man. Prosecutors must have been disappointed.

It mattered little, for on May 21, Warner, Udstuen, and Alan A. Drazek were indicted. That same day, Jim Thompson rode to Ryan's rescue before the Illinois Supreme Court. In a civil case that drew scant media attention but was perilous for Ryan, the Better Government Association had sued to recover for taxpayers the salaries paid to Ryan and his agents and the ill-gotten gains collected by them.

Big Jim strode into the supreme court room in Springfield for the first time in thirty-two years. He acted as an assistant attorney general on behalf of Ryan, who billed taxpayers $204,597 for the services of Thompson's law firm. This sum apparently was a bargain—the state held the firm's normal rate of $400 an hour to $200. (In a similar federal case that had been dismissed, CFR paid the legal bills, not the state.)

During oral arguments, a justice who was noted for falling asleep during oral arguments did so. BGA attorney Robert Atkins told the court, "These were ill-gotten gains and they belong to the treasury. They don't belong sticking to the hands of the defendants." Thompson argued that honoring such taxpayer-initiated suits would create a "parade of horrors," a landslide of frivolous lawsuits. "No decision of any state employee, any public official . . . would be safe."[7] To counter, Atkins cited a law review article advocating such taxpayer suits, co-authored by Jayne Carr Thompson, the former governor's wife.[8] Thompson smiled. The court ruled against the BGA.

In another court, Ryan had a legal setback. U.S. district judge Rebecca Pallmeyer banned the Chicago law firm of Altheimer and Gray from representing Citizens for Ryan because of a conflict of interest. Ryan's legal adviser Jeremy Margolis was the firm's head of litigation. Margolis also had represented Fawell, a co-defendant with CFR, on another matter. Thus, Altheimer and Gray now was in the position of defending its current client, CFR, against a former one, Fawell. The judge probably feared an Alice in Wonderland of testimony. Margolis: Fawell did it, not CFR. Fawell: But I only did what Margolis had approved. (Altheimer and Gray spectacularly collapsed in bankruptcy in 2003; the legal and political fallout rained for years and eventually smudged Ryan's defense.)

The marching band played on. Roger "The Hog" Stanley, identified only as "Vendor A" in the Fawell indictment, was indicted in a separate case in June and another in August. A judge increased his bond because he had concealed his assets and a second family in Costa Rica. Soon, Stanley flipped. Ryan must have been troubled: these guys keep flipping. To stop the flipping, he assigned Margolis to talk with the defendants, not a successful maneuver.

Fawell would die before he flipped, or so he and Ryan thought. The prosecution revealed that Stanley had provided Fawell free or cut-rate marijuana, prostitutes, and lodging in Costa Rica. The *Chicago Sun-Times* revealed that four of Ryan's children had testified before the grand jury under grants of immunity. Next, the feds alleged that Ryan had known his aides were illegally destroying documents as early as 1998. Through all of this, Ryan was trying to decide what to do about all the convicts on death row.

The problem was so torturous, and Ryan zigzagged through it so much, that he invited allegations of acting in bad faith. It is at least as likely that he was honestly anguished. On the night that Andrew Kokoraleis was executed, Ryan kept changing his mind about a reprieve as different aides bustled in and out of his office. Now Ryan said he would not consider a blanket commutation, then that he would, then again that he probably would not. He said he would not meet with the families of murder victims, then he did.

Speaking at the University of Oregon on March 2, 2002, Ryan said he would review every capital case and consider commuting some sentences. "A 99 percent accuracy rate isn't good enough. If government can't get this right, it ought not be in the business of passing such final, irreversible judgment."[9]

Wearing a beard and long hair, Lawrence C. Marshall looked exactly like what Ryan did not: the liberal criminal justice reformer. Marshall, a law professor, headed the Center on Wrongful Convictions at Northwestern University. He and other opponents of the death penalty instantly seized on the opportunity opened by Ryan and started filing clemency appeals for nearly everyone on death row.

Ryan's commission released its study on April 15, along with eighty-five recommendations to cleanse the system of incompetent lawyers, jailhouse snitches, and misconduct and errors by police, prosecutors, and courts. Of about 250 people sentenced to death in Illinois from 1997 through 2001, at least 115 would have been ineligible for execution had these safeguards been in place, the report said. Ryan duly forwarded the recommendations to the General Assembly. He added, on second thought, that he would not resume executions even if the legislature adopted every one of the eighty-five reforms.

Pretty soon he said that either all or none should have their sentences commuted. This position raised a question of why the Illinois Prisoner Review Board should bother holding hearings on the clemency petitions that Professor Marshall and others had filed for 157 death row inmates. Absurdly, the review board had scheduled just fifteen minutes each for the prosecution and defense in every case. Attorney General Jim Ryan, the Republican nominee for governor and a political enemy of George Ryan, unsuccessfully filed suit to stop the hearings.

Nine days of hearings opened on October 15, enraging prosecutors and murder victims' families alike. Tom Cross, a Republican state representative and a former prosecutor, explained the perspective of law enforcement. You live with a case for years, the trial takes maybe a couple of months, then you go through the appeals process, then you win on appeal and figure, at last, this case is closed. "All of sudden, along comes the governor and says, all right, that closure is no longer there and we are going to open it up. And there is a real sense of outrage."[10]

In practice, the review board allowed cases to be heard for a couple of hours, not thirty minutes. The board would make secret, nonbinding recommendations to Ryan. A typical case:

Gabriel Solache, a Mexican national, was convicted of murdering a couple and kidnapping their two children. "I confessed because I couldn't stand the beatings anymore," he told his appellate lawyer. Solache, with one hand handcuffed to a wall, was given only one sandwich to eat in forty hours. Blows to the head left him with permanent hearing damage and buzzing in his left ear. Solache did not speak English, but he was interrogated and forced to sign a confession in that language.

An assistant Cook County state's attorney retorted: "What's important here is that when defendants are faced with brutal facts, then certain things come about. Either all of a sudden [they're] mentally retarded, or all of a sudden [they claim] insanity, or if those are not available to you, then someone else must have done it and 'I must have been beaten.'"[11]

Ryan, watching a video feed in his office, noted that no prosecutor from any county in Illinois would give an inch, concede a single point, say, well, maybe here is something we should look at. Prosecutors, like the guys involved in Operation Safe Road. Look, see how rigid they are, how unfair.

Another case: Robert Jones was convicted of murdering a couple and raping the woman postmortem. Jones's mother, seated at the witness table, tearfully told the panel, "I am here today to plead for his life. His biological father was an abusive and dangerous man. He witnessed daily beatings against me. . . . We also lost a son that night. We are all victims here."

The murdered woman's father arose, stood at a lectern, and gazed poker-faced down at Jones's mother. "I can't forgive him."

"I'm not asking you to forgive him."

"I can't forgive him."

Again, "I'm not asking you to forgive him."

"I want him executed. I can't help it."

"I understand."[12]

After witnessing many scenes such as that, Ryan said he had nearly ruled out blanket clemency. He met with the families of murder victims in a ballroom of the governor's mansion in Springfield and at the Union League Club in Chicago.

"They just kicked the shit out of me," Ryan said. "Threw stuff at me, swore at me, and I got up and stormed out. And I understood their feelings. . . . They came up to me and said, 'I know that man's guilty because I sat under my kitchen table and watched those guys kill my dad and mother. I sat there and watched them; I know they're guilty. What are you gonna do about that?' . . . I just didn't know; I couldn't make up my mind."[13]

Ryan alluded to Rick Pueschel, who said, "I asked him, face to face, if he had any doubt that Jerry and Reginald Muhaffey were guilty of the murder of my parents—not just in the sense of a verdict but, in fact, in reality, in that they were the ones who swung the bats, swung the pistol, plunged the knife, violated my mother and shattered my father's skull [in 1983 in Chicago]. I knew that they were the ones who beat and stabbed me—then only 11 years old—happily believing they had killed me too. But did he? Ryan told me he had no doubts and no questions. He told me that he thought I would get what I was looking for."[14] (Pueschel's was not the only such case. U'Rica Winder, at age six, survived being stabbed while her mother, sister, and two others were killed in their Chicago apartment in 1986.)

If many cases were gut-wrenching, others were clear-cut. Late in 2002, Ryan issued four pardons that were nearly forgotten in the uproar over his pardons and blanket commutations of the next January. He went to Northwestern University to announce the pardon of Paula Gray of the notorious Ford Heights Four case. Gray, seventeen years old at the time, implicated four men from Ford Heights, south of Chicago, in a double murder and rape in 1978. Later she said the police interrogation was so intense that it put her in a mental hospital. She recanted her testimony before the cases went to trial. In response, prosecutors charged her with rape and murder along with the men and added a perjury charge. Sentenced to fifty years in prison, she served eight years before cutting a deal to testify against the four in new trials in exchange for her freedom.

Years later, she cooperated with Northwestern University journalism students investigating the case. The Ford Heights Four eventually were freed, and three other men confessed to the crimes. Gray's perjury conviction had been overturned, but the Cook County state's attorney appealed to reinstate it. Enough is enough, said Ryan, and pardoned her outright.

Stephen Bright of the Southern Center for Human Rights was among those who marveled that such cases "ultimately come to light not because of the police or the prosecution or the defense lawyers or the judicial system, but because a journalism class at Northwestern took it as a class project to see whether these people were guilty or not. If those students had taken chemistry that semester, those folks would have been executed."[15]

Ryan went to the University of Illinois at Chicago to announce his next three pardons: Rolando Cruz and Gary Gauger, two of the thirteen who had been exonerated from death row, and Steven Linscott, who had spent ten years in prison for murder before DNA evidence cleared him. The pardons erased the convictions from their records. "I wish them well. They've been through hell," Ryan said.[16] Perhaps he took a measure of satisfaction in the fact that Jim Ryan, while DuPage County state's attorney, had eagerly prosecuted Cruz in a notorious child murder case.

Meanwhile, the General Assembly did nothing about the proposed reforms. Legislators were struggling with a budget crisis, and it was an election year, and they were not about to invite accusations of being soft on crime. They did manage to pass a law making terrorism a crime punishable by death. Ryan vetoed it. They overrode his veto, the Senate unanimously.

Reporters visiting Chicago from New York or Washington or Los Angeles to cover the Ryan story were puzzled: why didn't Democrats in the General Assembly exploit the scandal, hold hearings, impeach Ryan, force him to resign? They did not understand Illinois politics. The Four Tops had Ryan exactly where they wanted him. Under such pressure, he was eager to make deals with them. Democratic recapture of the governor's seat after twenty-six years was all but certain anyway.

The legislature passed a state budget with a cigarette tax increase of forty cents a pack, $750 million in borrowing against an expected settlement from the tobacco industry, and assurances of pork. Ryan, of all people, proposed a freeze on some pork spending to offset cuts in social services. Democratic House Speaker Michael Madigan reportedly turned on Ryan in anger. "That's my money. You can't touch it."[17] (Madigan later denied saying that.)

An August poll by CBS 2/Survey USA showed that 61 percent of Illinois residents thought Ryan should resign, even though his term would expire in just five months. Ryan grew crankier and more hostile, even to members of his own party. He all but campaigned against Jim Ryan, the GOP nominee for governor, and Kristine Cohn, the candidate for secretary of state. Both had criticized him. No Republican named Ryan was about to be elected anyway, no matter how many billboards the attorney general erected with "Jim" in huge type and "Ryan" in small. On November 5, Democratic U.S. representative Rod Blagojevich was elected governor. Democrats swept the statewide offices.

Ryan spent election night in a Chicago hotel suite, his name not on any ballot for the first time in thirty-two years. He had passed the day clearing out his office and reading letters from mothers asking that their children on death row be spared. He reminisced about Governor Ogilvie, who had passed a state income tax because it was the right thing to do, even if it killed his career. Lura Lynn told him they needed to get the mice and spiders out of their house in Kankakee.

Later, Ryan threw a farewell party at the governor's mansion. Dan Rostenkowski flew in from Hawaii to make the scene. Mike Madigan was not there, with a good excuse—his wife was sick. Pate Philip was absent with a not-so-good excuse—he went hunting instead. Ryan told Jim Thompson that if he cried, he could not attend, but Thompson got teary-eyed anyway. He said Ryan had "the courage of a lonely voice protecting the poor and the reviled [death row inmates] even when the press turned against him."[18]

The Book of Life and the Book of Death

Public relations pressure was applied to influence Ryan's decision. Both Pope John Paul II and Bishop Desmond Tutu, the South African Nobel Peace Prize laureate, urged him to grant clemency. In Illinois, thirty-six men who had been released from death rows in thirteen states lit candles at Northwestern University Law School. Next, thirty-one of them marched thirty-seven miles from a state prison in Joliet to Ryan's office in Chicago. The "Dead Men Walking" relay took fourteen hours and ended by their trying to hand Ryan a letter, but an aide said he was out. Lawrence Marshall, who helped to organize the march, said, "If the governor thinks that he's going to be able to create two piles, the book of life and the book of death and confidently determine who belongs in which, history shows that he will make profound errors, fatal errors."[1]

The arts community put its oar in as well. Abby Mann, who won an Academy Award for the script of the 1961 film *Judgment at Nuremburg,* said he was writing a cable television drama about the dilemma facing Ryan. On New Year's Eve, the play *The Exonerated* opened in Chicago. Ryan had seen it in preview along with members of the National Gathering of the Death Row Exonerated. The play was written by Erik Jensen and Jessica Blank, based on interviews with former death row prisoners and their families. It starred Richard Dreyfuss, Danny Glover, and Mike Farrell.

Having met with families of murder victims, Ryan met with relatives of forty-five condemned prisoners on January 3, 2003, at Old St. Mary's Church in Chicago. Claude Lee had played football with Ryan at Kankakee High School. Lee, though a Democrat, had supported Ryan in the black community through decades of elections. Claude's son Eric had mental problems and had been dismissed from an institution to live with his father. Stopped for a traffic infraction, Eric fatally shot a Kankakee policeman in the face in full view of a busload of elementary school children. Inside the church, Claude Lee confronted Ryan. "My son shot and killed a policeman. No question that my son is guilty. What I want to know is, are you going to kill him?"

"God, I didn't even recognize Claude, he's aged," Ryan thought. He said, "Claude, that's a hard question. I don't know."[2]

Three days later, Alan Drazek pleaded guilty to a tax count related to laundering money for Don Udstuen and agreed to testify for the government. Four days after that, with four days left in his term, Ryan went to DePaul University Law School. Reporters from around the world wanted access, but Ryan insisted on making a statement, not in an auditorium or lecture hall, but in a standard law school classroom.

No inmate had ever been pardoned from death row while still appealing his case. Ryan pardoned four of them: Madison Hobley, Stanley Howard, Leroy Orange, and Aaron Patterson. Ryan said Chicago police had tortured confessions out of them, although that allegation had not been proved. (Decades of rumors and litigation about systematic torture by some Chicago police were later vindicated by a special prosecutors' study released in July 2006.) Democratic Cook County state's attorney Dick Devine belittled Ryan's pardons: "All of these cases would have been best left for consideration by the courts, which have the experience, the training, and the wisdom to decide innocence or guilt. Instead, they were ripped away from the justice system by a man who is a pharmacist by training and a politician by trade."[3]

The unprecedented pardons were startling enough, but the next day, Saturday, January 11, Ryan walked into Northwestern University Law School and into history. He had made sure that specially delivered letters to the families of murder victims were received before he spoke so that they got the news first. Capital justice was "haunted by the demon of error," Ryan said. "Because the Illinois death penalty system is arbitrary and capricious—and therefore immoral—I no longer shall tinker with the machinery of death," he said, borrowing words from the late Supreme Court justice Harry Blackmun. "I won't stand for it."[4] Using powers granted by the state constitution, he commuted the sentences of 163 remaining death row inmates to life in prison without parole and four others to forty years.

Devine complained again: "The governor, in his supposed search for the truth, spent hour after hour with defense attorneys, and not one minute with prosecutors."[5] Strictly speaking, this was not true—Ryan had been interviewed by Operation Safe Road prosecutors at length, four different times.

Thomas F. Roeser, a conservative activist and former Ryan supporter, was even more scathing. "He started to re-craft his image to appeal to a future jury pool. He switched from being a death penalty advocate to a vigorous opponent . . . which gained him huge publicity from the liberal media. . . . Since African Americans dominated death row, Ryan calculated he would make gains with any blacks on the jury. One large group remaining was Hispanic. Ryan became a darling of liberaldom nationally by going to Cuba."[6]

A friendly journalist asked Ryan if he had been thinking about his own legal trouble in deciding to grant blanket clemency. "No, I thought about my grandchildren, and the story of one Death Row prisoner who was born a cocaine addict, fed beer in a baby bottle, was beaten constantly by his prostitute mother and wound up killing someone. How do you raise a kid like that? It is not an uncommon story on Death Row."[7]

Operation Safe Road aside, Ryan's action was attacked as an act of moral vanity. He had substituted his own judgment for that of police, jurors, and judges. He short-circuited due process and caused terrible pain to victims' survivors. Nor were the commutations purely a boon for all the convicts released from a sentence of death. Some whose cases had been on appeal actually might have won retrials, lesser sentences than life without parole, or even exoneration. Further, the release of the worst sociopathic killers into the general prison population created problems for prison administrators. In solitary cells on death row, the inmates had certain privileges such as unrestricted access to a telephone; in the common cellblocks, they shared cells, felt at sea, and were apt to inflict or to be targets of violence. The law enforcement community in general was aghast at Ryan's action.

On the whole, though, Ryan's blanket clemency was lauded. Nelson Mandela called him, as did President Vicente Fox of Mexico (three Mexican nationals were among those spared). Few of us would object to being lionized, and Ryan certainly did not. He appeared on the *Oprah Winfrey Show* and other national television programs. He spent the next two years while awaiting trial traveling the lecture circuit as a sort of elder statesman, speaking out against capital punishment, his rhetoric steadily escalating. At Michigan State University, he declared, "Our system in Illinois is rotten to the core, arbitrary, capricious, unjust, racist and unfair to the poor and also to the families of the victims."[8] A Republican, supposedly conservative, was saying this.

Two polar views: Ryan acted from sincere moral conviction, or he cynically tried to seize the moral high ground in anticipation of his indictment. My position is not "the truth lies somewhere in between" so much as it is that both poles misunderstand how Ryan reacted primarily as a politician. His critics were right—he was not a philosopher, not given to introspection and casuistry. Instead, he saw a broken system that he had some power to fix. He did what politicians usually do, created a blue-ribbon commission to study the problem. The commission worked for two years and made sweeping recommendations. Ryan said, in effect, okay, General Assembly, I've done my job; now you do yours. Three times he tried to get reform legislation passed, and three times the legislators said, "Forget it." No election opponent was going to call them soft on crime. The clock was ticking, and Ryan was almost out of time. He had not failed the system in reforming capital justice; rather, the system had failed him. He had just one recourse left, the constitutional power to grant clemency. Ryan was never shy about seeking and exercising power. Now the system had put him in the position of a jury of one. "Even if the exercise of power becomes my burden, I will bear it," he said in announcing the three December 2002 pardons.[9] This one time, the exercise of power really was a burden. Later, he reflected, "When somebody is indicted, they hand them an indictment that says 'United States of America versus *you.*' Or 'The State of Illinois versus *you.*' That is pretty awesome. That includes the state treasury and all the manpower they can muster. Pretty awesome powers, and in a lot of cases it is abused. All in the name of good government and 'tough on crime.'"[10] He did not say so, but he likewise viewed Operation Safe Road as an abuse of power in that name. The politician never perceived Operation Safe Road with the moral clarity with which he understood capital punishment.

Three days after Ryan's commutations, his Democratic successor was inaugurated as governor. Just about his first act in office was to fax a letter. "Dear Mr. Fawell: Effective immediately, you are hereby terminated as the chief executive officer of the Metropolitan Pier and Exposition Authority. Sincerely, Rod R. Blagojevich, Governor."[11] Fawell had been on paid leave from his $195,000-a-year job since his indictment.

If one of Blagojevich's initial acts in office was to fire Fawell, one of Ryan's last acts was to document his own achievements. The state constitution requires an outgoing governor to report to the General Assembly on the condition of the state. Ryan did so with a taxpayer-paid seventy-eight-minute videotape, plus a fifty-page booklet, praising all the marvelous things he had done. "George Ryan's single term as governor of Illinois will survive the first draft of history as written by the media," said the videotape's narrator, Robert Newtson, Ryan's chief of staff.[12]

Ryan spent his last few days in the governor's mansion with Jim Thompson as his guest. Thompson remembered that two of his dogs were buried on the grounds. Ryan, heading to his successor's inauguration, remarked, "This morning, I awoke content with my decision [on capital punishment], but I also feel like I worked all day on a farm doing manual labor."[13] He knew the feeling from working on his grandfather Bowman's farm in Iowa as a boy.

The night after he left office, Ryan's campaign fund paid $619 for a dinner meeting at a restaurant on Navy Pier and $176 for another dinner meeting in Florida at the same time. Such payments indicated once again Ryan's apparently blithe unawareness of reality. Federal attorneys were highly curious about the expenditures of CFR.

Ryan's son, Homer, had given him a light truck for Christmas. George and Lura Lynn took some time off, driving to Florida and New Orleans. Then they headed to Los Angeles to discuss a movie project with Abby Mann, although nothing came of that. Ryan's trips had the advantage of getting him out of state during the Fawell trial.

The trial opened on the day the new governor took office. Fawell was impenitent. The prosecution called numerous witnesses under immunity who also would testify later in Ryan's trial. Fawell's pal Richard Juliano was forced to admit that he obtained no-show jobs for his wife, Erica, through businesses that got contracts from Ryan. Fawell's defense attorney Edward Genson asked, "Did she do any work?"

"No."

"Did you return the money?"

"No."[14]

Genson said Fawell was just an ordinary guy doing ordinary things in Illinois politics—the same defense that Genson offered later for Larry Warner and that Dan Webb offered for Ryan. Fawell "didn't have a machine," Genson said. "He didn't create anything. He didn't invent anything. He filled a niche. He took over a job."[15] There was more than a grain of truth in this defense.

Prosecutors countered that Fawell had one basic principle: "Screw you, taxpayers."[16] There was truth in this as well.

Fawell's boyhood friend Larry Hall, godfather to Fawell's daughter, avoided looking at the defendant as he testified that he had secretly taped conversations for the government. As a secretary of state official, Hall had traded low-digit license plates for campaign contributions. After testifying, Hall suffered a heart attack and had two angioplasties.

Now it was revealed what was in that Zip drive that Andrea Coutretsis had wanted to destroy and that her angry ex-husband, Dean Prokos, gave to the government. When printed out, the contents amounted to 555 pages listing all the political favors that Ryan had done for people since 1991. At the top was Warner, with seventy-three low-digit license plates, twenty-three contracts, and thirty-seven patronage jobs. Fawell's "master list" had the virtue of thoroughness. Included was his mother, Beverly Fawell, who got secretary of state office help for her state Senate primary campaign in 1994. Genson said, "The poor guy is being indicted for helping his mom."[17]

The jury was out a week. Fawell and Citizens for Ryan were convicted on March 19. CFR had to forfeit $750,000. Chief prosecutor Patrick Collins said, "Corruption has tangible consequences, in this case more tragic than any other public corruption case I've been associated with. And the notion that through a wink and a nod that this is what everybody does in the state of Illinois is offensive."[18] Offensive to him, maybe, but not to many others.

Ryan said, "I respect the jury system. However, today's verdict saddens me. I do wish Scott well during the trying days ahead. He is a bright and talented young man, and this will be a tremendous strain on him and his family."[19] All the proceedings were tantamount to a dress rehearsal for the Ryan-Warner trial. But at the time, Ryan took heart from the belief that his protégé would never testify against him.

Five days later, Fawell was divorced. Two months later, Fawell's girlfriend, Coutretsis, was indicted for perjury before the grand jury, becoming the sixty-third, but not the last, defendant in Operation Safe Road. (Officially, the U.S. attorney listed seventy-nine defendants as of April 2006, but the investigation produced three more indictments as late as July 2007.) On June 26, 2003, Judge Rebecca Pallmeyer sentenced Fawell to seventy-eight months in prison. At his request, he went to a federal prison camp in Yankton, South Dakota, that offered treatment for alcoholism. Inmates who complete such treatment may be given a reduction in sentence.

On August 27, Ron Swanson was indicted on seven counts of perjury for lying to the grand jury after receiving immunity. He had clouted a consulting contract to land a new prison in Grayville after secretly learning from Ryan that Grayville had been selected. This was the first indictment relating to Ryan's actions as governor, not just secretary of state. With Swanson indicted, Ryan took the precaution of hiring Dan Webb as his own attorney. As Fawell went to Yankton, Roger Stanley reported to federal prison in Leavenworth, Kansas, and Ryan unveiled his official gubernatorial portrait in the Capitol. Thompson and Dan Rostenkowski attended the ceremony, of course. Ryan told Blagojevich that he could look forward to the dedication of his own portrait. "I hope somebody shows up," Blagojevich said, looking at all the luminaries around Ryan. "You've got family, haven't you?" Ryan needled.[20]

The depth and breadth of the ninety-one-page indictment on December 17 surprised even Ryan's enemies. Ryan pleaded not guilty on December 23. Thompson made a point of taking him to dinner that night at Gibson's, a popular Chicago steakhouse, to show that his friends would stand by him. From prison, Fawell sent Ryan a Christmas card: "You know in your heart that we have nothing to be ashamed of. But they [prosecutors] have all the cards."[21]

U.S. attorney Patrick Fitzgerald said, "The state of Illinois was taken advantage of by Ryan and his greedy friends."[22] The essence of the case alleged that Ryan and Warner conspired to fix many of the major contracts in the secretary of state's office. In return, Ryan and his family members received illegal cash payments, gifts, vacations, and personal services. Of the twenty-two counts, four applied only to Warner, the rest to both or to Ryan alone. Ryan faced charges of racketeering conspiracy, mail fraud, making false statements, income tax fraud, and filing false tax returns. He was sixty-nine years old; Warner, sixty.

Citizens for Ryan was nearly broke, having spent more than $2.4 million on legal fees for Operation Safe Road defendants. The Friends of George Ryan Fund, a charitable trust, was created. Ryan promised to disclose the donors, then reneged. (A charitable trust, unlike political committees, need not so disclose.)

It raised less than half a million dollars. Not to worry, said Thompson; his firm, Winston and Strawn, would defend him for free. Warner, with no such offer, retained Genson.

The Friends of George Ryan Fund quoted Webb on its Web site: "The federal government has cobbled together a number of unrelated, innocent acts. There is nothing in here more than the fabric of what goes on in Illinois politics." Webb predicted Ryan would be acquitted for three reasons:

1. After five and half [sic] years, the government does not have one single witness that will testify that Ryan received corrupt payment as charged.
2. When the jury sees him testify as a man who has spent 40 years in public service [actually, 37] and who is the only governor in history to take it upon himself to fix a broken down death penalty system, the jury will agree that the character of this man does not fit with the charges.
3. If George Ryan did what the government alleges, he would be a man of financial means. Webb said that Ryan lives from month to month on pensions and Social Security, he has no stocks, no bonds and lives in a modest home in Kankakee.[23]

Ryan said he did not consider the impact his blanket commutation might have on a potential jury. His defense attorney, though, obviously considered it.

In January, Ryan, Lura Lynn, and Lawrence Marshall went to Park City, Utah, for the screening of *Deadline* at the Sundance Film Festival. That documentary by Katy Chevigny and Kirsten Johnson highlighted Ryan's pardons and commutations. In April, Ryan flew to Geneva, Switzerland, to address the United Nations Human Rights Commission on capital punishment. Yet it seemed that Ryan could never bask in the moment. The next day, Stanley pleaded guilty to one count of perjury and cooperated with the government.

And then the unthinkable happened. Fawell flipped.

17 Custer and the Indians

The distance from Scott Fawell's minimum-security prison cell in Yankton, South Dakota, to the federal courthouse in Chicago is 594 miles. That round-trip journey took Fawell twelve weeks early in 2004. The government shuttled him by airplane and bus to prisons in different cities, including a week's stay in an isolation cell at the maximum-security facility in Terre Haute, Indiana—an additional 199 miles east of Chicago. There, Fawell enjoyed a view of the death chamber.

Travel under the auspices of the U.S. Bureau of Prisons is unpleasant in any case. Regulations stipulate that prisoners be moved in leg irons and handcuffs attached to a belly chain. Fawell made such a trip just for the sake of a brief appearance at a Chicago court proceeding. Having a suspicious mind, Fawell concluded that the feds were trying to torture him into testifying against Ryan. He said that the ordeal only made him more stubborn against cooperating. Prosecutors in the U.S. attorney's office in Chicago later cited that attitude of Fawell's in their own defense—the Bureau of Prisons did that to him, not us! We had nothing to do with mistreating him, if he was mistreated! Most likely, the prosecutors were truthful. The Bureau of Prisons is among the most independent and arbitrary of federal bureaucracies. Convicts called such peregrinations—absurd roundabout travels before scheduled court appearances—"diesel therapy." Such therapy did not work with Fawell, no matter who ordered it.

In fact, though, Fawell had started thinking about flipping just a few weeks after hearing the Yankton cell doors clang shut behind him. All for the love of his girlfriend, he said.

One thing the Ryan scandals had lacked was sex, except for one of the counts against Dean Bauer, the former inspector general. A secretary of state agent at Joliet gave fake IDs to lingerie models younger than twenty-one. That agent was the son-in-law of one of Ryan's neighbors. Bauer shut down the investigation. In the spectrum of Operation Safe Road crimes, even the media saw that one as trivial.

Now, with Coutretsis, the scandals had a femme fatale. For the love of Fawell, she dumped her husband, destroyed evidence, gave him a place to live when his wife threw him out, lied to a grand jury, and faced time in prison. For the love of Coutretsis, to save her from a likely prison sentence and the possible loss of custody of her two small children, Fawell agonizingly betrayed the man he loved like a father, George Ryan. This is a charming story but far from the whole truth.

Shortly after Coutretsis was indicted, her former husband, Dean Prokos, threatened to seek custody of their children if she went to jail. She panicked and on December 3, 2003, pleaded guilty to perjury. Her attorney had an idea: Why don't you try to get Scott to flip? If you give them Scott, he will give them George, and then maybe a grateful government will not sentence you to prison. Before Christmas, Coutretsis visited Fawell at Yankton. She later testified that it took many months to flip him. The record shows that it took a few weeks, except for the formalities. For one thing, on February 10, 2004, the imprisoned Fawell and the imperiled Coutretsis were hit with new indictments.

They were charged with rigging a McCormick Place bid by giving secret inside information to a lobbyist. The contract in question was worth $11.5 million to supervise the $780 million expansion that Ryan had pushed through the legislature. As an aside, the government said Fawell and Coutretsis had charged taxpayers for more than a hundred nights they spent at a McCormick Place hotel. Fawell found other convenient uses for McPier funds. He leased an electronic device concealed as a clock to detect whether visitors were wired with hidden recorders or transmitters. In other words, he rigged a bid even while he knew he was under investigation for Operation Safe Road.

Soon Fawell was on the phone with Coutretsis. "It's kind of like, you know, Custer and the Indians. It's kind of like, OK, I fought the Indians once and now there's 400 of them coming over the hill and it's just me. It's kind of like do I fight them again or do I just wave the flag?"[1] He asked that she seek counsel from his mother, Beverly, and brother, Jeffrey, an attorney. There followed some hard words and hard feelings. His mother and brother were unconvinced that she had Scott Fawell's best interests foremost in mind.

On March 4, Coutretsis pleaded guilty to one count of mail fraud. On March 19, Fawell pleaded not guilty to five counts of mail fraud and one of wire fraud. This was the arraignment for which Fawell had been jerked around to different prisons. On September 14, Fawell changed his plea to guilty. He had already given the feds a forty-five-page statement, just the start of his cooperation. Upon his conviction a year earlier, Fawell had insisted that witnesses lied about him to get leniency from the government and that he would never do that to Ryan.

Fawell left Yankton once again to testify at a sentencing hearing for Coutretsis on October 28. Judge James Holderman called the hearing to gauge how instrumental she had been in flipping Fawell. Fawell said she had lied just to protect him, holding his nose with both hands to avoid crying. Prosecutors said their sentencing recommendations for both were contingent on how helpful they were in upcoming trials. Sentencing was delayed. Fawell was scheduled to be the first prosecution witness against Ryan when his trial was to open in March 2005. Even some of Ryan's enemies were impressed by how tough the government played this game.

With various delays, jury selection for the trial did not begin until September 19, 2005. Apart from any legal and moral issues raised, the trial loomed as a spectator sport, a tournament of brilliant lawyers.

The United States attorney. Patrick J. Fitzgerald was born in Brooklyn, the son of Irish immigrants. He attended Regis High School, a Jesuit school in Manhattan for gifted students, went on to Amherst College, and was graduated from Harvard Law School in 1985. Everybody talked about how hard he worked. He ran with Chicago's legal community in a five-kilometer Race Judicata, showered, and then, instead of socializing with his colleagues, went back to the office to put in more hours. Within seven months of taking office in Chicago, he won approval to hire twenty-five more prosecutors, raided Cook County offices in search of ghost payrolling, arrested insurance tycoon Michael Segal, launched an investigation of pay-for-play Illinois pork barreling, subpoenaed Mayor Daley's city records relating to organized crime figures, subpoenaed Illinois Gaming Board records not once but twice, and indicted Fawell and Citizens for Ryan. True, Chicago was what the Pentagon calls a "target-rich environment," but Fitzgerald was just getting started. Nobody could figure out his politics. "One day I read that I was a Republican hack, and another day I read I was a Democratic hack, and the only thing I did between those two nights was sleep," he said.[2] Some people took heart in the revelation that he was human and did need to sleep. Critics did not question his integrity but said he was so relentless he could not distinguish a minor regulatory infraction from a major felony. Such criticism followed him when as a special prosecutor he indicted I. Lewis Libby, chief of staff for Vice President Dick Cheney, in a national security case.

The lead prosecutor. Fitzgerald's top assistant, Patrick M. Collins, might have been Fitzgerald's brother. Both were six-foot-two former schoolboy athletes in their early forties; both still looked like short-haired high school student council presidents. The main difference was that Collins grew up in Chicago, not New York. As a boy, Collins sometimes walked picket lines with his father, a union printer at the *Chicago Tribune.* Collins cut lawns to pay tuition at a Catholic high school. After graduating from Notre Dame, he worked for an investment firm in New York for a couple of years, then returned to attend the University of Chicago Law School. Collins was a poker-faced, tenacious investigator. An FBI agent called him "an FBI agent in AUSA [assistant U.S. attorney] clothes"—high praise, as those acquainted with the frequent mistrust between police and attorneys will understand.[3] Back in 1998, U.S. attorney Scott Lassar doubted that

Operation Safe Road would be big enough to warrant a huge commitment of federal time and money. Collins insisted otherwise and was proved right. Like Fitzgerald, Collins tended to divide the world into good guys and bad guys and was sensitive to criticism that prosecutors were overzealous.

Ryan's defense attorney. Dan K. Webb retained the same boyish looks as the prosecutors, although he was now sixty years old. A farm boy from downstate Illinois, he perfected an aw-shucks demeanor that often, but not always, swayed juries. Webb talked Loyola University Chicago into letting him start law school a year early and never did earn an undergraduate degree. His lack of an Ivy League law degree hardly curtailed his career as a corruption-fighting U.S. attorney and then as a partner in Jim Thompson's law firm. *Corporate Crime Reporter* ranked him as the best white-collar criminal defense attorney in the nation.[4] Thompson's endorsement was even more expansive: "He is the best trial lawyer in America."[5] Whatever his talents, Webb could rack up billable hours approaching an astounding three thousand a year, or more than fifty-five a week, every week, at hundreds of dollars an hour.

Larry Warner's defense attorney. Edward M. Genson hardly looked like Fitzgerald, Collins, and Webb—he was short and overweight with shaggy curls and a scruffy beard—but all four men shared a similar life story, the working-class boy who climbed to the pinnacle of a profession. Genson's father, a Russian Jew, was a bail bondsman and precinct captain who raised his family on Chicago's South Side. Genson was hardly ten years old when he started hanging around criminal courts with his father and knew at once that he wanted to be a lawyer. Genson, now sixty-three, had suffered most of his life from dystonia, a neurological disorder most prevalent among Ashkenazi Jews. It made Genson walk with a limp, gave him painful muscle spasms, and caused his head to bob constantly. Critics suggested that Genson's condition mysteriously worsened whenever he sought a jury's sympathy. He got around on a motorized scooter and hobbled into court with a cane. While questioning witnesses, he sat on a high wooden stool, legs dangling and cane wielded like a classroom pointer. Genson said that he arose daily at 3 A.M. and, in the thick of a major case, worked from 8 A.M. to 10 P.M. As often with Genson, it was hard to separate fact from bluster in this claim. Certainly he prepared thoroughly for cross-examinations. Many of his clients were alleged mobsters and disgraced politicians. Often they were convicted, but retaining Genson in the first place signaled that they wanted no plea bargain and would fight to the last unpersuaded juror, the last unbroken bone. So it was with Warner.

The judge. Rebecca R. Pallmeyer was born in Japan, the daughter of a Lutheran missionary. She grew up in Minnesota, by reputation the home of squeaky-clean government. After sentencing Fawell the first time, she said, "There may be a culture of corruption in Illinois. This may be business as usual. Call me naïve, but this was news to me."[6] Pallmeyer earned a law degree at the University of Chicago in 1979 and aimed from the start to be a judge, not a litigator. Illinois senator Carol Moseley Braun sponsored her for the federal bench in 1997. Pallmeyer's courtroom style was informal, as federal courts go, and she was always courteous and even-handed. Sometimes attorneys on both sides wondered whether she was tough enough to preside over such a high-stakes trial. Pallmeyer had the mannerisms of twirling her hair on her finger and covering her mouth with her hand, looking uncomfortable. It seemed that she disliked saying no to anybody. She said the Ryan-Warner trial would start in March, no matter what, no more delays. Then, Webb pleaded for a delay because he was busily defending Philip Morris in a federal case against tobacco companies. If Pallmeyer refused, Ryan would have to find another lawyer. Warner and Genson did not much care—Genson kept filing motions to sever Warner's trial from Ryan's anyway and complaining that Warner was being denied his right to a speedy trial. Overnight, Warner changed his mind, deciding to help his friend Ryan by joining the request for a delay. Prosecutors were angry; Pallmeyer was incredulous. She demanded to know why Warner switched. "Quite frankly, it's none of your business," Genson told her.[7] Pallmeyer caved and granted a delay until September. Thompson pumped Genson's hand in congratulations. However, as the trial unfolded, attorneys on both sides discovered how steely Pallmeyer's will could be.

Prosecutors suggested, subtly but unmistakably, that Ryan's blanket clemency for death row prisoners was designed to overshadow his impending indictment. "[A]fter Ryan became aware that activities of the SOS Office that he led were being investigated, he had good reason to engage in what could be perceived as good (or 'courageous') acts." Further, the jury should "know of the speaking fees that Ryan has collected and put in his bank account as he travels about lecturing on the subject of the death penalty."[8]

The defense hit back just as hard. "According to the government, George Ryan's work to reform the death penalty in Illinois is irrelevant; but if this Court should disagree, then Ryan's actions *must* be part of a nefarious plan to 'influence the jury pool' and finance his defense through 'speaking fees' [emphasis in original]. These bizarre accusations are truly outrageous."[9]

Pallmeyer held firm on two points from the outset. The defense would say nothing about Ryan's emptying of death row, and the prosecution would say nothing about the Guzman-Willis accident that killed six children. Either matter might prejudice the jury.

Both sides grumbled a bit and settled into the tedious process of choosing a jury, an art that has become a quasi-science. Genson hired a focus group, conducted a mock mini-trial of Warner, and asked for a verdict. They convicted him.

Webb's firm, Winston and Strawn, hired jury consultants. All attorneys agreed on a forty-four page questionnaire, asking each potential juror 145 questions. Pallmeyer made them trim it to thirty-two pages and 110 questions. Only about half the jury pool answered that they knew about Ryan's stand on the death penalty. Most were only vaguely aware of the federal investigation of him. One remembered that Ryan once had botched an award presentation at a football banquet, confusing the names of Dick Butkus and Mike Ditka. Never mind capital punishment. Butkus and Ditka—that is serious.

Then, in Pallmeyer's court on the twenty-first floor of the Dirksen Federal Building in downtown Chicago, 301 potential jurors were interviewed one at a time, sometimes for as much as forty minutes. The defense tended to ask, "Considering that other people have pleaded guilty in this case, do you believe in guilt by association? Would you have a problem saying no to the government?" The prosecution tended to ask, "Do you have opinions on the death penalty? Are there any factors in your personal life that would bias you one way or the other?"

It took a week and a half to seat twelve jurors and six alternates. They were average working people—a hospital aide, an at-home day-care manager, a self-employed contractor, and such. They were warned that the trial would last four months—an inaccurately optimistic prediction. For the first weeks of the trial, Webb's jury consultant sat with a kind of scorecard, marking each juror's reactions as prosecutors made their points. Much of the trial explored the arcana of state personnel policies, contracts, and leases and of federal anticorruption statutes. Aside from yawns, most jurors usually showed no reaction at all.

A friend of mine once accompanied me to the Ryan trial, rather in the spirit of visiting a tourist attraction. She knew nothing about the courtroom layout but instantly distinguished the defense table from the prosecution table. She said she could tell by the cut of their suits. Defense attorneys' suits were expensively tailored, while the prosecutors' were off the rack. Prosecutors made about $150,000 a year, hardly more than top law school graduates were getting to join blue-chip firms. Webb's normal fee was $750 an hour.

Many mornings, Ryan would say hello to the homeless people and beggars on Dearborn and Adams streets, sometimes dropping some money out of sight of the media, before entering the courthouse. He took lunch with Lura Lynn in the second-floor cafeteria, where the jurors also ate. Perhaps he thought this gesture would help him seem like an ordinary guy. At trial, Ryan sat implacably at the center of the defense table, facing the jury, never missing a minute of testimony, glaring at his accusers behind large eyeglasses. He was a bit hard of hearing and one day went to Radio Shack and bought a cheap amplifier with a cord to his ear. Pallmeyer explained to the jury that he was not listening to a radio. Ryan scribbled notes furiously, ending each day with a stack of papers several inches high. He said he was keeping careful notes because he was talking to people about a possible book or movie deal. Thompson said that was fine but suggested the real reason Ryan wrote so much was that it was "therapeutic." It helped him focus, get through the pain.

18 My Head in a Vise

$\mathbf{T}$wo Scott Fawells testified against George Ryan. The first was cocky, snide, wisecracking. The second was subdued, sometimes tearful. Fawell was the prosecution's first witness, an unusual "star witness" who obviously despised the prosecutors. He took the witness stand grinning at Larry Warner, seated at a defense table behind Ryan's table, and pointing at Edward Genson, his former lawyer. Fawell tried making eye contact with Ryan, who just stared at his notebook.

Prosecutor Patrick Collins asked Fawell why he had agreed to testify. "I happen to love Andrea and you guys got my head in a vise," he said.[1] As Collins led him through the details of sweetheart contracts for Ryan's cronies, Fawell sneered and made faces. Fawell had some cause for his ill humor. Since Coutretsis had pleaded guilty, she was denied visits at Yankton. During Ryan's trial, Fawell was housed at a federal prison in downtown Chicago, where Coutretsis was allowed only the standard once-a-week and every-other-weekend visits. About the only privilege Fawell won was a direct flight from South Dakota to Chicago, avoiding the weeks-long meanderings of the year past. Also, Fawell was permitted to change from prison clothes to a business suit for testimony.

Fawell first testified on Thursday, September 29, 2005. As usual, court recessed for Friday and the weekend. A different Fawell appeared on Monday. His lawyer, Jeffrey Steinback, had persuaded his client that unless he cooperated, prosecutors could revoke their deal of seeking clemency for him and his girlfriend. Fawell was more down-to-business, though still reluctant to implicate Ryan and Warner in wrongdoing.

The prosecution projected on a screen a photo of six men posing before Cinderella's Castle at Disney World—Ryan, Warner, Fawell, Cook County Republican chairman Manny Hoffman, Chicago Bulls executive Joseph O'Neil, and insurance tycoon Richard Parillo (who had set up the Friends of George Ryan Fund.) Even Fawell allowed that "six grown men at Disney World" looked a bit ridiculous. The defense objected to showing this photo as prejudicial, but then, the defense was objecting to almost everything. The government's point was that Ryan often jetted off to sports events, resorts, and casinos on trips paid for by his pals. Ryan always carried wads of cash, yet over ten years he had withdrawn just $6,700 from his accounts and never visited an automated teller machine. After hearing obscure details about Warner's contracts, the jury seemed to grasp this fact at once.

Collins knew that defense attorney Dan Webb would try to suggest that Fawell's testimony could not be trusted because he had cut a deal to get leniency. To blunt such a challenge, on Fawell's fourth day on the stand, Collins questioned him at length about his motives.

Collins: After your trial [and conviction in 2003], were you angry?
Fawell: To put it mildly.
Collins: Do you believe some witnesses had lied?
Fawell: I know they did. . . .
Collins: Is it your belief that this prosecution has asked you to make up stories?
Fawell: No, you haven't asked me. . . .
Collins: Sir, at the time you entered into this written plea [on the McPier case], what was the agreement?
Fawell: That Andrea would avoid jail time, which was obviously the most important thing in the world to me. That's why I'm here, for good or bad, that's why I'm here.
Collins [not about to let that statement stand alone]: And what was your understanding regarding your own sentence?
Fawell: That my second sentence would run concurrent with my first one, and I'd potentially get a six-month reduction in my original sentence.[2]

Next, Collins brought up Coutretsis's visits to Yankton. Fawell sat silently, poured himself a glass of water, took a few sips, and blinked back tears. Judge Pallmeyer called a timeout, and as jurors filed out of the room, Fawell stood and turned his back to them, wiping away tears. When the jury returned, Collins put it on the record one more time: "Have you ever lied to help the government?" Fawell: "No."

Homer Ryan was allowed to attend the trial because, unlike his sisters, he was not a potential witness. Flushed with anger, he asked a reporter why nobody was investigating the government's strong-arm tactics in forcing Fawell to testify. "I'm just frustrated," he said. "They tore my dad up for eight years."[3]

Webb began his cross-examination, asking what the defense asked every witness: Did you ever see Ryan take a dishonest dollar to influence a governmental decision? Always, the answer was no.

The next day, Fawell broke down again. He was asked about a letter he had written the judge who was to sentence Coutretsis for her perjury and fraud convictions. Pallmeyer called another recess while Fawell stared at the floor, removed his glasses, and wiped his face.

As a rule, Fawell appeared more comfortable when answering questions from the defense than from the prosecution. He said he did not believe that he and Ryan committed any crimes and he had no "bomb" to drop on Ryan. Collins treated him as an adverse witness when he got him back on re-direct examination. Moreover, he seized on what he saw as a Webb blunder. Webb questioned Fawell about the motives of secretary of state employees selling Ryan's fund-raising tickets. Collins demanded that Pallmeyer now permit him to ask about the Ryan ticket sales underlying Ricardo Guzman's CDL.

Like Banquo's ghost, the Reverend Scott Willis appeared in court to witness a hearing that Pallmeyer called on Collins's motion. "To some people, this is about documents and contracts, and still for us this is about people," Willis told reporters.[4] Webb told the judge that Collins was frantically trying to rescue his case after the big mistake of calling Fawell as his first witness. Genson shouted across the room that he would demand a mistrial, but both defendants already had repeatedly called for a mistrial. Pallmeyer ruled that the prosecution could bring up sanitized references to an accident in Wisconsin.

Scott and Janet Willis showed up again at the next day of trial, after attending their fortieth high school reunion over the weekend. It was the first time since 1998 that the couple had been in the same room with Ryan, who gave no sign of recognition but admitted later that he had noticed them. "There needs to be accountability. For justice, for my children," the reverend said, although "there is no personal delight or joy in seeing somebody go to jail."[5]

Fawell spent ten days on the stand before both sides were done with him. A marshal escorted him from court, but he soon returned at the rear doorway with his bad-boy grin, waving to Warner and his wife, Cindy. Then he waved to Ryan and kept at it until a sour-faced Ryan finally waved back.

For fans of dramatic courtroom scenes as rendered by Hollywood and television, Fawell's appearance was about as good as it got as the trial stretched on over another 173 days. Even during Fawell's testimony, the jury was idle much of the time while lawyers wrangled over legalities in sidebars and in Pallmeyer's chambers. The judge frequently apologized to the jury for the delays and promised to speed things up, but she remained disinclined to tell the lawyers to cut it off. Being lawyers, they would keep arguing until she stopped them.

In sum, this is how the two sides presented the case.

Count one, Ryan and Warner: A pattern of racketeering including mail fraud, money laundering, extortion, and obstruction of justice.

Prosecution: Ryan and Warner broke the law to enrich themselves and their friends.

Defense: Ryan is a statesman and humanitarian. Warner is an aggressive businessman who made money legally. The government cannot prove its charges.

Count two, Ryan and Warner: A scheme to defraud, including mail fraud relating to the motor vehicle stickers contract awarded to American Decal Manufacturing Company, and various other payments, gifts, and services.

Prosecution: Ryan and Warner caused the mailing of a state check to ADM for a contract rigged to benefit Ryan, Warner, Don Udstuen, and Ron Swanson. Part of the scheme was assigning the awards of low-digit license plates to Warner and others.

Defense: Proper bidding procedures were followed. ADM's metallic security mark was necessary for visibility and safety. The other interactions were legal.

Count three, Ryan and Warner: Mail fraud relating to a secretary of state lease awarded to Warner in Joliet.

Prosecution: Ryan rigged a lease on a crumbling building in which Warner had a hidden interest. Taxpayers paid $296,485 above market-rate rents.

Defense: Proper procedures were followed, and the Joliet site was a good one. Our expert witness proves that the leases in question actually were good deals.

Count four, Ryan and Warner: Mail fraud relating to Warner's lobbying for IBM in seeking the secretary of state's mainframe computer contract.

Prosecution: Warner shook down IBM, and Ryan helped to rig the contract.

Defense: Everyone, including independent experts, agreed that IBM's system was best.

Count five, Ryan and Warner: Mail fraud relating to Warner's laundering IBM payments through Alan Drazek's American Management Resources.

Prosecution: Secretive transactions prove fraudulent intent.

Defense: These were legal and ordinary transactions.

Count six, Ryan: Mail fraud relating to securing a secretary of state lease for Harry Klein in South Holland.

Prosecution: Ryan cost taxpayers an extra $175,225 by moving a CDL facility from Lake Calumet to an inferior site in South Holland just to benefit Klein.

Defense: Proper procedures were followed, and South Holland actually was a better site.

Count seven, Ryan and Warner: Mail fraud relating to Warner's lobbying for a contract for Viisage Technologies to digitize driver's license records.

Prosecution: Ryan gave Warner's client Viisage a $20 million contract after failing to arrange a merger of Viisage and a firm represented by another Ryan friend, Al Ronan. Swanson secretly made $36,000 on the deal for doing nothing.

Defense: Ryan's actions actually forced Viisage to lower its price. The digitizing plan showed Ryan's efforts to reduce licensure fraud.

Count eight, Ryan and Warner: Mail fraud relating to a secretary of state lease for Warner in Bellwood.

Prosecution: Ryan fixed a lease on property in which Warner had a hidden interest, costing taxpayers an extra $428,909.

Defense: See count three.

Count nine, Ryan and Warner: Mail fraud relating to a secretary of state lease for Warner at 17 North State Street, Chicago.

Prosecution: Warner secretly made $382,000 for brokering this rigged deal.

Defense: See count three.

Count ten, Ryan: Mail fraud relating to Swanson's clouting a lobbying fee for a state prison in Grayville.

Prosecution: Ryan gave Swanson inside information that won Swanson a bogus $50,000 fee.

Defense: Ryan committed an error of judgment, not a crime. He did not know Swanson would misuse the information.

Count eleven, Ryan: False statements to the FBI about free vacations at Klein's estate in Jamaica, the South Holland and Joliet leases, and Warner's appointment to the McPier board.

Prosecution: The governor lied to federal agents even after they showed him every courtesy, allowing him to choose the time and place of the interviews (a hotel room away from the media).

Defense: We don't know what Ryan said because the FBI did not tape the interviews or keep detailed notes. Klein had no receipts or other proof that he gave cash to Ryan. The McPier matter was a trivial slip of memory.

Count twelve, Ryan: False statements to the FBI about the Joliet lease and Ryan's personal financial relationship with Warner.

Prosecution: See count eleven.

Defense: See count eleven; Ryan received legitimate gifts from Warner.

Count thirteen, Ryan: False statements to the FBI about receiving four $500 checks from Anthony De Santis.

Prosecution: See count eleven.

Defense: See count eleven; De Santis's checks were legal.

Count fourteen, Warner: Attempted extortion of American Decal Manufacturing.

Prosecution: Warner told ADM to hire him for $5,000 a month or lose its state contract.

Defense: The fix was in, but not for ADM and Warner. Jim Thompson originally tried to fix this contract for 3M.

Count fifteen, Warner: Mail fraud relating to money laundering on the ADM contract.

Prosecution: Warner mailed a check to Drazek's American Management Resources as part of this fraudulent scheme.

Defense: See count two.

Count sixteen, Warner: Mail fraud relating to money laundering on the IBM computer system contract.

Prosecution: See count fifteen.

Defense: See count two.

Count seventeen, Warner: "Structuring" $14,000 in bank withdrawals to avoid federal reporting requirements on sums exceeding $10,000.

Prosecution: Over seven years, Warner regularly made withdrawals of $9,000 to $9,600 to elude the $10,000 threshold.

Defense: Warner made legal withdrawals of his own money.

Count eighteen, Ryan: Filing false tax returns relating to the use of CFR funds, Phil Gramm presidential campaign payments, and the De Santis checks.

Prosecution: Ryan filed amended tax returns for 1995–98, knowingly understating his income from ill-gotten gains.

Defense: Accountants handled these matters for Ryan; they made some minor mistakes. Personal use of campaign funds was legal at the time.

Count nineteen, Ryan: Tax fraud relating to an amended return for 1995.

Prosecution: In 1998, Ryan filed an amended return listing an adjusted gross income of $120,542, knowing the amount was much larger.

Defense: See count eighteen.

Count twenty, Ryan: Tax fraud relating to an amended return for 1996.

Prosecution: In 1998, Ryan filed an amended return listing an adjusted gross income of $137,908, knowing the amount was much larger.

Defense: See count eighteen.

Count twenty-one, Ryan: Tax fraud relating to an amended return for 1997.

Prosecution: In 1998, Ryan filed an amended return listing an adjusted gross income of $106,486, knowing the amount was much larger.

Defense: See count eighteen.

Count twenty-two, Ryan: Tax fraud relating to an amended return for 1998.

Prosecution: In 1999, Ryan filed an amended return listing an adjusted gross income of $102,640, knowing the amount was much larger.

Defense: See count eighteen.

This naked outline obscures many of the complexities and nuances of the case. In essence, the prosecution lacked a smoking gun but subjected Ryan (to mix metaphors) to death by a thousand cuts. Ryan raised what might be called the "Checkers defense," after Richard Nixon's celebrated "Checkers speech" of 1952. Nixon, the Republican vice presidential nominee, was under fire for personal use of a slush fund. Nixon saved his place on the ticket with a dramatic televised address that asked, in effect, If I'm a crook, how come I'm not rich? (Checkers was the family dog.) Similarly, Ryan asked, If I'm a crook, how come my only substantial asset is my house?

The defendants did not coordinate their defenses. Early on, Genson, gesturing toward Webb, told the judge, "We don't talk." Warner's defense was that he was a legitimate businessman unjustly dragged into court with Ryan as the government sought to smear both men.

After Fawell, the trial droned on through twelve more witnesses before former senator Phil Gramm took the stand on November 17. At this point, Ryan lost his cool. Gramm testified that he knew some of the Illinois campaign money went to political consultants but not that it went to Ryan and his aides. He never would have approved such payments—"It is basically that it's a difference between love and prostitution. . . . You are not looking to buy support."[6] Ryan went down to the media "bullpen" in the lobby and growled, "I was paid about $11,000" as a consulting fee "and I earned every penny of that. . . . Mr. Gramm referred to me as a prostitute, and I really feel that I absolutely have to respond." He suggested that Gramm declined to seek reelection in 2002 because he was complicit in the bankruptcy of Enron, the Texas-based energy trading firm. "Perhaps investigators should revisit the Enron matter and the role that the Gramms played in the demise of Enron, if any. If Sen. Gramm wants to use the word 'prostitute,' perhaps he should look within."[7] Gramm's wife, Wendy Gramm, was a member of Enron's board of directors, and the corporation contributed campaign funds to the senator.

Ryan stormed off without answering questions. Webb had said in court that day that Ryan would take the stand to defend himself after the government rested—indeed, both Webb and Ryan often said they looked forward to his testifying. But Ryan's outburst against Gramm enhanced Webb's doubts that Ryan could keep his temper in court under prosecutors' questioning. Better to keep Ryan quiet and have the judge issue a routine instruction that jurors cannot hold a defendant's refusal to testify against him. For their part, prosecutors objected that Ryan's media appearance was meant to intimidate future witnesses—"They and their families can be publicly attacked outside the courtroom."[8]

The lawyers themselves sometimes lost their cool. In his cross-examinations, Webb liked to push the edge of courtroom propriety, then react with a posture of "Who, me?" affronted innocence when challenged. Assistant U.S. attorney Zachary Fardon complained to Pallmeyer, "Mr. Webb is running roughshod at the truth-finding process. He's the most effective lawyer in this room but in that process he is blowing a tremendous amount of smoke at these jurors." Genson sneered, "If this is the worst Mr. Fardon has seen, he hasn't lived." Webb said the defense had to "fight and claw" its way through questioning because the government kept "teeing up" witnesses.[9] Pallmeyer told the attorneys to put their motions in writing and then get some sleep. Few would envy her job of trying to keep in line aggressive, crafty attorneys for the prosecution and defense teams, both of them among the best in the country. As for the attorneys, if they thought the trial could hardly get more rancorous, they were mistaken.

Don Udstuen took the stand for three days in December, telling the sordid story of Ron Swanson's handing him $4,000 in a men's room. According to Udstuen, Swanson said, "You know I always take care of George"—the first testimony implying that kickback money went to Ryan himself. Further, Udstuen said, Warner had told him back in 1991, "I'll take care of George." The defense pounded on the fact that Udstuen did not recall that remark for prosecutors until 2005 while he was negotiating a plea bargain. Webb was merciless:

Webb: How many different people have you lied to and deceived?
Udstuen: A lot.
Webb: Is it more than five hundred?
Udstuen: I don't know. It's a lot. . . .
Webb: By this point in your life, had lying and deceiving people almost become hard-wired in your brain?
Assistant U.S. attorney Joel R. Levin: Objection, your honor. Argumentative.

Pallmeyer: Sustained. . . .

Webb: Was this the first day of your life you decided to be truthful?

Levin: Objection. Argumentative.

Pallmeyer: I'll allow it.[10]

And so on.

It fell to Genson to inject a note of levity. Coughing as he began his cross-examination, he was handed a glass of water by Collins. "It's not poison, judge," Collins assured Pallmeyer. Genson took a sip and said, "Wouldn't it be funny if I clutched my chest and fell over?"

19 A Real Schnorrer

When those on the defense team finally got their turn to drive the bus, they nearly ran it off the road. The government rested its case on February 2, 2006, eighteen weeks after Patrick Collins made his opening statement. George Ryan's defense figured it needed to blunt the prosecution's assertion that from June 1993 through December 2002, Ryan had withdrawn only $6,703.08 from his checking and savings accounts, all the while living like a high roller. He was always jetting off with his buddies to sporting events and gambling resorts, even to "fat farms" in Florida and California. From three to six times a month, Ryan visited casinos, gambling $100 to $300 each time on blackjack or craps. Usually he wagered $25 a hand, sometimes $50. He tipped generously, peeling bills off a thick wad. In one year, 1997, Ryan and Lura Lynn cashed only $77 in state lottery winnings. That Larry Warner withdrew $144,000 in cash from personal bank accounts that year was more than coincidental, the prosecution alleged. It was circumstantial evidence that Ryan was getting kickback money.

At first, the defense tried to argue that Ryan's daily, walking-around cash came from proper reimbursements from Citizens for Ryan. Ryan's secretary, Vicki Easley, had testified for the government on January 12. She said that CFR paid Ryan thousands of dollars every year for money he had spent on campaign-related travel and other expenses. Dan Webb's assistant, Timothy McCaffrey, insisted that these reimbursements were a legitimate source of cash. The government's retort was obvious—how did Ryan manage to pay cash for those costs in the first place, before being reimbursed? Indeed, questionable payments from CFR to Ryan over four years totaled about $80,000, not reported on his taxes. Personal use of campaign funds then was legal, provided the money was reported and taxed as income.

The defense tried to portray the tax charges as a mere accounting squabble. In a typical Webb maneuver, he hauled eight volumes of tax laws and regulations into court and demanded to know how Ryan could be expected to understand them all. Ryan had, after all, submitted amended tax returns, indicating good faith. The government observed that Ryan amended his returns only under intense federal heat.

In general, things had not been going well for the defendants. During the lunch break on January 5, Warner fell on a sidewalk and was taken to a hospital, causing a recess in the trial. That night, Cindy Warner's parents, both in their eighties, were sideswiped by a truck while driving in Chicago; they were treated at the same hospital. Warner returned to court after the weekend break with stitches in his lip, bruises under his eyes, and cuts above his nose.

Ryan's lawyers hoped to keep his daughters off the stand. The government agreed to stipulate to their written testimony, read to the jury, about money they got from CFR for little or no work. However, Michael Fairman, Lynda's husband, was called to testify. An avid gambler, he had met Lynda when she worked as a cocktail waitress at a riverboat casino in Joliet. Shortly after their marriage, Fairman borrowed $5,000 from Warner. Fairman had told a grand jury he had repaid the loan. At trial, he admitted he had not, saying he had misspoken to the grand jury from sheer nervousness. He also acknowledged that he did nothing to earn $55,000 from CFR.

There seemed no end to convenient uses of CFR funds. Deb Detmers, former CFR finance director, confirmed that she did political work on state time. Detmers recalled being dressed down by Fawell during the 1994 campaign over $100,000 mysteriously missing from the accounts. Fawell later apologized. It happened that Ryan had kept that $100,000 as a nest egg in case he lost the election.

Needing a break badly, Webb called Vicki Easley back to the stand as a defense witness shortly after the prosecution rested. The defense thought it had found an explanation for the cash always in Ryan's pockets—why, his grateful employees gave him cash gifts every Christmas! Nearly everyone in the Springfield and Chicago offices, from department heads to janitors and interns, voluntarily chipped in. During the secretary of state years, the annual kitty amounted to $1,500 to $3,000; during the gubernatorial term, $3,000 to $4,000, except in 2002, the last year, when it was $12,500. The Christmas gift card listed all who had contributed. At least in one year, 2001, Ryan made a point of computing the average donation from each of thirty-four staffers. On cross-examination, Easley said she never told a grand jury about the Christmas cash. During a break in the trial, Ryan remarked to a friend, "It's too bad they don't try these cases on the merits of the law instead of trying to destroy somebody's reputation."[1]

Of course the jurors were silent in their reactions, but in the court of public opinion, Ryan took a beating over this revelation. He looked like a greedy and venal boss, a big man squeezing the little people under him to cough up cash. A janitor, Donald Skoda, testified that he received $50 checks as Christmas gifts from CFR each year. Then he turned around and gave $25 of it back to Ryan. The *Chicago Tribune* editorially noted, "There's a Yiddish word that eloquently describes a brazen freeloader. Schnorrer. George Ryan was a real schnorrer."[2]

Perhaps some Hollywood stardust might help the defense. Webb called Mike Farrell, who played B. J. Hunnicut in the television series *M*A*S*H,* and Sister Helen Prejean, whose book inspired the film *Dead Man Walking.* Both had worked with Ryan in opposing the death penalty. They were not permitted to mention the death penalty, only a "major policy issue." Prejean said, "I would call [Ryan] a man of honesty and integrity because I found in him a man who was willing to look honestly at issues, public policy issues, even if it meant change and growth in himself. I haven't encountered that often, but I would just like to say I did encounter it in him." The jury gave no sign of recognizing who Farrell and Prejean were. Collins allowed himself a rare moment of humor: "This is obviously a very serious proceeding, but as a product of Catholic school education, it's every schoolboy's dream to cross-examine a nun."

"Be on your P's and Q's or sister Godzilla will haunt you for the rest of your life," Prejean shot back.

"That's already being done, sister."[3]

The defense even called as a character witness the doorman to Ryan's Chicago apartment building. Prosecutors merely asked Farrell, Prejean, and other character witnesses whether they knew anything about Ryan's personal finances or Illinois state contracts. They did not. Comments from jurors after the trial indicated that they viewed these character witnesses as a waste of their time. For that matter, jurors insisted that neither the death penalty nor the Guzman-Willis accident ever came up in deliberations.

The defense believed it had at least one more major weapon in its arsenal. It called to testify, of all people, a United States attorney.

Edward E. McNally earned his law degree from Notre Dame. As a Yale undergraduate, he belonged to Skull and Bones, one of the least secret "secret societies" on any campus, a fabled establishmentarian citadel whose members included both presidents Bush. McNally joined Altheimer and Gray, the Chicago law firm then representing Ryan and CFR. He was present when the FBI interviewed Ryan. Indeed, Ryan had wanted Senator Peter Fitzgerald to sponsor McNally for U.S. attorney in northern Illinois; McNally had worked for the senior George Bush. After the terrorist attacks of September 11, 2001, McNally left Chicago to become general counsel of the Office of Homeland Security. When that office became a full-fledged cabinet department, McNally was named senior counsel to the assistant attorney general for the criminal division.

In November 2005, during the second month of the Ryan trial, under circumstances still mysterious, McNally took a 120-day appointment as the interim U.S. attorney for the southern district of Illinois. U.S. attorney Ronald J. Tempas had resigned to become an associate deputy attorney general in Washington. Speaker Dennis Hastert and other Republican leaders never commented on their role, if any, in arranging McNally's appointment.

On February 16, 2006, he testified as a witness for Ryan. A high-stakes, prolonged criminal trial is an intense crucible; people on both sides can get emotional. Lawyers barely tried to mask the anger that McNally precipitated.

He began by saying he was so disturbed by FBI tactics during the February 5, 2001, interrogation of Ryan that he wrote a fourteen-page memorandum about it afterward. FBI agent Raymond Ruebenson (who had been the government's last witness) did not always take notes on what Ryan was saying, according to McNally. When he complained about it at the time, the government team just stared at him and said nothing.

Prosecutors could scarcely believe that one of their own was undermining their case. They noted that McNally's former firm, Altheimer and Gray, had been kicked off the Fawell case and related cases for conflicts of interest. The firm had made about $1.7 million from Ryan-related witnesses, many of whom worked for Ryan at the same time that CFR paid their legal bills.

Pallmeyer sent the jury out of the room as the lawyers battled for hours. Prosecutors said McNally's memo had been so detailed, he might have secretly taped the interview. Collins's assistant Zachary Fardon had telephoned McNally two weeks before, asking whose initials were at the bottom of that memo. McNally did not answer but instead called that person—a secretary and potential witness—the next morning. "He's on notice that she's a potential witness and calls her the next morning," Fardon told Pallmeyer. "It is incredibly probative of where this man's coming from and where his loyalties are." McNally said he merely was responding to an e-mail from that secretary about another matter the day before. "The government is out to destroy him," said Webb's assistant, Bradley Lerman. "I'm actually astounded by it. I'm stunned."[4]

So here was a United States prosecutor, formerly an attorney for Ryan, who had worked for a law firm dismissed from related cases for conflicts of interest, testifying against the United States. That situation might have been complicated enough to confound a jury, but the plot grew even thicker. Altheimer and Gray went bankrupt in 2003. As a former partner, McNally was liable for some of its debt. The court-appointed administrator of the bankruptcy was represented by Winston and Strawn, the law firm of Webb and Jim Thompson, the firm that was defending Ryan. About sixty equity partners in Altheimer and Gray had agreed to a settlement for $23 million in debt. Five former partners refused to settle. Winston and Strawn sued four of them. The fifth, McNally, was not sued.

If Collins and his team were angry before this news appeared in the *Chicago Tribune,* now they were enraged. On February 23, Pallmeyer excused the jury once again. "This is a huge financial conflict of interest," Fardon told her. "It's a significant bias issue in terms of Mr. McNally's motive to curry favor, to play nice with Winston & Strawn when they call him as a potential witness in this case." Ryan's lawyers swore they knew nothing about the matter; the bankruptcy was being handled by an entirely different team of lawyers in the huge firm. Prosecutors grumpily took them at their word, at least on the record, but Fardon added, "The one person who did know that he had this financial hammer over his head with Winston involved is the witness, Ed McNally."[5] If Webb's team did not know about it, McNally certainly did, and ethically he should have disclosed it, Fardon said.

In the end, the government did not recall McNally to the stand but instead read his sworn statement to the jury. McNally acknowledged that a Winston and Strawn bankruptcy lawyer gave him a two-month extension on the settlement issue partly due to his Ryan trial testimony. In a separate statement to the press, McNally said he testified under subpoena and never believed that doing so would benefit him financially. Ryan's lawyer Bradley Lerman said McNally was still negotiating settlement proposals, and if a settlement agreement failed, he would be sued.

During the time the lawyers were fighting over McNally, Ryan and Warner decided not to testify at trial. The ritual was duly performed. Pallmeyer called them before the bench, reminded them of their right to testify, and took their statements. Webb said, "I have given him my recommendation that he not testify because I don't believe the government has proved its case beyond a reasonable doubt." Collins replied, "Our judgment on this side, judge, [is] that Mr. Ryan is not testifying because his testimony would do more harm than good to his case."[6] At that, Ryan's family, seated in the front row of the gallery, audibly groaned. Collins ignored them, but he could hardly ignore it when Lura Lynn went on television that night.

At an office in the Winston and Strawn suite, Lura Lynn spoke in turn to each of the Chicago-area media outlets. Reporters agreed to restrict their questions to the impact of the trial on her family, not the proceedings as such. She said, "We really believe that this whole thing started from his commutation of the prisoners on Death Row and his stand on the death penalty. There's nothing there that he ever did that was illegal, and this is the only thing we can think of that created this whole thing."[7] (Ryan himself took care never to make that explicit claim in public.)

Collins stormed into court the next morning and demanded that Pallmeyer issue a gag order. He accused Webb and the Ryans of trying to influence the jury through the media—of course, the jurors were instructed to pay no attention to media reports, but they were not sequestered and such news might seep into the jury room. Webb denied orchestrating the interviews and said Lura Lynn still had First Amendment rights. The judge issued no gag order but implored everyone not to criticize the proceedings or impugn motives.

Four days later, Pallmeyer actually did impose a gag order on the lawyers, defendants, and their family members. She had just dismissed a juror for personal reasons unrelated to the case. The *Chicago Sun-Times* suggested the juror was excused because of continual conflicts with other jurors. Pallmeyer suspected that somebody from Ryan's side had leaked this item. She declared "Enough is enough" and issued the gag order. Court documents released later alleged that this juror worked crossword puzzles and read a romance novel in the jury box. Two jurors asked to move their seats because she snored. The juror told Pallmeyer she had been diagnosed with diabetes in December and often felt tired. Ostensibly for that reason alone, the judge dismissed her.

By the time of the gag order, the show was nearly over. Lawyers had called 117 government witnesses, defense witnesses, and rebuttal witnesses. Jurors were excused on February 27 as the lawyers took a week to prepare closing arguments and tussle over instructions to the jury.

Defense lawyers wanted to send the jury a sixty-eight-page verdict form. Pallmeyer said, "If I were a juror and got this verdict form, I would cry," and threw it out.[8] She also insisted that the government's eighty-eight-page indictment was too complex to send to the jury. At her orders, prosecutors edited it, first to seventy pages, then to twenty-nine.

Barely had the government begun its closing argument on March 6 when Webb moved yet again for a mistrial. A prosecution exhibit contained the words "mud flap." Webb said the term might remind jurors of the Guzman accident—he had lost a mud flap/taillight assembly from his truck—and thus bias them against Ryan. For the first time in nearly six months, Pallmeyer publicly showed anger. She continued Webb's motion and all but dared him to press it. Standing, she snapped, "I'll expect everybody to be ready to pick another jury next week if that's appropriate. I myself have this job for life and I will be happy to start this over again Monday morning."[9] With that she turned, black robe swirling, and marched to her chambers.

Of course the idea of starting over from scratch and going through another six months of this travail horrified everybody, including Pallmeyer. Scott and Janet Willis listened from the gallery as lawyers debated the semantics of "mud flap." The jury came back and arguments resumed. In the coming weeks, Pallmeyer would have numerous occasions to ponder whether she really would be happy to pick another jury.

20 Twelve Years of Christmas

Judge Pallmeyer launched the closing arguments with a request of the lawyers. "I really hope that you are going to be courteous to one another with respect to objections. I really don't want sidebars during the closings. . . . I think if there is anything at all we can do to avoid that, please don't object unless you honestly believe that failure to object will result in a mistrial."[1]

Assistant U.S. attorneys Joel R. Levin and Laurie J. Barsella opened the summations with a kind of world-weary air as they trudged through acres of testimony and documents. Levin concentrated on Ryan, Barsella on Warner. "In short, Ryan sold his office," Levin said. "He might as well have put a 'for sale' sign on the office. . . . When this 12 years of Christmas finally comes to an end and Mr. Ryan leaves office in early 2003, what you find when you look at his bank records is he starts withdrawing cash on a regular basis like everybody else."[2]

Barsella quoted Webb as saying that "providing benefits to supporters is part of politics, not a crime. . . . [But] there is a line between political activities and crime. And George Ryan didn't just cross over that line; he obliterated that line."[3]

After a day and a half of the prosecution's summation, Webb got his turn and perhaps demonstrated why clients are willing to pay him $750 an hour. On a large screen facing the jury, he projected in foot-high letters, "Beyond a Reasonable Doubt." Where Levin and Barsella were earnest and down-to-business, Webb was animated and passionate. Walking constantly about the courtroom, sometimes using the microphone and sometimes not, he was by turns charmingly folksy and indignantly sarcastic. Webb was not gifted with a powerful voice—it was rather scratchy—but he modulated his tones like an actor for seven hours over two days. He pronounced Washington as "Warshington" and government as "guvimmint" in the dialect of the rural Midwest (as did Ryan). Ryan seldom looked up from his notebook while the government lawyers were talking, but now he stared transfixed at Webb's performance.

You [the jury] might say, "I don't like what he did. I even think the government has proven that he had some bad judgment. He made mistakes." But that's not enough. You may even say, "I think he's guilty," but did they prove it? . . .

They literally tore apart this man's life. For seven years they did this. They talked about doing 650 interviews of people. They subpoenaed every document, every event, everything this man has done in his life. . . . [N]o witness testified that George Ryan accepted anything from anybody to perform his official acts. . . .

I heard Mr. Levin yesterday talk about 12 years of Christmas and "for sale" signs and Ms. Barsella talking about kingdoms and fiefdoms. . . . [I]f you want to use rhetoric, how about this: Seven years of hell. Because that's what he has been through.[4]

Webb observed that seventeen of the witnesses had some kind of agreement to receive favorable treatment from the government and therefore had motives to lie, or at least slant their testimony. He walked the jury through every charge against Ryan, portraying each as a legitimate transaction, a trifling issue, or an honest mistake. He had the toughest time trying to explain away Ryan's lying about getting free vacations at Harry Klein's place in Jamaica. Here Webb seemed to stumble and get tongue-tied:

Now, I'm going to suggest to you—because Harry Klein was not my witness—that there is a little bit more to this story than Harry Klein let us—let—told us. Because remember that villa, that was actually not just a personal residence. That villa was actually—was owned by two families. . . .

And so Harry Klein puts [Ryan's] check into the business account, and he gives cash back to George Ryan. The net impact of that is that Harry Klein's wife is happy because George Ryan [being a guest] didn't pay, and Harry Klein makes sure his business partner doesn't get cheated. That—that's what—Harry Klein testified to this. Now, you can say that's just a screwy, goofy way to do something. . . .

Now, the government says, "No, [Ryan] didn't [tell the truth] because he did not tell the government that he gave—that he got cash back."

Well, you know what? I am in a courtroom with a man on trial for a criminal felony, and so I am going to get literal here? I am going to. You know what the evidence establishes? They didn't ask him that question. They didn't.

Just so you know, the evidence is clear in the record. [FBI agent] Mr. Ruebenson has acknowledged it. They never asked George Ryan, "Did you get cash back?" They never asked him.[5]

Webb kept pounding on how circumstantial all the evidence was—there was no direct evidence, for instance, that Dean Bauer ever told Ryan about the secreted items from the 1993 Libertyville raid. (Bauer had called Ryan immediately after that raid, but there was no direct evidence of what he said.) "So the government says, 'Oh, I'll bet you that Dean Bauer must have told George Ryan that.' Well, you can't guess a man into a federal felony conviction."[6]

A paralegal from Webb's firm had been assigned to observe the jurors and note whenever one nodded off. All were wide awake now, and one, Evelyn Ezell, nodded and murmured in obvious agreement with Webb. Ryan, his wife, his six children, and other family members all watched Webb intently. When he was done, they looked at him with open admiration. Jim Thompson did, too.

Edward Genson spoke next on Warner's behalf and noted ruefully that the jurors already had listened to thirteen hours of closing arguments. Genson has a gift for making phrases and described the government's interviews of witnesses against his client as "an American Idol for stool pigeons."[7] The first thing of substance he said was, "Larry is not a public officer, he's not a public official, and this isn't an election. . . . Larry doesn't belong here. Larry made a bunch of money, but he's a private citizen. . . . Larry doesn't belong here."[8]

To that repeated theme, Genson added, "[T]he problem is you don't know what a crime is yet. The problem is you don't know what the law is yet. The problem is, the problem is, it's so—it scares me so that you might have made up your mind without the law. . . . [Y]ou don't know what the law is."[9] Perhaps Genson knew what he was doing—it was true that the judge had not yet instructed the jury about applicable law—but insulting the jury is not usually a recommended legal maneuver. He took care not to insult the court: "We have probably the hardest-working, most sincere Judge anyone has ever worked before."[10]

Pallmeyer recessed the court with Genson scheduled to finish the next morning. As people filed out, the Reverend Scott Willis, who had watched Webb's summation, sought out Patrick Collins. He grabbed Collins's arm and asked anxiously, "Are we OK?" Collins could not look him in the eye. "After what Webb had done, I didn't think we were OK. I couldn't tell him yes. I couldn't tell him anything. It was a huge motivator, though." Collins and his team took the elevator down to the U.S. attorney's offices and pulled an all-nighter.[11]

Collins's final summation, which started the next afternoon, was a lawyerly masterpiece. He struck exactly the right note of appearing somehow humble yet outraged, rational yet passionate. Even Jim Thompson made a point of congratulating him.

> Now, ladies and gentlemen, what you also got in the ten hours of [defense] argument is what I'll call the extreme makeover. . . . [Y]ou heard from both defense counsel that their clients are victims, that this [prosecution] table and this process victimized Mr. Ryan, victimized Mr. Warner. . . .
>
> Mr. Ryan wants to say we charged federal crimes that were just politics. Mr. Warner wants to say we charged him with crimes when he was just a legitimate businessman doing business.

Ladies and gentlemen, that's not what the evidence has shown. This wasn't politics and it wasn't business. It was crimes. . . . And Mr. Webb and Mr. Genson both had different words to say it, and they wanted to trivialize the case, and Mr. Genson's characterization was on many occasions, "So what?" Mr. Webb said, "Who cares?" . . . [T]he good news is, I believe for this process, the "Who cares" question gets to be answered by you.[12]

Collins projected on the screen Fawell's notorious "let's get someone in there who won't screw our friends" memo of 1995. "This is the memo, Government Exhibit 01–019. Ladies and gentlemen, please, at least some of you, write that exhibit down and please take a good look at this document." Many of the jurors dutifully scribbled the number. "This is the Magna Carta, this is the Constitution of the way George Ryan and Scott Fawell did business."[13]

He mocked Webb's defense of Ryan's cash back from Klein: "Let's get literal. No, folks. Let's get real. That's a lie. That wouldn't pass muster with my four-year-old, folks. That's a lie."[14]

As for the "seven years of hell," Collins said, "investigations take longer when people lie. Investigations take longer when they hide transactions."[15]

Near the end, Collins indulged in a bit of theatrics. "I don't want to be cute here, and I had to borrow some money from Mr. Fardon to make up $77. [He held up $77.] But, ladies and gentlemen, in 1997 this is how much cash the record shows that George Ryan used, pennies a day."[16]

Collins's peroration mentioned every juror's occupation:

You decide whether there's a tangible consequence to corruption. Not us, not how the prosecutors think, you decide. The people who raise our families, the people who work and build our homes, the people who served our country and work at stores, the people who work in our shipping business, the people who work as technicians, the people who work in the post office, the people who work as office managers, the people who work in offices, the people who teach kids, the people who work in Home Depot, Walgreens, the truck drivers, the heavy equipment folks, the offices, the people who tend bar, the people who work for grocery stores, you guys decide. You guys decide: Is this politics, or is this a crime?[17]

Next, the judge took ninety minutes to read 148 pages of legal instructions to the jury. One of them, a victory for the prosecution, was called by lawyers the "ostrich instruction." A defendant could "know" about wrongdoing if he had a strong suspicion of it, yet deliberately shut his eyes for fear of what he might learn—put his head in the sand. However, the defense managed to limit this instruction strictly to the allegation of using state resources for political campaigns.

After the weekend, on March 13, 2006, twenty-five years after Dan Webb had warned Jim Edgar that the secretary of state's office was corrupt, twelve years after six Willis children died, eight years after the U.S. attorney declared that Ryan was not a subject of Operation Safe Road, thirty-eight months after Ryan emptied death row, and twenty-seven months after Ryan was indicted, the jury began to deliberate.

Allison S. Davis, an African American lawyer and developer in Chicago and a mentor to a young politician named Barack Obama, speculated about the outcome of the trial while Fawell was still on the stand. "George will walk," Davis predicted, because there were seven black jurors. (After several changes, the final jury included three blacks.) "The black community believes O. J. [Simpson] was guilty but set up by a lying, racist cop, Mark Fuhrman. Every black family has had experience with lying, racist cops. So they don't trust cops and prosecutors. Plus, George let everybody off death row."[18] Events proved Davis wrong—the jury nearly did tear itself apart, but not over racial issues, at least not overtly.

During the trial, a source told me that at a bar association luncheon at 321 South Plymouth Court, Chicago, Pallmeyer privately remarked that she was going to get this case out of her court. If somebody wants to appeal the verdict, that is their right. If I am overturned, I have been overturned before. But I am getting this case out of my court. I thought, "That's interesting, but no way could I ever confirm that statement for this book." But then Pallmeyer implied as much, in circumspect legal language, from the bench. During repeated appellate filings, the defense grew progressively tougher on Pallmeyer for her alleged determination to avoid a mistrial at almost any cost.

Certainly she was faced with terribly difficult decisions. The trouble started as early as March 20. Juror Evelyn Ezell wrote Pallmeyer a note: "Do I have to accept being called derogatory names, shouting profanity, and personal attacks? Can you please address this issue because this has been going on for the last couple of days."[19] Two days later, eight other jurors sent their own note: "One juror, Evelyn, is either intellectually incompetent to handle the task, or she has ulterior motives behind her actions. . . . Evelyn is either unable to understand the instructions or is blatantly refusing to adhere to them. . . . She is intentionally antagonistic, goads others into verbal fights, and when all else fails, gets physically aggressive in a juvenile attempt to intimidate whomever she is arguing with."[20] This note, written by juror Leslie Losacco and signed by her and seven others, asked Pallmeyer to remove Ezell from the jury.

Pallmeyer called in the lawyers for two closed meetings in one day. Something serious obviously was happening, because U.S. attorney Patrick Fitzgerald himself showed up. Pallmeyer told the jurors to treat one another with dignity and respect and to keep deliberating. Some jurors felt insulted, that they were being treated like children.

Actually, the jurors' letters were hardly news to Pallmeyer. In her chambers, she sometimes could overhear jurors shouting in Room 2107. The scene inside that jury room was even more contentious than the letters told. The jury split into factions that sometimes caucused on different floors. [21]

During the trial, other jurors called Ezell "Church Lady" because she remarked once that homosexuality is an abomination. She was the wife of a minister and worked as the office manager of a roofing company. During deliberations over counts against Warner, she twice stated that Warner was not on trial there; other jurors stared at her incredulously.

After the second note had been sent to Pallmeyer, one juror, Denise Peterson, arrived the next morning armed with a printout of an article from the American Judicature Society's Internet site. That was improper—jurors are not supposed to consider anything except what was presented at trial. Citing the article, juror Peterson, a substitute kindergarten teacher, told Ezell that she could be dismissed for not deliberating in good faith. Another juror said, "No, read the one on bribery, because George Ryan was taking bribes and the only way you [Ezell] can vote the way you're voting is that you've got to be getting paid."[22] Peterson said, "No, we don't need to. We've got her right there. We've got her where we want her." Supposedly, Peterson then laughed at her, and Ezell and another female African American juror wept. (Peterson later denied there was such a reaction.) Ezell eventually told the court that she started to write another note to Pallmeyer that day but stopped from fear that other jurors would not let her send it.[23]

Later on the day when Ezell was confronted with possible dismissal from the jury, she cited five reasons why Ryan should be convicted on a count of lying to the FBI. Another juror said he had thought of only three such reasons and thanked her. Ezell said at once that her words had been twisted and she would not vote to convict on that count. At that point, other jurors asked her to her face if she were taking bribes. She denied it.

Of course the jurors could not talk with the media during the trial, but they might talk after a verdict was reached. For that reason alone, *Chicago Tribune* reporters started compiling personal information about them—their phone numbers, addresses, employers, marital status, and such. In the Internet age, such data are easily gotten. The reporters' motive was to scoop other news outlets in obtaining the first jury comments. A conspiracy theory soon developed that the *Tribune* deliberately tried to derogate the jury because the paper editorially supported Ryan's stand on the death penalty.

On March 24, the paper headlined that one of the jurors had concealed his criminal record. A question on the jury form asked, "Have you had any particularly good or bad experience or contact with the Illinois Secretary of State's

Office or any other state governmental agency?" Robert Pavlick checked "no," although he had a felony DUI conviction while Ryan was secretary of state. Likewise, Pavlick answered "no" to "Have you, or has any close friend or relative ever been charged with or accused of a crime?"

The next day, the *Tribune* reported that a female juror had been arrested on felony drug charges, although she was acquitted, and misdemeanor assault and child neglect charges, although those charges were dropped. At least once, she had been arrested under an alias, "Thora Jones." Later, the court learned that she was under an outstanding 1996 arrest warrant for driving on a suspended license. This juror turned out to be Ezell, although the public did not know then that other jurors had tried to oust her. Later, Ezell said she was a recovering alcoholic and the arrests dated from when she abused alcohol.

Following the *Tribune* reports, Pallmeyer quickly dismissed Pavlick and Ezell for concealing their criminal records, then began interviewing other jurors. She also directed the U.S. attorney's office to run criminal background checks on the remaining jurors. Lawyers for Ryan and Warner did their own "public records" searches on the jurors. Not all the jurors were ideal citizens, nor had they answered the questionnaire completely. One juror was convicted of DUI in the 1960s and spent three days in jail. Another failed to disclose a domestic violence arrest. Two others had filed for bankruptcy. One of the alternates who replaced a juror had pleaded guilty to buying a stolen bicycle in Peoria in 1983.

Even before the judge bounced Pavlick and Ezell, Ryan's lawyers filed another motion for a mistrial, arguing against impaneling two alternate jurors after eight days of deliberations. The next day, Pallmeyer did that very thing, seating two alternates and ordering the jury to start over. Once again, she read the 148 pages of jury instructions. She said she still might declare a mistrial if she saw the proceedings were unfair.

The press estimated the cost of Winston and Strawn's free defense of Ryan at $20 million. Probably nobody outside of Winston and Strawn partners knows the actual number. At any rate, the prospect of a mistrial or a hung jury had to disconcert the firm, even if either outcome was better, from Ryan's standpoint, than a conviction.

Then the fitness of another juror—the foreman, in fact—was questioned. At 10 A.M. on April 17, foreman Sonja Chambers sent word to Pallmeyer that the jury had reached a verdict. Within minutes, Pallmeyer's courtroom was filled, the crowd abuzz with excitement. They waited for two hours, unaware that Webb and Genson were in the judge's chambers, beseeching her to disqualify Chambers. She had checked "no" when asked whether she had been involved in any court proceedings.

Genson had earlier told the judge that Chambers was divorced in 1992, fought her ex-husband over child custody, remarried, and then sought orders of protection against her second husband in two counties and filed again for divorce. Genson acknowledged that this record might belong to another Sonja Chambers, not juror Chambers. Sure enough, it turned out to belong to a Sonja T. Chambers, not juror Sonja Y. Chambers, who was not divorced until 2004. No matter, now argued the defense lawyers, juror Chambers still had lied about being divorced. Indeed, she had sought a protection order against her husband, charging physical abuse. Genson and Webb asserted that Pallmeyer had set the standard that lying on the questionnaire about brushes with the courts was grounds for dismissal; therefore, they insisted, she should dismiss Chambers.

Further, Chambers apparently had lied about improperly discussing the case outside of court. "Dennis" operated a coffee kiosk in the commuter rail station used by Chambers. Dennis called a talk radio station on March 28 and said that a female juror chatted with him one morning when he asked her about a news report that the ousted Ezell was claiming to be Ryan's only friend on the jury. Pallmeyer interviewed Chambers three different times. Her denial of having talked with Dennis grew steadily more convoluted. The judge said she was inclined to believe her denial.

Pallmeyer summoned Chambers anew over the divorce matter. Chambers said the divorce question was under the heading "Criminal Justice Experience," and she did not believe a divorce and a lawsuit were criminal matters.[24] Pallmeyer accepted that explanation. Moments later, Pallmeyer stepped into the courtroom to receive the jury's verdicts. She read them silently, then aloud. Lawrence E. Warner, guilty on all counts. George H. Ryan Sr., guilty on all counts. Ryan sat stone-faced with his hands folded on the table, glaring at the jurors as each was asked in turn whether that was his or her true verdict.

With the gag order now lifted, Ryan could say whatever he liked, but his statement for the cameras was bland: "I believe this decision today is not in accordance with the kind of public service that I've provided to the people of Illinois over 40 years. And needless to say, I am disappointed in the outcome. But I feel confident in our appeal, and there will be an appeal."[25]

Warner said, "The logic was if they find George guilty, then I must be guilty. . . . Basically what this says is someone in an elected public office cannot have friends."[26]

Ryan took his family to dinner at McCormick and Schmick's restaurant in Chicago. He told a friendly journalist, "Life is going to be tough, but I have no feeling of guilt."[27] He seemed blithely unaware that sentencing judges want to hear expressions of contrition from convicts.

One of the jurors auctioned on eBay a purple blouse she wore during the trial and sold it for $99. When she said she would sell her notes next, Pallmeyer ordered all the jurors to turn in all their notes. Just kidding about selling them, the juror said.

21 A Mutating Virus

Lura Lynn Ryan served on the Abraham Lincoln Bicentennial Commission, so she and George drove to Washington, D.C., in July 2006 for commission meetings. They also toured Civil War battlefields and other historic sites. On the way home, Ryan called the editor of his hometown newspaper and said, "I expect the verdict will be turned around in due time. I've always felt that way. . . . The trial came up with the wrong result. It is going to be corrected."[1] His attorney Dan Webb chewed him out, and Ryan finally stopped talking with the media after that.

The feds held off sentencing those who had flipped against Ryan until after the Ryan trial. In May 2006, Judge Pallmeyer sentenced Don Udstuen to eight months in prison, eight months of home confinement, and a $30,000 fine for tax fraud. The dominoes steadily tumbled. Alan Drazek was sentenced to two months in prison and a $15,000 fine after serving as middleman in the Warner-to-Udstuen payoffs. Scott Fawell was sentenced to thirty months in prison for the rigged McPier bid, but it would be concurrent with his previous sentence for secretary of state corruption, and prosecutors were still seeking to have that sentence reduced by six months. Fawell's aide Richard Juliano was sentenced to three months in a work-release program and four years' probation. Andrea Coutretsis was sentenced to four months in prison for the McPier fraud, concurrent with a previous sentence of four months for lying to the grand jury. Michael Tristano, former chief of staff to the Republican leader of the Illinois House, was sentenced to 366 days in prison and a $120,000 fine for assigning civil servants to do political work (not an Operation Safe Road case, but parallel).

Ryan and Warner arrived in Pallmeyer's court for sentencing on September 6, their lawyers having failed repeatedly to persuade her to declare a mistrial for jury irregularities such as juror Denise Peterson's "homespun jury instruction" about deliberating in good faith. "Half of the jurors made material misrepresentations on their questionnaires. . . . These jurors distinguished themselves by their willingness to engage in blatant misconduct and by their failure to follow the simplest and clearest instructions from the Court."[2]

The lawyers' language was unusually vivid, reflecting the bitterness of the long case. Prosecutor Patrick Collins once told Pallmeyer in her chambers, "I went into this trial with the utmost respect for Mr. Webb. I had heard he is the greatest lawyer in America, and I heard he is a former U.S. attorney and that his word is his bond. That is not the way this trial has transpired. We have been lied to."[3] The language in official court papers was hardly more restrained. The government lambasted "the defendants' scorched-earth posturing" and their "egregious misconduct and arrogance."[4] The defense said that a government brief proved "that even the most skilled advocate cannot muster an apology sufficient to absolve the irregularities surrounding these proceedings."[5]

The Reverend Scott and Janet Willis asked to address Pallmeyer at the sentencing hearing. She declined but invited them to write a letter. Mrs. Willis wrote:

> In the years since [the accident], both my husband and I have struggled with depression. While my husband battled thoughts of suicide, I battled to keep my sanity. My parents have also had their battles. My mother taught the four boys piano so we went to their house twice a week. She has battled depression ever since the accident. . . . Incredibly, even after our accident, [Ryan] permitted the fundraising scheme to continue. . . . Had there been an admission of guilt from Mr. Ryan, right from the start, the air would have been cleared. All of us have waited patiently for justice.

Scott Willis wrote:

> [S]ix children were innocent victims resulting from a political scheme to raise campaign money. . . . Janet and I have prayed not to have a bitter or revengeful spirit. . . . My wife and I have a strong desire to forgive Gov. Ryan but it must be on an honest basis: sorrow and admission. Even a 6-year-old boy knows when he's done wrong he needs to be truly sorry, and admit it. Then forgiveness and mercy can be graciously offered. That would be our joy.[6]

Amy Moody, one of the surviving Willis siblings, wrote, "I wish that George Ryan would have cared as much about the lives of innocent children as he has claimed to care for convicted criminals."[7]

The court received 102 letters asking for leniency for Ryan and Warner. Six lawyers for Ryan and four for Warner showed up at the sentencing. Pallmeyer granted two of the defense motions, dismissing two counts against Ryan and one against Warner. She said there was insufficient evidence that Ryan knew that Swanson would scam Grayville, or that Ryan clouted the secretary of state lease in Chicago for Warner.

Collins asked Pallmeyer to impose a stiff sentence. "Judge," he said, "like a mutating virus that finds a way to thrive regardless of the environment, corruption in Illinois has proven difficult to deter."[8]

Webb asked for a light sentence that would "properly punish George Ryan but still gives him a few years left with his family before he dies."[9] Ryan was seventy-two.

Ryan addressed the court, saying, "[T]here is [sic] failures which I feel regret and personal shame about. The jury's verdict speaks for itself in showing that I simply didn't do enough. Should have been more vigilant. Should have been more watchful. Should have been a lot of things, I guess."[10]

Sentencing guidelines called for seventy-eight to ninety-seven months in prison. Pallmeyer said, "The one thing that Mr. Ryan has not, sadly, had, until perhaps a few moments ago, is any apparent introspection or sense of remorse."[11] She imposed seventy-eight months. Ryan was to go to prison on January 4.

Edward Genson said of Warner, "When I met him he was 60 going on 50. And today he is 67 going on 70. . . . He drinks now when he never drank before. He could go and lift weights, in those days, three days a week. Now he can't lift himself out of bed. He goes to a psychiatrist for depression."[12]

Unlike Ryan, Warner openly expressed contrition. "Your honor, I repent. I am sorry as heck. . . . I have been punished for it for the last seven or eight years. And when I tell you I haven't had a night's sleep in all that period of time, I am pretty sure I am right. . . . I have served my sentence already, basically, because I have been living in hell for the last seven years. I have seen everything I have ever worked for crumble and go away."[13]

Warner's daughter, Laura, wrote the judge a letter. Pallmeyer said, "[I]t was, I think, the longest letter I have ever gotten of that nature. And I want you to know, I read it twice, and I was moved especially by your comments that you and your dad share one, big damaged heart. That touched me deeply." The sentencing guidelines' range was forty-one to fifty-one months. Pallmeyer imposed forty-one months plus "the $75,000 fine that's at the top of the guideline range."[14] In addition, Warner would pay $431,348 in restitution and $1.7 million to satisfy both defendants' restitution and forfeiture obligations. The judge would recommend Warner's assignment to Yankton, South Dakota, to take advantage of an alcoholic rehabilitation program there. (An assistant U.S. attorney recently had remarked in an unrelated case in Chicago, "It used to be when it came to sentencing, people got religion. Now they tend to get alcoholism."[15])

The lawyers went down to "Camp Ryan," the forest of cameras and microphones in the lobby, but Ryan managed to escape. The new chief judge of the district court was James Holderman, formerly a member of Winston and Strawn whose wife still worked for the firm. Holderman allowed the Ryans and Warners, accompanied by Jim Thompson, to use the freight elevator and a basement door out of the courthouse. Thus, the cameras were denied their shots. The news media demonstrated once again why they deserve their reputation for superficiality. Reporters kept demanding that U.S. attorney Patrick Fitzgerald comment on this outrage against the public's right to know. Fitzgerald kept saying he knew nothing about it.

In another coincidence that might make a self-respecting novelist blush, Ryan and his prosecutors ended up in the same restaurant that night. Ryan's party was seated in Athena in Chicago's Greektown when the U.S. attorney's team walked in. The two sides locked eyes and half-heartedly waved. Then the government lawyers turned and walked out.

As in a good-news, bad-news joke, Ryan received both on November 29, 2006. All six Ryan children and their families had been home for Thanksgiving and Ryan was cutting up some leftover ham for bean soup when he got a call from one of his lawyers. A panel of the Seventh Circuit Court of Appeals ruled that Ryan could remain free on bond pending his appeal—such appeals bonds are usually denied. "I'll tell you one thing. There is a God," Ryan said.[16]

In Springfield that same day, the General Assembly Retirement System board voted unanimously to strip Ryan of his annual $197,000 pension because he was a felon. He could apply for a refund of the $235,500 he had contributed to the fund over his career. A month later, Ryan sued to keep the portion of his pension earned before he became secretary of state, as he had been accused of no crimes in that time. That suit failed.

Ryan's appellate brief before the Seventh Circuit was scathing:

> The district court's singular desire to bring this case to a verdict led it to commit an avalanche of errors that deprived Warner and Ryan of a fair trial before an impartial jury. These errors undermined the legitimacy of the verdicts, which are contaminated by outside influence and divorced from meaningful group deliberations. . . . The court, however, failed to see "any great harm" because "[i]f I am wrong, it will not be the first time I was reversed, and I am not afraid to be reversed [quoting Pallmeyer's comments in chambers]."

Also, "Ezell did not refuse to deliberate, she simply disagreed with the other jurors."[17]

The government responded, "During these proceedings, Judge Pallmeyer expressed, *no fewer than twelve times,* her view that the defendants' right to a fair trial was paramount and that, if fairness could not be achieved, she would not hesitate to declare a mistrial and start the trial over, despite the amount of time that had gone into the trial"[18] (emphasis in original).

When the appellate judges ruled, sixteen months after Warner and Ryan's convictions, they conveyed an air of impatience with the defense arguments. In a fifty-five-page opinion, Judges Daniel Manion and Diane Wood allowed that "the trial may not have been picture-perfect." After thirty pages, they said, "Moving, at last, away from the jury issues . . ." In the end, "We conclude that the district court handled most problems that arose in an acceptable manner, and that whatever error remained was harmless."[19]

The dismissive tone of the majority opinion made the dissent seem even more stinging. Judge Michael Kanne said that his colleagues' description of the trial as less than picture-perfect was "a whopping understatement by any measure." Kanne listed eighteen trial irregularities, some "unremarkable" while others would be "totally astounding in any case." For instance, "in the most high profile case in Chicago in recent memory, there was no thought of sequestering the jury. . . . [A]n apparent holdout juror was purportedly threatened by other jurors with a charge of bribery. . . . [A] majority of the jurors had provided false answers under oath [on the questionnaire] and could face criminal prosecution. . . . [D]uring the course of interrogations [about the questionnaires], the jurors were granted immunity from prosecution by the U.S. Attorney." Kanne concluded his nineteen-page dissent by saying, "I have no doubt that if this case had been a six-day trial, rather than a six-month trial, a mistrial would have been swiftly declared. It should have been here."[20]

Manion had been appointed by President Reagan in 1986, Wood by President Clinton in 1995, and Kanne by Reagan in 1987. The fact that the press took care to note this history is a telltale that our courts are increasingly viewed as political creatures—a trend dating at least to the *Bush v. Gore* case that decided the presidential election of 2000. However, little, if anything, could be inferred from the political provenance of these three judges.

Ryan and Warner had raised six defense arguments:

1. The verdict was tainted by the jurors' use of the legal article introduced by juror Denise Peterson.
2. The dismissal of juror Evelyn Ezell was an arbitrary removal of a defense holdout.
3. Seating two alternate jurors after eight days of deliberations was improper.
4. Certain evidence was erroneously excluded.
5. Prosecutors failed to identify a racketeering "enterprise" under federal racketeering laws.
6. Section 1346, the honest-service clause of the mail fraud statute, is unconstitutionally vague. (This was the clause that Jim Thompson had championed against Otto Kerner thirty-six years earlier.)

In addition, Warner said that his trial should have been separated from Ryan's, and Ryan claimed that certain grand jury testimony violated his lawyer-client privilege.

The only legal ground broken by the appellate judges was their decision that a state may indeed function as a racketeering enterprise. As for Section 1346, the judges noted that eight different federal cases have upheld it, although, admittedly, "the rationales have differed."[21]

Some of the jurors said they felt vindicated by the appellate decision. Leslie Losacco, who had drafted the letter asking Pallmeyer to bounce Ezell, said, "It's a shame that [defense attorneys] feel the need to come after jurors with false allegations in a desperate attempt to get their client off. I now understand why people despise most defense lawyers."[22]

The judicial ruling meant that Ryan and Warner were within seventy-two hours of having to report to prison. At once, Jim Thompson sped to the Dirksen Federal Building. That same day, August 21, 2007, the court granted Thompson's request for time to plead for an en banc hearing by all eleven circuit judges. Meanwhile, the defendants remained free on bond. En banc reviews of a three-judge panel's decisions are seldom granted, as Thompson acknowledged—but "this is an extraordinary case."[23]

Thompson had clouted three of the eleven onto the appellate bench. Joel M. Flaum, who had just stepped down as chief circuit judge after six years, had been an assistant U.S. attorney under Thompson. Ilana Diamond Rovner had served as deputy governor to Thompson. Ann Claire Williams got her start as an assistant U.S. attorney under Dan Webb. Thompson suggested that Flaum would recuse himself because his wife worked for Winston and Strawn; whether Rovner or Williams would withdraw from the case would be up to them, he said.

Friends told Patrick Collins, who had left the U.S. attorney's office for the private sector, that the fix was in and Thompson would clout an en banc review. Collins did not believe it and was proved right. On October 25, the circuit court refused the petition in a 6–3 decision. Flaum and Rovner recused themselves, while Williams joined the dissent along with Kanne.

Once again, the dissent was stinging. It was written by Judge Richard A. Posner, one of the nation's foremost public intellectuals, author of more than thirty books. Posner focused on the length of the trial, an issue not raised by the defense. He scolded Pallmeyer's conduct of the trial, although she was not named.

> We agree with the panel majority that the evidence of the defendants' guilt was overwhelming. But guilt no matter how clearly established cannot cancel a criminal defendant's right to a trial that meets minimum standards of procedural justice. . . . [H]armlessness is not the test of reversible error when a cascade of errors turns a trial into a travesty. . . . [A trial judge's] discretion can be abused, as it was in this case, resulting in a distended trial. The trial should not have taken anywhere near the six

months that it did take. . . . [T]he longer the trial, the less likely the jury is to be able to render an intelligent verdict.[24]

Posner has a reputation for stating provocative opinions, and perhaps he thought the overlong-trial issue would be one to attract the U.S. Supreme Court's attention. Thompson immediately asked for an appeal before the Supreme Court. The U.S. solicitor general scoffed, "Applicants [for appeal] do not challenge the trial's length, and for good reason—they bear much of the responsibility for it."[25]

Jim Thompson summoned his driver to take him, Ryan, and Ryan's family in a van to the federal prison in Oxford, Wisconsin, on November 7, 2007. Thompson went down fighting, pleading for Supreme Court justice John Paul Stevens to allow Ryan out on bond while the high court considered whether to take the case. Stevens, who as a young attorney made his name by exposing corruption in the Illinois Supreme Court, handled matters from the Seventh Circuit. On November 6, Stevens declined the request. Thompson did get one last break for Ryan—the Bureau of Prisons agreed to jail him in Oxford, instead of Duluth, Minnesota, to be nearer his family.

Larry Warner went quietly to prison in Littleton, Colorado, with no media coverage. Ryan, on the night before his 254-mile drive to Oxford, met reporters on his Kankakee front lawn, impenitent to the end: "Tomorrow I embark in a new journey in my life. I do so with a firm faith in God and my family. We will continue in our fight. I will report to the federal corrections facility in Oxford, Wis., as ordered. But I do so with a clear conscience. As I have said since the beginning of this 10-year ordeal, I am innocent."[26]

He went inside and packed his medicines and eyeglasses. That, along with his wedding ring, was all that he was permitted to take into prison. He would be issued steel-toe shoes, tan shirts, and khaki pants.

The expected nest of reporters and cameramen awaited at Oxford. Prison officials allowed Ryan to enter the camp by a side entrance, thus avoiding the media. A prison spokesman said the move was necessary for security and that Ryan would get no other special treatment. He would share a four-bed room with a single toilet and work at menial jobs for pennies an hour.

There were no more deals that George Ryan could make, no backroom compromises. Nor were there more public speeches or cheers from the crowd. The former governor of Illinois was federal prisoner number 16627-424. He likely would not be released until he was seventy-nine years old.

Conclusion

> All political lives, unless they are cut off in midstream at a happy
> juncture, end in failure.
> —British statesman J. Enoch Powell, in *Joseph Chamberlain*

Four questions about the legacy of George H. Ryan Sr.

Why did he empty death row?

Judging another person's motives can be easy, but substantiating the judgment is hard. I have speculated about Ryan's motives in this book. Nobody denies that Ryan was emotionally tormented to the bottom of his soul by ordering the execution of Andrew Kokoraleis. Still, a widespread school of thought holds that Ryan's moratorium, pardons, and blanket commutation sought three things: first, applause from liberals, especially the liberal news media—conservatives distrusted him and were not about to support him anyway; second, approval from the electorate; and third, at least grudging admiration from prosecutors because Ryan displayed moral courage.

None of these points survives a scrutiny of the record. However delighted were liberals, they had no influence on a U.S. attorney's office in a particular case, and Ryan seemed genuinely surprised by the warmth of the liberal embrace of him, a lifelong Republican. As for the electorate, public opinion polls on the death penalty fluctuate over time, but in general, a solid majority of Americans supports it. When he emptied death row, Ryan had retired from politics anyway. As for prosecutors, they tend to support the death penalty and hardly would be more sympathetic to a defendant who overturned it.

Never mind, say Ryan's critics, the real point is that his intended audience was simply the liberal minority-group members who make up much of the Cook County jury pool. Most death row convicts were African American or Hispanic. The argument that Ryan intended to sway such a jury was advanced by Thomas F. Roeser, a conservative, and Allison S. Davis, a liberal. The record shows that Dan Webb at least considered the impact of Ryan's actions on a potential Cook County jury.

Such a view of Ryan's motives overlooks two factors. First is the tremendous liberation that politicians experience when they no longer have to face the voters. Ryan was not running for reelection and therefore could act on how he truly thought and felt. Most voters would not endorse his decision. Ryan might as well have chanted "Free at last, free at last, thank God Almighty I'm free at last" and could go where his gut led him.[1] Perhaps the clemency powers granted the governor by the state constitution are overbroad, but that issue has nothing to do with Ryan's employment of those powers.

The second factor is that Ryan was convinced he was innocent and thus had no need to snooker a jury. I asked Ryan whether there came a moment when he knew he would be indicted. He insisted that he never thought he would be indicted until Webb called him with the news. At first I thought Ryan was just maintaining a posture of innocence because his conviction was still under appeal. But the more I studied the man and his career, the more it seemed clear that he really did not believe his activities were criminal. Blanket clemency was not meant to deter or defeat an indictment because he never thought an indictment or conviction would happen. Such a proposition seems dubious until one contemplates the human capacity for self-delusion.

Lawyers debated legalities. Ryan's convictions were extralegal: prosecutors sent some innocent people to death row. Now they want to send me, an innocent man, to jail.

But how could Ryan and his cronies think they could get away with all those scams for all those years?

I have argued in this book and elsewhere that Chicago and Illinois are especially corrupt and that corruption and reform are phenomena of class, ethnic, partisan, and even religious conflicts. Larry J. Sabato, a professor at the University of Virginia, coauthor of *Dirty Little Secrets: The Persistence of Corruption in American Politics,* and a kind of all-purpose political commentator, told me that the "unholy trinity" of corrupt states are Illinois, New Jersey, and Louisiana. If that is so, I asked Sabato, what distinguishes those states from others? His reply amounted to "a culture of corruption." But "culture of corruption" is a slogan, not an explanation. Ryan himself used that slogan in testifying before the Federal Motor Carrier Safety Administration. If there is such a culture, what constitutes it?

Sabato answered, "Corruption is nurtured by the political culture, which depends heavily on what average voters will tolerate from their elected officials. Through the generations, corruption has become strongly associated with politics in New Jersey, Illinois, and Louisiana, and sadly, people just expect the two to go together like love and marriage. Until that changes, I expect this deplorable condition to continue in all three states. Contrast them with Oregon, for example, where clean politics is a given, and wholly expected by the people. The electorate punishes any one or any party that does not live up to those expectations."[2]

Richard A. Juliano, Scott Fawell's former top aide who flipped against Fawell and Ryan, gave as good an explanation of the culture of corruption as any. Juliano met Hubert H. Humphrey when he was five years old, and his dream had always been to work for a president. In 2001, he had a high position in President Bush's Department of Transportation. In August of that year, the feds subpoenaed him in Operation Safe Road. Then the terrorist attacks of September 11 occurred, and his meeting with the feds was delayed. Juliano ended up flying seventeen times from Washington, D.C., to Chicago to discuss the case and had to resign his federal job.

> There was a mentality of blurring the line between government and political resources, using government resources as an advantage of incumbency . . . just another resource to be used, and Mr. Fawell, who was running the campaign, was very conscious of trying to hold down the [campaign] budget. . . . [H]is priority was for TV commercials, or radio commercials, which are very expensive. . . . [H]is instructions to me were very explicit. . . . [A]nything that belonged to state government that could be used for political purposes, he wanted them used.

Juliano was still in law school when he worked for the 1994 Ryan campaign, although he was paid by the secretary of state's office.

> I largely kept the two worlds separate. There was the political world, it was the practical world in which you get things done, you're running this campaign, you're really accomplishing something. There's a law school, it's very academic, it really has very little to do with becoming a lawyer. . . . Nobody ever came to me and said, where's your state work? What are you doing? The system was designed in such a way that those questions were never asked. We were conditioned by Scott Fawell to basically consider all of these to be minimal transgressions, at least in the beginning. This goes back to the first of the three campaigns in 1990 [then 1994 and 1998] when there was some of this going on, but not to the degree later. . . . [Fawell] conditioned us to believe that as long as the media didn't find out about it, in which case we would have a political problem, that it would be OK, and that there was a lot of other stuff going on in Chicago [city government] that was a lot worse than this. . . . His way of rationalizing it . . . was, [this was] what everybody did in Illinois politics; he said explicitly, Illinois is different. . . . [In the 1998 gubernatorial campaign] the sense of urgency became much greater, and the sort of things that [Fawell] wanted us to do, that he explicitly told us to do, became much more egregious, and the goal was to win the election. As long as we win the election, everything else will take care

of itself. . . . Over time, to an extent, I kind of became the good cop to his bad cop. . . . He would be the abrasive one, pound the table and all that sort of thing, and I would smooth everything over in the political community after that. . . . Winning this election . . . ultimately is the only thing that was really important; you don't want to be a loser. . . . I was the first witness in the Fawell trial, January of '03, six days, two days of direct [examination], four of cross. . . . I half-expected him to get up from the table and come up and punch me in the face at some point. . . . [A] big rationalization that Scott used to use, particularly in the early years—who's going to care? Why should federal law enforcement, why should they ever care about office supplies and things like that?[3]

I largely kept the two worlds separate. The system was designed in such a way that those questions were never asked. Minimal transgressions. As long as we win the election, everything else will take care of itself. You don't want to be a loser. Who's going to care?

It happened that Patrick Fitzgerald cared about office supplies and things like that, if few others in Illinois did.

In fact, the causes of political corruption need not be so mysterious. A substantial body of academic research finds that ordinary people, believing themselves to be ethical, as did Juliano, will do unethical things to advance the interests of their social group. People who do unethical things often do not see them as such, or see them as minimal, especially when done in pursuit of a higher end. "Most fraud within institutions takes place through the willing cooperation of many otherwise upstanding individuals who have no psychological predispositions to be criminals. . . . [T]he perpetrators rationalize away their responsibility. . . . People engaged in corruption, the academic researchers suggest, create a kind of psychological atmosphere in which what they're doing seems normal or even honorable."[4]

Of course, the psychological pressures on Ryan's secretary of state employees were not always that subtle. Their incentives included wanting to keep or advance in their jobs by selling thousands of dollars worth of Ryan tickets twice every year.

Meanwhile, the boss has strong reasons not to clean things up. The noted political scientist Edward Banfield observed, "[T]he boss must—if he is to keep his organization from falling to pieces—'look the other way' to avoid seeing the inevitable corruption. If he saw it he would have to put a stop to it, and if he had to put a stop to it, he would weaken both his personal political position and the whole structure of governmental power."[5] Perhaps this disincentive is another explanation of Ryan's seeming blindness to the crookedness of his public offices.

"Personal political position" and "the whole structure of governmental power" are powerful gods whom few wish to offend.

Put together historical features of Illinois politics, psychological pressures to get along and go along, and the larceny in human hearts, you get a George Ryan.

For all that, was Ryan unfairly prosecuted and convicted? Have we criminalized politics? Is that largely why there seems to be so much political gridlock? Have reformers gone too far?

The idea that politics is now criminalized and popularly despised has some respectable support. Two scholars conducted research over several years indicating that many Americans judge political maneuvering as corrupt even when it is not, on its face, illegal.[6] Another scholar warns that "contempt for ordinary politics, an attitude we see underlying many of our current scandals, is a corruption even more dangerous than stealing money from the public till."[7]

Ryan's defenders describe him as a 1950s man governing in a twenty-first-century world. He grew up in machine politics, then the rules changed and he did not keep up. This defense has been raised for Ryan, Dan Rostenkowski, and many other political felons. As Jim Thompson put it:

Part of it is the gradual transformation of practices that people always accepted as legal into illegal practices over the years. You hear that defense sometimes in criminal cases, that it was just politics or it's business as usual, we've always done this. Well, heh! Nowadays that's not always a very safe defense. But sometimes these offenses grow out of older, politically accepted customs. And the other thing that has made a difference is the way the news media has changed the focus and the spotlight on politics . . . so that things that were overlooked or accepted before are now crimes, and some politicians haven't been smart enough to understand the difference. And prosecutors get more inventive and push the envelope. Juries today have been conditioned by the media to be much more sensitive to this kind of stuff than they were in the old days.[8]

The problem with this theory is that Ryan was convicted under old laws, not new ones—racketeering, mail fraud, tax fraud, false statements. Patrick Collins was sensitive to charges that prosecutors were so eager to "get" Ryan that they scoured the law books for pages that they might stick on him. "The stuff that we are charging is stuff that third-graders know is wrong." Collins mentioned again what particularly seemed to stick in the craw of the U.S. attorney's office, Ryan's getting cash back from Harry Klein for his bogus checks for Jamaican vacations. "As a prosecutor, when you get somebody falsifying information, that's your bread and butter to show the jury that they knew what they were doing is wrong."

Collins added that he recently had bumped into a state representative who told him, "You guys are doing great stuff. You wouldn't believe how down in Springfield, everybody thinks everybody's wired." If politicians are more wary of lawbreaking now, Collins insisted, "I would categorically reject that this is a bad thing."[9]

That said, it remains troubling that Ryan was convicted of seven counts under the "honest service" clause of the mail fraud statute. (At the sentencing hearing, prosecutors said they were not trying Warner for dishonest service, the reason being that he was not a public official. Technically, that was correct, but Judge Pallmeyer had already dismissed honest-service counts in Warner's indictment for that very reason.) The honest-service prosecution had been pioneered by Thompson in jailing former governor Otto Kerner. An honest-service assault was further championed by Thompson's protégé, Dan Webb, in the Operation Greylord investigation of Cook County judges in the 1980s.

Then, wham! The U.S. Supreme Court ruled in 1987 that there is no such thing as "intangible rights to honest and impartial government." Mail fraud, the court said, applies only when people are cheated out of money or property. Justice John Paul Stevens was so angered by this ruling, *McNally v. U.S.,* that he read parts of his dissent from the bench, a rarity with the Supreme Court.

The justices declared in *McNally* that if Congress wanted to establish a right to honest government, it must say so. Which it did, just a year later. In 1988, the late senator Paul Simon of Illinois and others sponsored a bill to outlaw "a scheme or artifice to deprive another of the intangible right of honest services." In the inscrutable way of Congress, it was passed with little debate and tacked on to a "war on drugs" bill. It became known as Section 1346 of the mail fraud statute.

As early as 1980, Jed S. Rakov, later a federal judge in New York, wrote, "To federal prosecutors of white-collar crime, the mail fraud statute is our Stradivarius, our Colt .45, our Louisville Slugger, our Cuisinart—and our true love. We may flirt with [other laws] and call the conspiracy law 'darling,' but we always come home to the virtues of [mail fraud], with its simplicity, adaptability, and comfortable familiarity. It understands us and, like many a foolish spouse, we like to think we understand it."[10]

Not just the criminal defense bar but many civil libertarians and some judges worry that Section 1346, along with wire fraud and racketeering laws, invite prosecutors to overreach. The Racketeering Influence Corrupt Organization Act covers anyone involved in a "racketeering enterprise" who commits two "predicate acts" within ten years. Almost any activity that involves mail or phones can be an alleged fraud. One judge in a federal appellate case in 1981 remarked that the use of "mail fraud as a catch-all prohibition of political disingenuousness . . . subjects virtually every active participant in the political process to potential criminal investigation and prosecution."[11] More recently,

Judge Richard A. Posner of the Seventh Circuit in Chicago observed in 1999, "A century of interpretation of the [mail fraud] statute has failed to still the doubts of those who think it is dangerously vague." There was one appellate ruling in New York in 2002—"The plain meaning of 'honest services' in the text of Section 1346 simply provides no clue to the public or the courts as to what conduct is prohibited under the statute."[12] However, that decision applied narrowly to just that one case.

Collins said, "The Seventh Circuit [appellate court] has now said where the line for honest services is for us. We have to show personal gain, so it's not sort of this amorphous situation." He referred to a 1998 case involving a former Chicago alderman, *U.S. v. Lawrence S. Bloom*. "The defense bar, juries, the Seventh Circuit are there to hold us to that, if we overreach. . . . If we were losing cases and judges are saying, you know, this doesn't pass muster, if this wasn't the Bloom standard for honest services," then accusations of prosecutorial abuses might have merit, Collins said.[13]

Daniel Scott, a criminal defense lawyer in Minneapolis, offered a typical rejoinder. Under honest-service fraud, he said, "the government could bring a case in which a public official failed to reveal which way his daughter told him to vote. . . . It is an impossible standard for any defendant to get past. . . . Finding amateurs is as good as finding professionals for your stats [prosecutors' conviction statistics]."[14]

Perhaps all might agree that good prosecution is not the same thing as good government. Another approach to reconciling these arguments is to consider both a "corruption tax" and a "prosecution tax" on society. Public corruption causes injustices and inefficiencies—costs that society pays to the extent that such corruption exists. Excessive or improper prosecutions also impose costs of injustices and inefficiencies. Which tax is more onerous is largely a matter of individual views.

For the Reverend Scott and Janet Willis, however, the question is not abstract.

What is the historical importance of George Ryan?

As reviewed earlier, Ryan's emptying of death row was not purely a moral sunburst. Some convicts actually might have gotten better deals had their appeals been allowed to proceed toward a possible retrial, reversal of sentence, or exoneration. The release of the most evil killers into the general prison population under life sentences without parole also created serious problems for prison administrators.

Moreover, Ryan's clemency actually might have facilitated additional murders in Illinois by voiding the deterrence effect of the death penalty. Ryan said he does not believe in the deterrence theory, a theory that has been debated for centuries. In June 2005, two academics at the University of Houston published a study that included these findings:

> In January 2000, the Governor of Illinois declared a moratorium on executions pending a review of the judicial process that condemned certain murderers to the death penalty. In January 2003 just prior to leaving office the Governor commuted the sentences of all those who then occupied death row. We find that these actions are coincident with the increased risk of homicide incurred by Illinois residents for the 48-month post event period for which data were available. The increased risk is associated with an estimated 150 homicides during the post-event period.[15]

So, in this view, Ryan indirectly caused 150 Illinoisans to be killed over four years. Such a development would be a painful confirmation of Lord Powell's dictum that "all political lives . . . end in failure."[16]

Actually, not even the authors of that study, advocates of the deterrence hypothesis, say their findings are that clear-cut. Dale O. Cloninger and Roberto Marchesini also wrote:

> *Deterrence is neither served by executing an innocent person nor by failing to execute a guilty one.* . . . There existed sufficient questions in sufficient number of death row cases to cause [Ryan] pause. A necessary prerequisite for deterrence is a common and universal perception that the judicial process is unbiased, fair and accurate. Otherwise, executions may engender more violence not less. Likewise, for the threat of an execution to generate a deterrent effect, citizenry must be convinced that executions will occur when warranted. The mere presence of a death penalty does not in and of itself provide a measurable deterrence effect.[17] (emphasis in original)

That is, even if the deterrent effect is real, Ryan found a system so wrecked it provided no deterrent. If the system is wanton, arbitrary, and capricious, then the deterrence effect and also the issue of retributive justice are negated. Deterrence and retribution are the only arguments for the death penalty, aside from bloodthirstiness.

Terry Cosgrove, leader of the pro-choice lobby Personal PAC and no particular fan of Ryan's, said, "He changed the terms of debate across the world on the death penalty."[18]

An ordinary man from an ordinary midwestern city changed the terms of a worldwide debate on a crucial moral issue. Our culture celebrates the physical courage of athletes and warriors. Maybe we should honor more the moral courage that can be displayed by ordinary, even sinful, people.

Notes
Selected Bibliography
Index

Notes

The following abbreviations are used for frequently cited sources in the notes:

CST   *Chicago Sun-Times*
CT   *Chicago Tribune*
DH   *Daily Herald* (Arlington Heights, Ill.)
DJ   *Daily Journal* (Kankakee, Ill.)
GHR   George H. Ryan Sr.
JRT   James R. Thompson
USvWR   *United States vs. Lawrence E. Warner and George H. Ryan,*
                Sr., U.S. District Court, Northern District of Illinois, Eastern
                Division, 396 F. Supp. 2d 924 (N.D. Ill. 2005)

Introduction

1. Savageau and D'Agostino, *Places Rated Almanac.*
2. "Ryan's Legacy Shines Brightly Abroad," *DJ,* April 22, 2006.
3. "Ryan Defends Clemency Plea in '70s for a Kankakee Killer," *CT,* September 1, 1998.
4. Michelle Stoffel, "Final Farewell," *The DePaulia,* November 2006, DePaul University, Chicago.
5. Kurtis, *Death Penalty on Trial,* 3.
6. Ibid., 3–5.

1. See Kankakee for a Dime

1. *Journal of the [Illinois] House of Representatives,* June 11, 1974, 7061.
2. GHR, interview with the author, January 22, 2007.
3. "This Lady's Done It All," *DJ,* February 6, 2003.
4. "Transcript of Proceedings—Sentencing," *USvWR,* September 6, 2006, 69.
5. GHR, interview with the author.
6. Ibid.
7. Ibid.
8. Ibid.
9. "New First Lady Ready to Step into Spotlight," *CST,* January 11, 1999.
10. Michael Sneed column, *CST,* May 6, 2001.

2. Smell the Meat a-Cookin'

1. Hartley, *Paul Powell of Illinois,* 192.
2. David Kenney, "Gov. Stratton's Passage."
3. Paul Simon, as told to Alfred Balk, "The Illinois Legislature: A Study in Corruption," *Harper's,* September 1964, 72.

4. Merriner, *Grafters and Goo Goos*, 161.

5. See Merriner, "Conservative Angels," *Illinois Issues*, February 1996.

6. See Merriner, *Grafters and Goo Goos*, 177–78.

7. JRT, interview with Richard Norton Smith, in *Evenings to Remember*.

8. Ibid.

9. Barnhart and Schlickman, *Kerner*, 297.

3. What Can I Do for You?

1. GHR, interview with the author.

2. Henry Hyde, interview with the author, April 4, 2007.

3. "Blair Reelected Speaker after Long Battle," *CT*, January 11, 1973.

4. Quoted in Walker, *Maverick and the Machine*, 61–62.

5. Ibid., 238.

6. Ibid., 242–43.

7. "Son of Clout Spreads His Wings," *CT*, June 28, 1975; Netsch was quoted in "Behind the Blizzard of Bills—the Uncommon Seven" in the same issue.

8. JRT, interview with Smith.

9. "At the Crossroads," *CT*, March 17, 1985.

10. "Pay Boosts Called Setback to Nation," *CT*, December 3, 1978.

11. Robert H. Newtson to GHR, "Confidential Memorandum," Ryan Papers, Box 14, "Memos" file, September 24, 1979.

12. Newtson to GHR, "Confiedential [*sic*] Memorandum #2," Ryan Papers, Box 14, "Memos" file, December 17, 1980.

13. See Merriner, "Before the Robots Marched on Springfield."

14. GHR, speech to the Illinois Municipal League, Ryan Papers, Box 11, Folder 6, "Speeches," n.d.

15. Newtson to GHR, "Confidential Memorandum," Ryan Papers, Box 14, "Memos" file, June 30, 1980.

16. "Thompson to Decide Soon on State Secretary," *CT*, November 12, 1980.

17. JRT, interview with the author, September 7, 2006.

18. William Dart, interview with the author, August 29, 2006.

4. I Push This Button Right Here

1. GHR, interview with the author.

2. JRT, interview with the author.

3. GHR, letter, in Ryan Papers, Box 11, Folder 15, "ERA," May 23, 1980.

4. "The Big Top in Springfield," *CT*, June 20, 1982.

5. "ERA Backers Invade House, Halt Session," *CT*, June 17, 1982.

6. JRT, interview with the author.

7. "Ryan Aids Nursing Home Owner, Gains Thousands," *CST*, July 11, 1982.

8. Rich Miller, "Product of Corrupt Political Culture, Ryan Can't Acknowledge His Guilt," *Chicago Daily Southtown*, April 24, 2006.

9. "Ryan Aids Nursing Home Owner."

10. "A Troubled Nursing Home Gave Ryan Business: BGA," *CT*, July 11, 1982.

11. "Statement by Speaker George Ryan," in Ryan Papers, "Nursing Homes" folder, July 13, 1982.

12. "Thompson Gives Embattled Ryan a Hand," *CST*, July 15, 1982.

13. Ty Fahner, interview with the author, March 15, 2007.

14. "Time Out for Politics," *CT*, September 25, 1981.

15. William Dart, interview with the author.

16. "Talk of Candidate Change Clouds Ryan's Future," *Crystal Lake (Ill.) Morning Herald*, in Ryan Papers, Box 14, "Press Clippings" file, August 6, 1982.

17. "No Marshmallow," *CT*, September 25, 1982.

5. Cut Ribbons and Hand Out Money

1. "No. 2 State Job Has Little Glory and Less Respect," *CT*, October 11, 1996.

2. GHR, interview with the author.

3. JRT, interview with Smith.

4. Ibid.

5. "Legislators Vote to Save Sox," *CT*, July 1, 1988. See also "Miracle of '88 Led to This One," *CT*, October 26, 2005, and "White Sox Park: How the Fix Was In," *CST*, http://blogs.suntimes.com/sweet/2006/02white_sox_how_the_fix_was.html.

6. "Resolution," Bradley Board of Trustees, Ryan Papers, Box 11, Folder 6, n.d., n.p.

7. JRT, interview with the author.

8. Thomas F. Roeser (former Quaker Oats vice president for governmental affairs), interview with the author, August 14, 2006.

9. "TV Allegations Ripped by Ryan," *DJ*, October 5, 1990.

10. "Choices for State Offices," *CT*, October 15, 1990.

6. These Are My Guys

1. "The Man with the Golden Charm," *CT*, January 13, 1991.

2. "From Jack Who? To GOP's 800-lb. Gorilla," *CT*, July 4, 1993.

3. "Man with the Golden Charm."

4. "Government's Evidentiary Proffer as to Co-conspirator and Agency Statements," *USvWR*, December 23, 2004, 65. The source of the allegation was assistant U.S. attorney Patrick Quinn (not the Patrick Quinn who championed the Cutback Amendment), who was present at the meeting. O'Malley, testifying at Ryan's trial on February 6, 2006, at first denied that Ryan had made the remark; on cross-examination, he said he did not remember Ryan making any such remark in a threatening manner.

5. JRT, interview with Smith.

6. "Memo Suggests 'Licenses for Sale' Scandal Nothing New," Associated Press, May 30, 2000.

7. "Ryan's Office Knew in '93 of License Selling," *CT*, October 31, 1999.

8. The Libertyville episode provided one of six racketeering charges against Dean Bauer in a February 1, 2000, indictment. Bauer pleaded guilty to one

count of obstructing justice and admitted that the government could prove other misconduct at trial.

7. The One Guy Left in This Business

1. Belzer, *Sweatshops on Wheels*, 21, 42.
2. Russell Sonneveld, "Transcript of Proceedings—Trial," *USvWR*, January 4, 2006, 14520. This episode also was called "Racketeering Act Three" alleged in *U.S. v. Bauer*.
3. "Fawell Trial Zeros In on Ryan," *CT*, February 19, 2003.
4. "$100 Million Settlement in Van Horror," *CT*, August 27, 1999.
5. "Minister, Wife in Van Crash Leave Flock for a New Life," *CT*, May 1, 2000.
6. "Couple Have Faith in a Life beyond Grief," *CT*, December 28, 2000.
7. Scott R. Fawell, "Memorandum," *USvWR*, Government Exhibit 01–019, December 14, 1994. The quotes in the following paragraphs are also from this memo.

8. They Thought It Was Too Political

1. This and following GHR quotations are from the author's interview, except as noted.
2. GHR, letter to the editor, *CT*, June 29, 1994.
3. "Organ Donor Ads Help Ryan, Program," *CT*, April 6, 1998.
4. "'Joke' of State Lobbyist Law Ends When Edgar Signs Disclosure Bill," *CT*, August 5, 1993.
5. "Ryan Case Filled with Kankakee Connections," *DJ*, January 10, 2005.

9. Some Comic Book Character Called "The Fixer"

1. "Old Friends Had Clout, Used It," *CT*, May 23, 2002.
2. Regarding the usage of "clout": "Originally, a noun meaning improper political influence or the bearer of it or a verb meaning to exercise such influence; now a national generic synonym for power" (Merriner, *Grafters and Goo Goos*, 283).
3. James Covert, "Transcript of Proceedings—Trial," *USvWR*, November 10, 2005, 8110.
4. The breakdown included $834,000 from Viisage Technologies, $399,000 from American Decal Manufacturing, $1,000,000 from International Business Machines, $8,200 from American Temperature Control, $382,276 from an SOS lease in Chicago, $171,000 from a lease in Bellwood, and $387,000 from a lease in Joliet. See "United States' Position Paper as to Sentencing Factors," *USvWR*, September 1, 2006, 12.
5. Lawrence E. Warner, letter, "Government's Evidentiary Proffer," January 25, 1995, 33.
6. "Government's Evidentiary Proffer," April 1992, 19.
7. Warner, letter, *USvWR*, Government's Exhibit 02–013.

6. GHR, interview with the author.

7. "Execution Made Ryan Queasy," *CST,* June 12, 2001.

8. GHR, interview with the author.

9. Governor Jeb Bush of Florida suspended executions in that state on December 15, 2006; however, the suspension reflected questions about the lethal-injection method of execution, not the justice of the prisoners' death sentences.

10. GHR, interview with the author.

11. "McCormick Expansion Passes," *CT,* June 1, 2001.

12. "O'Hare Expansion a Done Deal," *CST,* December 6, 2001.

13. Steve Rhodes, "The Day Clout Struck Out," *Chicago,* August 2001, http://www.ipsn.org/rosemont/day_clout_struck_out.htm.

14. Michael Sneed column, *CST,* August 10, 2001.

15. "Ryan Won't Seek Second Term," *CT,* August 9, 2001.

16. The source of this anecdote requested anonymity.

17. Sheila Murphy, interview with the author, April 11, 2007.

15. If Those Students Had Taken Chemistry

1. Michael Sneed column, *CST,* January 27, 2002.

2. "Castro to Ryan: How About a Statue?" *CST,* January 27, 2002.

3. "Ryan, Castro Home In on Trade," *CT,* January 26, 2002.

4. Steve Neal column, *CST,* April 12, 2000.

5. Ibid., *CST,* April 5, 2002.

6. "Transcript of Proceedings—Trial," Dec. 8, 2005, 12222–23.

7. "Justices Hear Bid to Make Governor Return Salary," *CST,* May 22, 2002.

8. See Flaum and Carr, "Equitable Bill of Accounting."

9. "Ryan May Commute Death Sentences," *CST,* March 3, 2002.

10. "What Is Justice?," segment of *Deadline.*

11. "The Commission," segment of *Deadline.*

12. "Two Weeks of Hearings," *Deadline.*

13. GHR, interview with the author.

14. Rick Pueschel, letter to the editor, *CT,* September 18, 2005.

15. "Two Weeks of Hearings," *Deadline.*

16. "Illinois Governor Issues Three New Pardons as His Own Legal Problems Mount," *New York Times,* December 20, 2002.

17. "$1.5 Billion Pot Brims with Secretive Pork," *CT,* February 3, 2002.

18. Michael Sneed column, *CST,* November 24, 2002.

16. The Book of Life and the Book of Death

1. "Appeals Process in Illinois Includes the Exonerated," *New York Times,* December 17, 2002.

2. GHR, interview with the author.

3. Kurtis, *Death Penalty on Trial,* 8.

4. "Clemency for All," *CT,* January 12, 2003.

5. "Prosecutors, Survivors Rip Ryan," *CST,* January 13, 2003.

6. Roeser, "Failing Private Ryan," April 17, 2006, www.tomroeser.com.

7. Michael Sneed column, *CST*, January 13, 2003.

8. "G Ryan Condemns IL Judicial System as 'Rotten to Core,'" November 14, 2003, www.illinoisleader.com.

9. GHR's remarks of December 18, 2002, were published as "The Role of the Executive in Administering the Death Penalty," *University of Illinois Law Review* 4 (September 2003); see 1085.

10. "The Decision," segment of *Deadline*.

11. "Blagojevich Takes Over, Puts Deficit at $5 Billion," *CT*, January 14, 2003.

12. "Official Videotape Just Praises Ryan," *CT*, January 15, 2003. (Under the Blagojevich administration, these documents were not available in state archives.)

13. Mike Sneed column, *CST*, January 13, 2003.

14. "Ryan Aide Testifies Even the Shredder Used to Destroy Documents Was Stolen," *DH*, January 17, 2003.

15. Mark Brown column, *CST*, January 15, 2003.

16. "Feds Say Fawell Had 'Screw You' Attitude," *CST*, March 12, 2003.

17. "Indictment Targets Ryan Fund, Ex-aides," *CST*, April 3, 2002.

18. "Fawell Is Given 78-month Sentence," *CT*, July 1, 2003.

19. "Fawell Guilty of Corruption," *CST*, March 20, 2003.

20. "Ryan Hailed, Unveiled," *CT*, November 19, 2003.

21. "No 'Bomb' on Ryan, Fawell Says," *CT*, October 12, 2005.

22. "How Old Friends Helped Prosecutors Make Their Case," *DH*, December 18, 2003.

23. "Defense," n.d., www.georgeryanfund.com/defense.php.

17. Custer and the Indians

1. "Fawell Tune: What He'll Do for Love," *CT*, October 29, 2004.

2. "'Hurricane Fitzgerald,'" *CT*, October 30, 2005.

3. "Perseverance Pays Off in Hunt for Corruption," *CT*, December 18, 2003.

4. See "Webb, Keker, Weingarten, Sullivan, Bennett, Green Are Top White Collar Criminal Defense Attorneys, Survey Shows," *Corporate Crime Reporter*, May 27, 2003, www.corporatecrimereporter.com/05_27_03_pressrelease.html.

5. "Webb Set to Defend 'Ryan the Man,'" *CT*, December 19, 2003.

6. John Kass column, *CT*, July 2, 2003.

7. Steve Rhodes, "Devil's Advocate," *Chicago*, March 2005, 135.

8. "Government's Motion *In Limine* for an Order Excluding Evidence and Argument Concerning Defendant Ryan's Decisions Concerning the Death Penalty," *USvWR*, June 17, 2005, 10, 15.

9. "Ryan's Response to the Government's Motion *In Limine* Regarding Ryan's Decisions Concerning the Death Penalty," *USvWR*, July 8, 2005, 1.

18. My Head in a Vise

1. "Transcript of Proceedings—Trial," *USvWR*, October 28, 2005, 2719.

2. Ibid., October 11, 2005, 3694–3717.

3. "Fawell's Transition Is Complete," *CT,* October 12, 2005.

4. "Willis Points to Human Side in Ryan Trial," *CST,* October 22, 2005.

5. "Prosecutors Try to Show Ryan Linked to 'Nitty-Gritty,'" *CST,* October 25, 2005.

6. "Transcript of Proceedings—Trial," *USvWR,* November 17, 2005, 8934.

7. "Ryan Tees Off on an Old Ally," *CT,* November 18, 2005.

8. "Transcript of Proceedings—Trial," *USvWR,* November 21, 2005, 9129.

9. Ibid., November 8, 2005, 7640.

10. Ibid., December 12, 2005, 11779–11905.

19. A Real Schnorrer

1. GHR, remark noted by the author, February 6, 2006.

2. "Ryan's Christmas Spirit," *CT,* February 9, 2006.

3. "Transcript of Proceedings—Trial," *USvWR,* Feb. 14, 2006, 19994.

4. Ibid., February 16, 2006, 20536.

5. Ibid., February 23, 2006, 21325–21331.

6. Ibid., February 22, 2006, 21128.

7. "Feds: Lura Lynn on TV 'A New Low,'" *CST,* February 24, 2006.

8. "Transcript of Proceedings—Trial," *USvWR,* March 2, 2006, 22519.

9. Ibid., March 6, 2006, 22948. The document in question was a memorandum from secretary of state police director Giacomo A. Pecoraro to chief deputy director William H. Thompson, *USvWR,* Government Exhibit 38–001, November 16, 1994.

20. Twelve Years of Christmas

1. "Transcript of Proceedings—Trial," *USvWR,* March 6, 2006, 22826–27.

2. Ibid., 22836, 22990.

3. Ibid., March 7, 2006, 23098–99.

4. Ibid., 23145, 23149–50.

5. Ibid., March 8, 2006, 23359–65.

6. Ibid., 23392.

7. Ibid., March 9, 2006, 23509.

8. Ibid., March 8, 2006, 23475–76.

9. Ibid., 23478–79.

10. Ibid., 23486.

11. John Kass column, *CT,* March 2, 2007.

12. "Transcript of Proceedings—Trial," *USvWR,* March 9, 2006, 23675–77.

13. Ibid., 23678.

14. Ibid., 23707.

15. Ibid., March 10, 2006, 23829.

16. Ibid., 23849.

17. Ibid., 23869–70.

18. Allison S. Davis, interview with the author, October 7, 2005.

19. "Behind-the-Scenes Jury Turmoil Disclosed," *CST,* April 22, 2006.

20. "Transcript of Proceedings—Trial," *USvWR*, March 22, 2006, 24074–76.

21. The appellate court later stated (emphasis added), "Putting media accounts and testimony that the district court discredited to one side, there is no basis *in the record* to conclude that any deliberations took place when the jurors were separated from one another." U.S. Court of Appeals for the Seventh Circuit, *USvWR*, Nos. 06–3517 and 06–3528, "Opinion," August 21, 2007, 4, 506 F.3d 508 (7th Cir. 2007).

22. "Memorandum in Support of Losacco's Motion to File *Amicus Curiae* Brief and Brief," *USvWR*, May 3, 2006, 3.

23. "Consolidated Brief and Required Short Appendix of the Defendants-Appellants," *USvWR*, December 14, 2006, 15.

24. The questionnaire categories included, among others, "Demographic Information," "Family History," "Your Spouse/Significant Other Background," and "Criminal Justice Experience."

25. "Guilty of All Charges," *CST*, April 18, 2006.

26. "Warner: I Needed a Separate Trial," *CST*, April 18, 2006.

27. Michael Sneed column, *CST*, April 18, 2006.

21. A Mutating Virus

1. "Hope for a New Trial," *DJ*, August 7, 2006.

2. "Ryan's Reply in Support of His Motions for Judgment of Acquittal, New Trial, and Arrest of Judgment," *USvWR*, July 28, 2006, 7–9.

3. "Press Worried Ryan Judge, Lawyers," *CST*, May 3, 2006.

4. "United States' Position Paper as to Sentencing Factors and Its Consolidated Response to Defendants' Position Papers," *USvWR*, September 1, 2006, 4.

5. "Ryan's Reply in Support of His Motions," 1.

6. "Letters Full of Pain and Loss," *CT*, September 8, 2006.

7. "'My Heart Goes Out' to Willises," *CST*, September 9, 2006.

8. "Transcript of Proceedings—Sentencing," *USvWR*, September 6, 2006, 45.

9. Ibid., 66.

10. Ibid., 91.

11. Ibid., 95.

12. Ibid., 135.

13. Ibid., 150–52.

14. Ibid., 155.

15. "Warner Wants in Popular Program," *CST*, September 8, 2006.

16. Michael Sneed column, *CST*, November 30, 2006.

17. "Consolidated Brief and Required Short Appendix," 17, 23.

18. "Brief of the United States," *USvWR*, January 16, 2007, 34.

19. U.S. Court of Appeals for the Seventh Circuit, *USvWR*, "Opinion," 1–2, 31, 2–3.

20. Ibid., 55–57, 74.

21. Ibid., 42.

22. "Former Jurors Feeling Vindicated," *CT*, August 22, 2007.

23. "Ryan Loses Appeal but Remains Free," *CT*, August 22, 2007.

24. U.S. Court of Appeals for the Seventh Circuit, *USvWR*, "Order," October 25, 2007, 5, 6, 8, 12.

25. "On Emergency Application for Bail Pending Certiorari, Memorandum for the United States in Opposition," *USvWR*, Supreme Court No. 07A373, November 5, 2007, 32.

26. "Ryan Leaves for Prison," CT, November 7, 2007.

Conclusion

1. For this insight I am indebted to Rich Miller, publisher of *Capitol Fax* and the best political reporter in Springfield.

2. Larry J. Sabato, e-mail to the author, August 10, 2006.

3. Richard A. Juliano, "Exploring Public Corruption: Its Causes, Consequences, and Remedies," remarks noted by the author, University of St. Thomas, Minneapolis, Minn., February 27, 2007.

4. Mark Buchanan, "Our Lives as Atoms," May 29, 2007, http://donkeyod. wordpress.com/2007/ 05/31/chain-reactions/. Buchanan discussed in particular Anand, Ashforth, and Joshi, "Business as Usual."

5. Banfield, *Political Influence,* 257.

6. Redlawsk and McCann, "Popular Interpretations of Corruption."

7. Garment, *Scandal,* 303.

8. JRT, interview with the author.

9. Patrick M. Collins, interview with the author, November 6, 2006.

10. Rakov quoted in Merriner, "Did Gov. George Ryan Cost Us a Dime?"

11. Burrows, "Corruption in Government," 441.

12. Posner quoted in Merriner, "Did Gov. George Ryan Cost Us a Dime?"

13. Collins, interview with the author.

14. Daniel Scott, "Exploring Public Corruption," public remarks noted by the author.

15. Cloninger and Marchesini, "Execution Moratoriums," 967.

16. Ibid., 978.

17. Powell, *Joseph Chamberlain,* 151.

18. Terry Cosgrove, interview with the author, April 24, 2007.

Selected Bibliography

Books

Anechiarico, Frank, and James B. Jacobs. *The Pursuit of Absolute Integrity: How Corruption Control Makes Government Ineffective.* Chicago: University of Chicago Press, 1996.

Angelo, Phil, ed. *150 Years: People, Events and Moments That Touched the Kankakee Valley.* Kankakee, Ill.: Kankakee Daily Journal Co., 2003.

Banfield, Edward C. *Political Influence: A New Theory of Urban Politics.* New York: Free Press, 1968.

Barnhart, Bill, and Gene Schlickman. *Kerner: The Conflict of Intangible Rights.* Urbana: University of Illinois Press, 1999.

Belzer, Michael H. *Sweatshops on Wheels: Winners and Losers in Trucking Deregulation.* New York: Oxford University Press, 2000.

Biles, Roger. *Illinois: A History of the Land and Its People.* DeKalb: Northern Illinois University Press, 2005.

Blank, Jessica, and Erik Jensen. *The Exonerated: A Play.* New York: Faber and Faber, 2003.

Bone, Jan. *The Thompson Indictment.* Chicago: Public Interest Press, 1978.

Burnham, David. *Above the Law: Secret Deals, Political Fixes, and Other Misadventures of the U.S. Department of Justice.* New York: Scribner, 1996.

Cahan, Richard. *A Court That Shaped America: Chicago's Federal District Court from Abe Lincoln to Abbie Hoffman.* Evanston, Ill.: Northwestern University Press, 2002.

Davis, Angela J. *Arbitrary Justice: The Power of the American Prosecutor.* New York: Oxford University Press, 2007.

des Lauriers, Don, and Mardene Hinton. *Riverview Historic District 1866–1935: Tales of Villas, Bungalows, Parks and Drives.* Kankakee, Ill.: Kankakee County Historical Society, 1997.

Dow, David R. *Executed on a Technicality: Lethal Justice on America's Death Row.* Boston: Beacon Press, 2005.

Friedrich, Carl J. *The Pathology of Politics: Violence, Betrayal, Corruption, Secrecy, and Propaganda.* New York: Harper and Row, 1972.

Garment, Suzanne. *Scandal: The Culture of Mistrust in American Politics.* New York: Times Books, 1991.

Hartley, Robert E. *Big Jim Thompson of Illinois.* Chicago: Rand McNally, 1979.

———. *Paul Powell of Illinois: A Lifelong Democrat.* Carbondale: Southern Illinois University Press, 1999.

Healy, Gene, ed. *Go Directly to Jail: The Criminalization of Almost Everything.* Washington, D.C.: Cato Institute, 2004.

Heidenheimer, Arnold J., Michael Johnson, and Victor T. Levine, eds. *Political Corruption: A Handbook*. New Brunswick, N.J.: Transaction Publishers, 1989.

Howard, Robert P. *Mostly Good and Competent Men: The Illinois Governors*. 2nd ed. Springfield: University of Illinois at Springfield, 1999.

Johnson, Vic. *An Illustrated Sesquicentennial Reader: Kankakee County, Illinois, 1853–2003*. Kankakee, Ill.: Kankakee County Historical Society, 2004.

Kurtis, Bill. *The Death Penalty on Trial: Crisis in American Justice*. New York: Public Affairs, 2004.

Merriner, James L. *Grafters and Goo Goos: Corruption and Reform in Chicago, 1833–2003*. Carbondale: Southern Illinois University Press, 2004.

———. *Mr. Chairman: Power in Dan Rostenkowski's America*. Carbondale: Southern Illinois University Press, 1999.

Monroe, Dan, with Lura Lynn Ryan. *At Home with Illinois Governors: A Social History of the Illinois Executive Mansion, 1855–2003*. Springfield: Illinois Executive Mansion Association, 2002.

Morgan, Peter W., and Glenn H. Reynolds. *The Appearance of Impropriety: How the Ethics Wars Have Undermined American Government, Business, and Society*. New York: Free Press, 1997.

Pensoneau, Taylor, and Bob Ellis. *Dan Walker: The Glory and the Tragedy*. Evansville, Ind.: Smith-Collins, 1993.

Powell, J. Enoch. *Joseph Chamberlain*. London: Thames and Hudson, 1977.

Protess, David, and Rob Warden. *A Promise of Justice: The Eighteen-Year Fight to Save Four Innocent Men*. New York: Hyperion, 1998.

Roberts, Paul Craig, and Lawrence M. Stratton. *The Tyranny of Good Intentions: How Prosecutors and Bureaucrats Are Trampling the Constitution in the Name of Justice*. Roseville, Calif.: Forum, 2004.

Rose-Ackerman, Susan. *Corruption and Government: Causes, Consequences, and Reform*. New York: Cambridge University Press, 1999.

Sabato, Larry J., and Glenn R. Simpson. *Dirty Little Secrets: The Persistence of Corruption in American Politics*. New York: Times Books, 1996.

Savageau, David, and Ralph B. D'Agostino. *Places Rated Almanac*. Boston: IDG Books Worldwide, 1998.

Schafer, Tom. *Meeting the Challenge: The Edgar Administration, 1991–1999*. Springfield, Ill.: Office of the Governor, 1998.

Turow, Scott. *Ultimate Punishment: A Lawyer's Reflections on Dealing with the Death Penalty*. New York: Farrar, Straus, and Giroux, 2003.

Walker, Dan. *The Maverick and the Machine: Governor Dan Walker Tells His Story*. Carbondale: Southern Illinois University Press, 2007.

Articles, Manuscripts, Media

Anand, Vikas, Blake Ashforth, and Mahendra Joshi. "Business as Usual: The Acceptance and Perpetuation of Corruption in Organizations." *Academy of Management Executive* 19.4 (November 2005): 9–23.

Burrows, Edwin G. "Corruption in Government." In *Encyclopedia of American Political History,* edited by Jack P. Greene, 417–42. New York: Scribner, 1984.

Cloninger, Dale O., and Roberto Marchesini. "Execution Moratoriums, Commutations and Deterrence: The Case of Illinois." *Applied Economics* 38.9 (May 2006): 967–73.

Deadline. DVD. A film by Katy Chevigny and Kirsten Johnson. Chatsworth, Calif.: Home Vision Entertainment, 2004.

Federal Motor Carrier Safety Administration. "Evaluating Commercial Drivers License Program Vulnerabilities: A Case Study of the States of Illinois and Florida." Washington, D.C.: Government Printing Office, October 2000.

Flaum, Joel M., and Jayne A. Carr. "The Equitable Bill of Accounting—A Viable Remedy for Combatting Official Misconduct." *Illinois Bar Journal* 62.7 (July 1974).

Kenney, David. "Gov. Stratton's Passage through Political Patronage." *Illinois Issues,* April 1990, 26–27.

Merriner, James L. "Before the Robots Marched on Springfield." *Chicago Sun-Times,* April 16, 2006.

———. "Conservative Angels." *Illinois Issues,* February 1996, 30–33.

———."Corruption: Exploring Politics as Usual in the Windy City." *Chicago Sun-Times,* April 29, 2004.

———. "Did Gov. George Ryan Cost Us a Dime?" *Chicago Sun-Times,* February 19, 2006.

———. "Illinois Really Is More Corrupt." *Chicago Sun-Times,* March 11, 2007.

———. "'I'm Pro-Choice!' Says Gov. George Ryan. 'No, You're Not!' Says His Aide. 'Yes, I Am!'" *Chicago Sun-Times,* April 29, 2007.

———. "3 Governors Found Guilty—3 Claims of Political Prosecutions." *Chicago Sun-Times,* September 11, 2006.

Redlawsk, David P., and James A. McCann. "Popular Interpretations of Corruption and Their Partisan Consequences." *Political Behavior* 27.3 (September 2005): 261–84.

Ryan, George H. Papers. Illinois State Historical Library, Springfield.

———. "The Role of the Executive in Administering the Death Penalty." *University of Illinois Law Review* 4 (September 2003).

Shapiro, Bruce. "Ryan's Courage." *Nation,* February 3, 2003, www.thenation.com/doc/20030203/shapiro.

———. "A Talk with Governor George Ryan." *Nation,* January 8, 2001, www.thenation.com/doc20010108/shapiro.

Simon, Paul, as told to Alfred Balk. "The Illinois Legislature: A Study in Corruption." *Harper's,* September 1964.

Thompson, James R. *An Evening to Remember.* DVD. Springfield: Illinois State Historical Library, April 3, 2004.

Index

mail fraud, as legal issue, 22–23, 167, 174–76
Mandela, Nelson, 104–5, 128
Maquoketa, Iowa, 9
Marchesini, Roberto, 176–77
Margolis, Jeremy: as attorney for Citizens for Ryan and for Ryan, 79, 91, 92, 106; as private attorney, 69, 70, 107, 111, 115–17, 120–21
Marshall, Lawrence C., 121, 126, 132
Marx, Groucho, 13
McBroom, Amanda, 14
McBroom, Edward M., 2, 11, 14, 15, 24, 39
McBroom, Marden "Andy," 13–14
McBroom, Stanley, 12
McBroom, Vernon, 12
McBroom, Victor, 12
McNally, Edward E., 107, 151–53
Mendoza, Gonzalo, 61, 87, 92, 100, 105
Metropolitan Pier and Exposition Authority ("McPier"), 99, 113, 129, 163

Nourie, Ray, 14
nursing homes, 36–38

O'Brien, Thomas, 76–78
Ogilvie, Richard, 18, 19–21, 24, 53, 71, 86
O'Hare International Airport, 2, 97, 109, 112–15
Old Timers Club, 52–54
O'Malley, Jack, 54–55, 86, 183n4
O'Neal, Dave, 37–38

Pallmeyer, Rebecca R.: and Citizens for Ryan, 120–21; and Fawell, S., 131, 136–37; profile of, 136–37; and Ryan, 91, 153–55, 159–62, 166–69
patronage, political, 18, 55–56
Peterson, Denise, 163, 167
Philip, James "Pate," 44, 68–69, 86, 97–98, 102–3, 125
Porter, Anthony, 5, 6, 98–99
Poshard, Glenn 87, 89, 91–94, 96, 100–102
Posner, Richard A., 175–76
Powell, Paul, 17–18, 19, 22, 27
Power, Joseph A., Jr., 63, 85, 89, 93
Prejean, Helen, 150–51
Prokos, Andrea Coutretsis. See Coutretsis, Andrea

Quinn, James, 57–59
Quinn, Patrick, 30–31, 63–64, 67, 68, 183n4

Raynor, Tammy Sue, 87–89, 95, 106
Roeser, Thomas F., 90, 107, 127, 170
Roff, Laurie, 84, 85, 95
Ronan, Al, 68–69
Rostenkowski, Dan, 7, 117, 125, 131, 174
Ryan, Elizabeth "Nancy" (sister of G. Ryan), 10, 114
Ryan, George H., Sr.: and abortion, 89–90; and Cuba, 101–4, 119; health of, 45; as House Speaker, 32–36; as lieutenant governor, 42–45, 47–49; marriage of, 10–15, 11; pension of, 166; as pharmacist, 11, 14–15, 34, 36–38, 46; political persona of, 7–8, 23; scandals involving, listed, 95–96; as secretary of state, 49–51, 57–58, 63–69, 74–78, 185n1; and South Africa, 104–5; as state representative, 5, 29–33; and substance abuse, actions against, 67–68, 73–74, 118; youth of, 9–11. See also capital punishment; Citizens for Ryan; criminal case against Ryan; Friends of George Ryan Fund; governorship of Ryan
Ryan, George H. "Homer," Jr. (son of G. Ryan), 11, 73, 80, 129, 141
Ryan, Jeanette (daughter of G. Ryan), 11, 45, 74
Ryan, Jeanette Bowman (mother of G. Ryan), 9, 45–46
Ryan, Jim (no kin of G. Ryan), 110, 122, 124–25
Ryan, Julie (daughter of G. Ryan), 11, 80, 84
Ryan, Joanne (daughter of G. Ryan), 11, 84
Ryan, Kathleen (sister of G. Ryan), 10
Ryan, Lynda (daughter of G. Ryan), 11, 73–74, 83–84, 150
Ryan, Lura Lynn Lowe (wife of G. Ryan): and corruption charges against Ryan, 88, 153; marriage of, 10–11, 15; and political career of Ryan, 46, 47, 104, 163
Ryan, Nancy (daughter of G. Ryan), 11, 63, 84
Ryan, Thomas, Sr. (father of G. Ryan), 9, 14
Ryan, Thomas, Jr. (brother of G. Ryan), 3, 10–11, 14–15, 46, 57, 69–70

James L. Merriner, who has written about national, Illinois, and Chicago politics for three decades, is the author of five books about issues of public corruption and reform. An independent researcher, he is a former James Thurber Writer in Residence at Ohio State University and currently serves as president of the Society of Midland Authors.